Palgrave Studies in Green Criminology

Series editors
Angus Nurse
Department of Criminology and Sociology
Middlesex University
London, UK

Rob White
Department of Criminology
University of Tasmania
Hobart, TAS, Australia

Melissa Jarrell
Texas A&M University
Corpus Christi, TX, USA

Criminologists have increasingly become involved and interested in environmental issues to the extent that the term Green Criminology is now recognised as a distinct subgenre of criminology. Within this unique area of scholarly activity, researchers consider not just harms to the environment, but also the links between green crimes and other forms of crime, including organised crime's movement into the illegal trade in wildlife or the links between domestic animal abuse and spousal abuse and more serious forms of offending such as serial killing. This series will provide a forum for new works and new ideas in green criminology for both academics and practitioners working in the field, with two primary aims: to provide contemporary theoretical and practice-based analysis of green criminology and environmental issues relating to the development of and enforcement of environmental laws, environmental criminality, policy relating to environmental harms and harms committed against non-human animals and situating environmental harms within the context of wider social harms; and to explore and debate new contemporary issues in green criminology including ecological, environmental and species justice concerns and the better integration of a green criminological approach within mainstream criminal justice. The series will reflect the range and depth of high-quality research and scholarship in this burgeoning area, combining contributions from established scholars wishing to explore new topics and recent entrants who are breaking new ground.

More information about this series at
http://www.springer.com/series/14622

Hanneke Mol

The Politics of Palm Oil Harm

A Green Criminological Perspective

palgrave
macmillan

Hanneke Mol
Northumbria University
Newcastle upon Tyne
UK

Palgrave Studies in Green Criminology
ISBN 978-3-319-55377-1 ISBN 978-3-319-55378-8 (eBook)
DOI 10.1007/978-3-319-55378-8

Library of Congress Control Number: 2017939551

Cover credit: Hanneke Mol

Printed on acid-free paper

This Palgrave Macmillan imprint is published by Springer Nature
The registered company is Springer International Publishing AG
The registered company address is: Gewerbestrasse 11, 6330 Cham, Switzerland

For my father, Leo Mol

Acknowledgements

My heartfelt thanks to the people in Colombia who participated in this research and shared their views and stories with me, welcomed me to their homes, accompanied and supported me, and showed me the beauty of Colombia and the warmth, joy, and spirit of its people. A special thanks to Salomon and Mary, and Nixon.

For inspiring me, and for their continuous support and encouragements without which this book would not have come about, I would like to thank Phil Carney, Nigel South, Avi Brisman, Rob White, and Tanya Wyatt. Thanks also to David Goyes, for the feedback, conversations, and friendship ever since our paths crossed in Colombia.

Personal circumstances made 2016 a bumpy year. I am grateful for the love and support of Hans, my mum, Erwin and Jeanette, Susanne and Alex, and the many friends that helped me get through this difficult period. You were with me to enjoy and celebrate the good moments, and your presence and support during the tough ones has been tremendous.

My deepest gratitude and love for my parents: for your unlimited support, endless faith, for insisting that I follow my heart, dreams, and ambitions, and for helping me realize them. To my mother, thank you for always being there for us (and, in my case, *everywhere!*), you're the best.

To my father, thank you for your warmth, love, jokes, energy, for the dedication and perseverance you showed in all you did, and for all the beautiful memories. You are greatly missed. I dedicate this book to you.

Contents

List of Figures

1
Introduction

"*Wherever you find the palm oil industry, you find progress*" (Fedepalma 2002). This claim forms the essence of a promotional video that marked the 40th anniversary of Fedepalma, the National Federation of Oil Palm Growers of Colombia. The video opens with images and action scenes of sportsmen and women engaging in adventurous activities like paragliding, rafting, and mountain climbing, accompanied by the following words:

> This is the spirit of determined men, fearless in facing nature, powerful in surmounting challenges, endowed with a vision of progress and hope for the future, unwavering and committed to struggle. (Fedepalma 2002)

Immediately after, images of the palm oil industry follow, and the voiceover states:

> This is the same unbreakable spirit of those pioneering men who had the audacity to try the unknown, the courage to widen frontiers, and the vision that forged this legacy for Colombia. Palm oil: the future for all Colombians. (Fedepalma 2002)

H. Mol, *The Politics of Palm Oil Harm*, Palgrave Studies in Green Criminology, DOI 10.1007/978-3-319-55378-8_1

Worldwide, industry proponents legitimize, and actively promote, the continued expansion of oil palm cultivation by invoking the allegedly beneficent social, economic, and environmental impacts of the palm oil industry. Yet in Colombia, as elsewhere, the palm oil industry has been linked to practices that fit the most conventional definition and perceptions of crime, through to types of social and environmental harm that do not fit strictly legalistic definitions and understandings of crime. For its critics for that matter—from local inhabitants of zones of palm oil production to global NGOs—palm oil epitomizes imposition, ecological destruction, and (deepened) social, economic, and cultural dispossession. Against this background, this book develops a critical analysis of the perceptions, realities, practices, and constructions of harm linked to the production of palm oil in Colombia, contributing to greater understanding of the social and environmental harms associated with palm oil, the theorization of harm within green criminology, and to ongoing debate over the proper object of criminological analysis more generally. The analytical and theoretical approach put forward, and the green criminological perspective that informs it, will be introduced later in this chapter and taken up in more detail in the next. First, the main drivers of the global demand for palm oil, and the reasons why the industry has moved to the centre of political, academic, and environmental debate, will be outlined.[1]

The Global Palm Oil Economy: Drivers, Incentives, and Legitimations

Accounting for about one-third of the total volume of vegetable oil produced annually, palm oil—cultivated in the tropical climates of Asia, Africa, and Latin America—is the world's most consumed and traded, and highest yielding, vegetable oil (Pirker et al. 2016). The global land area currently under oil palm cultivation is approximately 17 million hectares (Pirker et al. 2016). With oil extracted from the pulp (crude palm oil) as well as from the kernel of the oil palm fruit (crude palm kernel oil), a range of products are elaborated. Palm oil is widely used as cooking oil; a component of margarine; an ingredient of food products from bakery to confectionery goods, ice cream, chocolates, pre-made meals, and so on; as well as a raw material for the production of cosmetics, paints, lubricants, and detergents.[2] But the industry is moreover booming due to the fact that, increasingly, the production of this vegetable oil has become geared to the growing demand for renewable (i.e. "green") energy. In the context of growing concern over diminishing crude oil reserves, fluctuating oil prices, and unease with the dependence on oil supplies from unstable production regions, alongside demands to reduce greenhouse gas emissions in order to mitigate climate change (EC 2009; Franco et al. 2010), its use for biodiesel production further adds to the surge of interest in palm oil.

In response to palm oil's manifold uses and the corresponding demand, the global area under oil palm cultivation has increased exponentially in recent decades. With 75% of global palm oil production traded internationally, and as an ingredient of one in two supermarket products, Oosterveer (2014: 1) points out that "palm oil has become a typically globalised agro-food commodity". Renewable energy targets, too, play an important role in such international trade. The European Union has set targets that require that by 2020, 20% of total energy use—differentiated according to member state—and 10% of each member state's fuel consumption in the transport sector, come from renewable energy sources (EC 2009).[3] As such targets cannot be met via domestic production alone, heavy reliance on imports from the Global South[4] is inevitable. Between 2006 and 2012, the consumption of crude palm oil in the EU increased by 40%, from 4.5 to 6.4 million tonnes: 3.9 million tonnes going into the production of food, cosmetics, and oleochemicals; 0.6 million to heating and electricity; and 1.9 million tonnes of palm oil were geared to biofuel production, comprising 80% of the total increase in imports in the stated period (Gerasimchuk and Koh 2013).

In view of the proclaimed socioeconomic and environmentally beneficent impacts that such imports would have for producer countries, the dependence on imports is considered largely unproblematic by industry proponents and in official discourse (Franco et al. 2010). However, as already indicated, depictions of palm oil as an environmentally sustainable form of development and a socially and economically beneficent activity are contested.

A Green Deception Mired in Controversy

The expansion of palm oil production in the Global South, driven (amongst other factors) by the demand for renewable energy feedstock in the framework of climate change mitigation, has been critiqued as a form of "CO_2lonialism" that exploits and destroys human and nonhuman life in regions where the industry operates (Hazlewood 2010). The environmental concerns that the palm oil industry is linked to include deforestation, soil erosion, and the climate change effects of land use change of forests, grassland, and diversified agriculture to agroindustrial monocultures (Danielsen et al. 2009; Carrere 2001; Fitzherbert et al. 2008). In fact, it has been indicated that land conversion to oil palm is more likely to result in an *increase* in net greenhouse gas emissions and a prolonged carbon debt, considering that the re-absorption of the carbon stored in forests and high-carbon soils—released into the atmosphere upon establishment of oil palm plantations—can take years, if not decades or centuries (Danielsen et al. 2009; Gibbs et al. 2008). This relates not only to direct land use change but also to the indirect land use change that results from the displacement of existing land uses (Franco et al. 2010). Gibbs et al. (2008) found that while land use change of degraded lands to oil palm could potentially lead to increased carbon storage, "carbon payback time" in the case of forest ecosystem conversion may range from 30 to 120 years.[5]

Other environmental impacts to consider are biodiversity loss and the contamination of air, water, and soils. The dominant modality of palm oil production takes the form of large-scale monocultures, i.e. plantations made up of orderly rows of a single crop, on a scale of up to thousands of hectares. Although to the untrained eye a monoculture may look like a forest, in reality these plantations do not remotely resemble the complexity, resiliency, and species diversity of forest ecosystems (Altieri 2009). Fitzherbert et al. (2008) for instance note that in comparison to other forms of agriculture, oil palm plantations hold particularly low levels of biodiversity and that there "appear to be few biodiversity-friendly management practices which could enhance the value of oil palm plantations for native species" (Fitzherbert et al. 2008: 543). Monocultures are also linked to water shortages and hydrological imbalances due to the excessive demands that plantations as well as processing plants place on water sources (Levidow and Paul 2010; McCarthy and Zen 2010).

Due to ecosystem simplification, disturbances in the replenishment of soil nutrients, and a consequent reduction in ecosystem resiliency, monocultures require the external input of fertilizers and—for being highly susceptible to disease and pest problems—the use of pesticides and herbicides (Altieri 2009). Through agrochemical runoff from plantations and the liquid wastes produced in the processing plants, the application of artificial fertilizers and agrochemicals has been linked to contaminated soils, groundwater, and rivers (McCarthy and Zen 2010; McMichael 2010). This causes harm to nearby flora and fauna, fish populations, and impacts negatively on the health of land and marine ecosystems more generally. It also poses direct and indirect risks to human health, either via direct contact with these products (e.g. affecting plantation workers) or via the consumption of contaminated water and fish. When the oil palm shells and empty fruit bunches that remain after processing the harvest are not returned to the plantation[6] but burned instead, the areas surrounding the production facilities risk being exposed to noxious odours and air (e.g. smoke and dust) pollution (McCarthy and Zen 2010).

Aside from its environmental impact, agroindustry establishment and expansion have also been indicated as major drivers of displacement, driving local populations off their land and threatening rural and forest-dependent livelihoods (Dauvergne and Neville 2010; Vélez 2010), often in disregard of established property rights and not uncommonly accompanied by violent means (Borras and Franco 2012; McMichael 2010). In the case of Colombian palm oil, critics scrutinize the palm oil industry for its alleged complicity in the dispossession of land and the displacement of traditional systems of subsistence and production. Those most affected are often already marginalized groups: indigenous, Afro-descendant, and peasant communities, whose food security and sovereignty, and enactment of cultural practices and belief systems, are under severe threat (Vélez 2010; Escobar 2008).

The displacement of (local) food production by the palm oil industry is emblematic of the "large-scale dispossession of peasant agriculture under conditions of a 'corporate food regime'" (McMichael 2009: 281) signified by the dominance of agribusiness in a market-led global restructuring of agricultural relations.[7] With the demand for renewable energy, this is also claimed to result in the diversion of food crops and agricultural lands previously devoted to food production; now increasingly directed to the production of fuels. Such practices have been blamed for rising food prices and exacerbated food shortages. The former UN Special Rapporteur on the Right to Food, Jean Ziegler, even referred to such policies and practices as "crimes against humanity" and "massacre (by) hunger" (Ziegler in Lederer 2007). Critics therefore reject the term "biofuels", which in policy discourse and by industry proponents tends to be used to refer to fuel produced from agricultural crops (e.g. oil palm, soybean, rapeseed, jatropha for the production of biodiesel; corn, sugarcane, sugar beet for the production of bioethanol), insisting on calling them "agrofuels" instead. Contrary to what the prefix "bio" appears to suggest, critics argue that the production of agrofuels does not so much sustain as *undermine* life. By referring to these fuels as "agrofuels", attention is drawn to their intricate relation to agriculture, food production, and agrarian social relations (McMichael 2010; Cerdas Vega 2009).[8]

Palm Oil as Economic, Social, and Environmental Opportunity

In sharp contrast with the above-presented points of critique, arguments in favour of palm oil production revolve around notions that the industry: plays a crucial role in meeting the rising global demand for food; supports affordable food prices; contributes to poverty alleviation by generating employment; stimulates rural development by investing in necessary social and economic infrastructure; and protects the environment and fragile ecosystems (RSPO 2013; Nestlé 2013; World Growth 2011). Sayer et al. (2012: 115) note that "oil palm is one of the most profitable land uses in the humid tropics", and an attractive economic opportunity for local people, corporations, and governments. That is, the proclaimed economic benefits of palm oil production are held to prosper both national economies and rural livelihoods. In view of controversy around palm oil's contribution to economic growth, social welfare, and rural development, Castiblanco et al. (2015a) conducted a statistical analysis to assess the socioeconomic impacts of palm oil expansion in Colombia. Although the study points to higher-than-average levels of land concentration, violence, and poverty for some production zones of palm oil, the authors were led to conclude that oil palm municipalities in Colombia "have [significantly] lower unmet basic needs indicators and have bigger fiscal income when compared to other municipalities where oil palm is not produced" (Ibid: 38).

It has moreover been noted that, alongside the employment generated to plantation workers of medium and large palm oil companies, the palm oil industry also contributes to rural development and livelihoods via the opportunities opened up to local smallholders that get involved in oil palm cultivation on their own land (Sayer et al. 2012; Castiblanco et al. 2015a, b). Contrary to reports that link the palm oil industry almost exclusively to land grabs, human rights violations, and the exploitation and impoverishment of rural populations, Rist et al. (2010) state that in the four locations included in their studies of Sumatra and Kalimantan, local willingness to cultivate oil palm was high, thus generating substantial economic benefits to small growers. Still, it is the *opposition* to palm oil, Rist et al. (2010) emphasize, which gets disproportionate coverage in the reports of NGOs.

In fact, the controversy surrounding the palm oil industry has led to concerns being raised about the perceivably "biased" accounts and rigid opposition (Rival and Levang 2015) resorted to by some palm oil critics. In view of the potential socioeconomic benefits of palm oil and local attitudes to the industry, Rival and Levang state: "local people dream first and foremost about paved roads, electricity, water supply, mobile phone networks, schools and dispensaries, even international airports. Living in harmony with nature by hunting and gathering forest products, far removed from the stress of the modern commercial world is the dream of the affluent urban westerner and not that of the "noble savage"" (2015: 39).

Vis-à-vis the alleged environmental consequences of palm oil production, it has been pointed out that notwithstanding the cases where deforestation has been driven by the establishment of oil palm plantations, overall, the relation between palm oil and deforestation is hard to pin down due to a lack of reliable data. Nor is this relation necessarily or primarily a direct one; even where the palm oil industry operates on deforested lands, it is argued that the corresponding deforestation may well have had its origins in factors wholly disconnected from subsequent oil palm establishment (Rival and Levang 2015; Fitzherbert et al. 2008). And even if the opportunity costs of environmental protection and conservation efforts are high for a business as profitable as palm oil, Sayer et al. (2012: 115) have stated that "this should be set against the reality that it is generally easier to secure conservation outcomes when people are prosperous". Without denying the low levels of native biodiversity within oil palm plantations and the risk that palm oil production results in net increases in carbon emissions, Sayer et al. furthermore state that both in terms of carbon emissions and biodiversity loss, palm oil outperforms other oil crops. In addition to "standing carbon stock" per hectare (Sayer et al. 2012), this also relates to the yields derived from oil crops and the associated surface of land thus needed to meet global demand. With yields of up to 4700 kilos of oil per hectare, oil palm is the highest yielding oil crop, compared to 720, 580, and 400 kilos of vegetable oil per hectare for rapeseed, sunflower, and soybean, respectively (Dangond Lacouture 2014).

Moreover, oil palm requires less fertilizer than other oil crops and a shift is underway to the "use of integrated pest management and leguminous cover crops", reducing the use of insecticides and herbicides (Fitzherbert et al. 2008: 543). This suggests that measures can be taken to lessen the pollution that the palm oil industry is associated with. On the topic of palm oil-related water contamination, too, while it is certainly true that the wastewater that is produced in the process of extracting the oil from the oil palm fruits has the potential to be highly contaminating, it has also been noted that, increasingly, purification systems are in place that allow treated water to be safely discharged into nearby water streams (Fitzherbert et al. 2008).

Colombian Palm Oil: A Source of Progress and Hope for the Future

In Colombia, agriculture is presented as one of five engines of development and economic growth[9] that can consolidate peace and "prosperity for all" (DNP 2011). Echoing the above-presented views of palm oil as a social and economic opportunity, palm oil production is framed as a key economic activity both in the national interest and for the well-being of local populations and environments. Documents produced by or written under the auspices of Fedepalma, highlight the range of industrial applications of palm oil and its corresponding high economic value. The crop is moreover considered to have rooted socially and culturally in Colombia's rural zones, bringing stability and increased opportunities for daily subsistence. Along such lines, it is argued that:

> Oil palm is not only agroindustrial activity and prosperity for Colombia. It is also history, culture, promise, well-being… It is, above all, compromise: with the people, with the land, with development. (Ospina Bozzi 2007: 5)

Over the last decade, the extension of oil palm plantations in Colombia increased annually with 8% on average (Mesa Dishington 2014). Both in extension and intensity of production (i.e. yields per hectare), the Colombian palm oil sector is perceived to have ample room for further growth. With little alteration, some 2.5–3 million hectares are held to be suitable for oil palm cultivation. Regarding the intensity of production, emphasis is placed on the need to increase yields from its current level of 3.1 tonnes of palm oil per hectare to 4.7 (Dangond Lacouture 2014; Mesa Dishington 2014). Although the two largest producers of palm oil, Malaysia and Indonesia, in 2013 accounted for roughly 76% of the global land area under palm oil production—Colombia's share that year being 2.2%—Colombia is the largest producer of palm oil in the Americas and ranks fifth globally (Fedepalma 2014). President Juan Manuel Santos in 2014 reiterated that his government is determined to support the continued growth of the palm oil sector, which is acclaimed for its commitment to bring peace and progress to Colombia (Santos 2014). Colombia's cultivated area has grown from approximately 150,000 ha in 2000

(Fedepalma 2005) to 477,000 ha by the end of 2013 (Fedepalma 2014) and is now approaching 500,000 ha.

Growth of Colombia's palm oil industry is significantly geared to the sector's capacity for biodiesel production. The Colombian government has implemented mandatory blending targets, tax exemptions, and subsidy schemes to incentivize biofuel production through palm oil (Castiblanco et al. 2015b). Colombia's National Planning Department, in setting out its policy guidelines for the sustainable production of biofuels in Colombia (DNP 2008), recognized that biofuel production can have positive as well as negative consequences for biodiversity and the environment. Accordingly, it is held that, with the adoption of adequate technological and environmental standards, biofuels can contribute beneficially to reductions in the use of fossil fuels; recuperation of degraded lands previously used for activities such as cattle ranching; and reduced greenhouse gas emissions (DNP 2008).

Nearly half of domestic palm oil production in Colombia is now geared to biodiesel (Mesa Dishington 2014). The domestic production of biodiesel has in fact increased to such extent that palm oil exports dropped significantly in recent years (Fedepalma 2014). When in 2000 Fedepalma presented its vision for the future, it expressed its intent to work towards—to paraphrase—an "ambitious but realistic" growth in the export rate from 20% to close to 80% (Fedepalma 2000). Indeed, between 1995 and 2006, Colombia experienced a steady rise in palm oil exports, increasing from 6% to 33% of total production (Ospina Bozzi 2007: 29). However, by 2013 total exports—with the European Union as the main export destination—had dropped to 16.3%,[10] although for reasons that do not solely come down to the increase in biodiesel production (see Chap. 6).

In Colombia, palm oil is not just seen as opportunity, but as an *alternative*. There are three dimensions in particular that stand out in terms of palm oil's depiction as an alternative crop in the Colombian context. As a productive alternative, palm oil is claimed to provide the stability and income security that local subsistence economies and annual crops purportedly lack (Ospina Bozzi 2007). The main factors underpinning the view of oil palm cultivation as a source of regular income and well-remunerated economic activity are that it is a perennial crop with an economic life of 25–30 years that, once producing, produces constantly, and that it lends itself to competition in the domestic and global market economy.

Second, and connected to the first point, palm oil is promoted as a legal alternative. Centred on the notion that palm oil is a lucrative commodity with the potential to incorporate large parts of the landless rural proletariat as well as smallholders into its production chain, the sector is viewed as a possible counterweight to immersion in illicit economic activity (e.g. coca cultivation) and involvement with illegal armed groups. As such, palm oil takes a central place in alternative development discourse and programmes as the Peace and Development Projects co-financed by the World Bank, the US-funded Plan Colombia,[11] and the Peace Laboratories of the European Union (Godnick and Klein 2009; Seeboldt 2010).

Third, as a more general feature of depictions of palm oil, the industry is presented as an environmental alternative. In view of its potential as a source of renewable energy, it is thereby argued that the land extensions needed to steer the economy away from fossil fuel dependence are far less if cultivated with oil palm compared to other oil crops; to replace 5% of global diesel production with biodiesel, palm oil is held to require five times less land than rapeseed production and ten times less than soybean (Ospina Bozzi 2007: 39; Dangond Lacouture 2014). In addition, the production model itself is deemed green, too, manifest for instance in Fedepalma's claim that "mature oil palms form true forest landscapes, inhabited by numerous flora and fauna species" (2006: 19). However, the extent to which animal and plant life in oil palm plantations resembles biodiversity levels in forests is subject to serious challenge. Wholly contrary to claims that oil palm plantations equate to true forests, there is evidence that "oil palm is a particularly poor substitute for either primary or degraded forests, and whereas any conversion of natural forest is inevitably damaging to biodiversity, oil palm plantations support even fewer forest species than do most other agricultural options" (Fitzherbert et al. 2008: 542).

The Politics of Harm Linked to Palm Oil Production

Clearly then, the harms (and beneficial impacts) of palm oil are contested. Without altogether denying the possibility that oil palm cultivation can indeed have positive effects on poverty alleviation and human and environmental well-being in rural zones, the green credentials and development rhetoric called upon to justify agroindustrial palm oil production require critical examination. From a green criminological perspective, this book offers an analysis of the perceptions, realities, practices, and constructions of harm in the context of Colombian palm oil production, with a specific focus on the industry's presence and operations in the southernmost part of its Pacific coast region. It has its basis in a qualitative study into the social and environmental harms of palm oil production, from a primarily interview-based ethnographic approach[12] for which fieldwork has been undertaken in Colombia between July 2012 and March 2013. To set out in an introductory way how this research took shape, what is innovative about it and what it endeavours to contribute to (green) criminology, let me start by narrating my engagement with the subject matter. This leads me from my initial encounter with the contradictory reality of palm oil *on paper* to my encounter with it *on-the-ground* when I first arrived to Tumaco, located in the department of Nariño.

In the convergence of a proclaimed shift to "sustainable development" and "green growth", a global economy that thrives by virtue of extractivist patterns of accumulation, and an enduring colonial logic, Tumaco has been converted into the centre of one of Colombia's four zones of palm oil production. The situation in this beautiful yet troubled region reflects with particular force the type of world(s) we live in, the privileges this generates to some, and the inferior treatment, exploitation, and dispossession thus brought upon others. Against this background, when starting my fieldwork in Colombia I aimed to investigate the confrontation between the pro-palm oil stance of public officials, industry representatives, and corporate actors on the one hand, versus the palm oil critical perspectives of local communities and NGOs supporting them in their struggles on the other hand. Of course, matters turned out to be more complex than this binary opposition, which changed my preconceptions and laid the basis for the harm approach here advanced.

My first visit to Tumaco was a rather unexpected one. Having arrived to Colombia in July 2012, late August 2012 I travelled to Pasto, the capital of Nariño, for an interview with the UNIPA, the umbrella organization of indigenous Awá in the Department of Nariño. While in Pasto, I visited Corponariño, the regional environmental authority. Half an hour (and one phone call) later, I was on my way out again with what looked like a promising step towards research access in Tumaco. The director at Corponariño's office in Pasto had arranged that Corponariño's coordinator in Tumaco would await me there two days later, to help establish contacts with local stakeholders.

Upon arrival in Tumaco, first I was taken to Cordeagropaz—a local organization that promotes the involvement of small growers in the cultivation of oil palm—and interviewed its Executive Director. This was followed the next day by an interview with a representative of Palmasur (*Palmeros del Pacífico Sur*), an association that represents and seeks to uphold the interests of small growers in the commercialization of their fruits. Thus, I was made aware of the extent of small grower involvement in the palm oil industry in Tumaco. However, during these days I also met with two community leaders that were highly critical of what they perceived as the imposition of oil palm plantations onto Afro-Colombian collective territory, small grower involvement included. Consequently, after my first visit to Tumaco I was struck by the local coexistence of what seemed to be a rather substantial support for the palm oil industry by small growers and the strong rejection of the industry by local critics within the same population. It challenged my somewhat binary view of the "push for" versus "opposition to" palm oil, and more than anything it challenges the link that often tends to be made between palm oil, violence, and coercive imposition.

What was I to make of agroindustry expansion through small growers on the one hand and the insistence by palm oil critics that this clashes with the biodiversity and cultural and territorial vocation of the region on the other hand? To make matters more complex still, where does Colombia's progressive Constitution in terms of the recognition of cultural and ethnic diversity fit in with all of this, and what about the collective land titles allocated to Afro-Colombian and indigenous communities in Tumaco over the past two decades? What to make of this in terms of harm, power, and legality? I became more and more convinced of the need for harm perspectives in criminology in a way that does more than merely expose and denounce the types of harm in contexts as these. Why and in what ways does the reality of harm experienced and articulated by palm oil critics differ from the reality of harm experienced and articulated by small growers of oil palm? How does each of these realities sit with hegemonic notions and practices of legality and what can critical criminology and a critical *green* criminology learn from an engagement with these realities?

What the above seemed to call for is an approach to harm explicitly connected to a view on power. Accordingly, the aim of this study has been to interrogate the mechanisms and relations of power that invest practices and discourses of harm. Thereby moving to the centre is the notion that harm is contested and that it is the analysis of the contestedness of harm that can advance debate over harm within criminology. I will elaborate on these notions in the next chapter. Suffice to clarify here that, although it is possible to attend to the contestation around harm through a focus on practices of resistance (e.g. Oslender 2007), this study engages the contestedness of harm in a much broader sense. While recognizing that such contestedness can be manifested through practices of resistance, and that resistance can offer valuable insights into conceptions of harm and the meanings ascribed to particular social relations, practices, and natural goods (e.g. water, McClanahan 2014), harm may well be endured and contested without engaging in overt or organized forms of resistance. Practices and understandings of harm can also be contested in the discourses, systems of production and subsistence, and everyday ways of being of those affected, which implicitly or explicitly challenge oppressive and exploitative power relations and dynamics and prevailing social, economic, and political arrangements.

The objectives of this book are twofold: (1) at the descriptive level, to provide an encompassing account of the different perceptions, practices, and lived experiences of harm in the context of palm oil production in Colombia's south Pacific coast region, and (2) at the theoretical level, to enhance the theorization of "harm" within green criminology. In view of the latter, the aim is not just to advance understanding of the power dynamics that *draw* the boundaries of harm and crime, but also shed light on the ways in which hegemonic notions and practices of legality are *kept in place* and hence operate to reproduce the status quo in ways that generate harm to human beings and the natural environment. In so doing, this book endeavours to contribute empirically and theoretically to the green criminological analysis of the extractive industries, encouraging green criminologists to engage with harm in more complex and nuanced ways.

Extractivism, Criminology, and the Emergence of Green Perspectives

Extractivism refers to the appropriation or the intensive exploitation of natural resources. The activities that first come to mind in this regard tend to be mining, and oil and gas exploration and exploitation. But agroindustry, forestry, and fishing can just as well take extractivist forms (Veltmeyer and Petras 2014a). The dynamics of extractivism are largely similar across these sectors (see, e.g., Giarracca and Teubal 2014); the difference lies mostly in the object of extraction: nonrenewable resources in the case of mining and oil and gas exploitation, versus renewable resources in the case of agrarian extractivism—even if extracted at a rate that exceeds the environmental capacity of renewal (Acosta 2013), thus depleting the resource itself or the ecological conditions upon which its extraction depends.

Extractivist agriculture is characterized by vast, capital-intensive monocultures that rely heavily on external inputs such as artificial fertilizers and agrochemicals, and the continuous development of "advanced" planting and harvesting methods as well as seed and crop technologies (increasingly, this involves genetic engineering). Rather than driven by principles of social and environmental well-being, such models are above all geared to continuously maximizing productivity (in harvested yields), profits, and efficiency. Harvests tend to be processed to only a limited degree in the region of cultivation, if processed at all before being transported. This means that the added value of production that results from the transformation of raw materials is usually realized outside the region where the agroindustry is situated (Grigera and Álvarez 2013).

As such, an international division of nature tends to confine countries like Colombia to the role of mere provider of raw materials, generally left with nothing other than social and environmental destruction while the profits and consumption of the final products are enjoyed elsewhere (Vélez and Vélez 2008; Cerdas Vega 2009). In Latin America, the current phase of extractivism is characterized by what is mostly a foreign direct investment-driven, export-oriented "reprimarization" of the economy (Grigera and Álvarez 2013); a colonial pattern of power thus permeates contemporary neoliberal globalization. However, an enclave economy model can also be at work *within* the geographical limits of countries, reducing regions like the Colombian Pacific to "internal colonies" (Mondaca 2017; see also Chap. 2).

Under extractivist modes of accumulation, agro-commodity chains are all but completely controlled by agribusiness, (further) pushing out smallholder and traditional (i.e. nonindustrial) systems of agricultural production (Veltmeyer and Petras 2014b; Giarracca and Teubal 2014). Although in the majority of cases the corporate control thus exerted over the extractive industries involves transnational capital, this is not necessarily the case, as the palm oil industry in Colombia illustrates.[13]

Of course, extractivism is not a new phenomenon but has been a mechanism of plunder and appropriation since colonial times, with the first phase of extractivism going back some 500 years with the conquest and subsequent colonization of the Americas (Alimonda 2011; Acosta 2013). Since then, extractivist modes of accumulation have passed through different stages (Veltmeyer and Petras 2014b; Moore 2000). As such, apart from continuity there are also new dynamics at play in view of which Latin America has been experiencing a renewed cycle of extraction, commodification, and degradation of its natural wealth in recent decades (Seoane 2012).[14]

The impetus to scale up investments in the extraction of a set of primary commodities that are particularly lucrative now and towards the future is significantly driven by the renewable energy sectors. The world over, the production of primary commodities such as oil palm, soy, jatropha, sugar cane, and corn, is intensified and redirected to visions of clean energy. However, as Seoane asserts: "This is not about greening the economy, but on the contrary, about making the green into an economic matter; which is to say, to treat or subordinate the environmental to the logic of the market" (2012).[15] Seoane notes that an ever more extensive and unprecedented intensification of the commodification of nature and life is not only destroying local environments, territories, and populations in the Americas but is also threatening the continuity of life *as such* (Seoane 2012). This resonates with wider critiques that insist on the huge social and environmental costs of extractivism, most notably exacerbated social inequality, the destruction of livelihoods, the breakdown of communities' social fabric, and environmental degradation (Acosta 2013; Veltmeyer and Petras 2014). Extractivist patterns of accumulation are held to constitute the type of capitalist development that is characterized by Harvey (2003) as "accumulation by dispossession" (see also Grigera and Álvarez 2013).

The need for criminology to address the crimes, harms, and injustices bound up with natural resource exploitation is increasingly recognized, and so is the awareness of the need for such analyses to address the cross-boundary operation of "the politics of power, harm and justice" (Walters 2010: 314) and the fact that the negative impacts of global patterns of production and consumption tend to disproportionately weigh down on the Global South (White 2011). Although still a relatively understudied area within criminology, more research into the dynamics and consequences of extractivist practices is emerging. Walters (2011), for instance, provides a critical analysis of the political economy of GM food, bringing into focus the corruption, economic exploitation, livelihood dispossession, and environmental damage linked to this type of corporate domination of agriculture. Reflecting on rural realities in the Global South, Rojas-Páez (2017) scrutinizes the "historical injuries" that the colonized peoples of the world have had to endure at the hands of the extractive industries; while Gutiérrez-Gómez (2017) sheds light on the neoliberal policies and practices conducive to crime and harm related to extractivist gold mining in Colombia. What these types of criminological analysis have in common is that they address harmful practices that are to a large extent *lawful*. Inevitably, this raises questions regarding the "appropriate" boundaries of the discipline.

Harm, Crime, and Criminology: Politics with a Vengeance

Passas and Goodwin (2004: 2) note that, as criminologists, "we have set our priorities wrongly by overlooking misdeeds whose consequences are even more threatening than what is legally designated as crime". The authors point to the existence of practices that are "lawful but awful". Whilst not officially defined as illegal or criminal, these practices have devastating outcomes for humans and environments and should be of concern to criminology. It would, however, according to Passas & Goodwin, be too far off "to stretch the concepts of crime and criminality to cover these practices" (2004: 3). I coincide with the view that it is not helpful to blur the concepts of crime and harm but that there is nevertheless scope for criminologists to scrutinize the boundaries drawn between "crime" and the type of harmful practices that for various cultural, political, and economic reasons are socially accepted or tolerated.

By way of introduction to what will be discussed in more detail in Chap. 2, it is worth reflecting briefly on the debate on harm within critical criminology. In 1970, Herman and Julia Schwendinger addressed "the 30 year controversy about the definition of crime" (1975: 113).[16] This "controversy" refers to the discussion stirred up in the late 1930s and 1940s by Sutherland (1940) and Sellin (1938), who questioned the extent to which the criminal law forms an appropriate basis for criminological analysis. Tappan (1947), a foremost critic of attempts to broaden or otherwise rethink the scope and focus of criminological analysis, responded as follows:

> Vague, omnibus concepts defining crime are a blight upon either a legal system or a system of sociology that strives to be objective. They allow judge, administrator, or – conceivably – sociologist, in an undirected, freely operating discretion, to attribute the status "criminal" to any individual or class which he conceives nefarious. This can accomplish no desirable objective, either politically or sociologically. (Tappan 1947: 99)

The Schwendingers (1975), taking up this debate 30 years later, concurred with critiques of criminal law definitions of crime. However, other than Sutherland (1940), who had extended the definition of crime to violations of civil and administrative law, the Schwendingers argued against the acceptance of *all* legal definitions of crime as handed down by the State, whether this be by criminal law or another form of law. They did so from the view that such acceptance implicates criminologists in the reproduction of the existing inequitable social order.

Another 45 years have passed since the Schwendingers' contribution. Although harm perspectives now assume a more central place and broader acceptance within criminology, harm still remains a contested object of criminological analysis, and suggestions that the study of social harm could be pursued within the (new) discipline of "zemiology" (see Hillyard et al. 2004) are much debated. Within critical criminology, there are various positions vis-à-vis the boundaries of a criminologically relevant conceptualization of harm: some advance a focus on crime-equivalent harm, thereby to different degrees moving away from the legal framework traditionally adhered to in criminology (i.e. domestic criminal law); others insist on abandoning the concept and the discourse of crime altogether, to advance a focus on social harm instead; and lastly there are those that question the move away from the concept of crime, insisting on the link between crime and deviance (rather than between crime and harm), the ontological reality of crime, or a combination of the two. In Chap. 2, these positions will be discussed in more detail.

The existence of substantial disagreement on *whether* criminologists should engage broader notions of harm, and if so, *how far* the disciplinary boundaries of criminology can or ought to be pushed in this regard, are far from trivial definitional matters. Tensions about the subject matter of criminology and divergent conceptualizations of harm are *political* tensions. Indeed, as Reiman has stated, "this is politics with a vengeance. Politics openly, necessarily, insinuates itself into the heart of criminology" (2007: 236). And as if this politics had not been complex enough already, adding to the discussion, from the 1990s on a growing number of critical criminologists began to insist explicitly on the inclusion of a crucial dimension that thus far had been missing from criminology's conceptual framework and analytical focus: the natural environment and nonhuman species.

Towards a Green Frame of Reference

One of the areas of criminological scholarship where harm perspectives assume centrality is green criminology, although research into environmental crime may also be informed by strictly legalistic understandings of crime (White 2011). Furthermore, alongside the critical perspectives to which this book seeks to add, there are also more mainstream explanations of the causes of environmental crime and appropriate responses to such crimes. As South (1998) observes, green criminology is neither a theory nor a unified field of theorizing, but a "sensitizing perspective" that builds on diverse theoretical positions. Broadly defined, green criminology engages the ways in which human society relates to, acts upon, and interacts with the nonhuman in ways that generate harm and crime against humans, animals, and the natural environment at large (Halsey and White 1998; Cazaux 1999). In addition, green criminology also involves the analysis of environmental law and regulation (White 2008) and more recently attention has been drawn to the *criminogenic effects* of environmental harm as warranting more thorough attention. Approaches along the latter line rest on the notion that, in a variety of ways, environmental harm can be a cause of crime; resource scarcity for instance can be conducive to social conflict, violence, and property crime (Potter 2014; Lynch and Stretesky 2014).[17]

Some of the topics that from the 1990s began to be addressed within the contours of an emerging green criminology were not entirely new to the discipline. One example is the study of the illegal disposal of hazardous waste as a case of corporate crime facilitated by a vulnerable regulatory structure and an at times blurred line between corporate and organized crime (Szasz 1986). Yet it was felt that the nature and extent of environmental harm as an endemic feature of current political economic and sociocultural arrangements, asked for the type of analysis that could critically engage these themes beyond a crimes of the powerful analytical framework (Halsey 1997; Halsey and White 1998). This paved the way for a much more explicit criminological engagement with the interconnection between social and environmental issues, the systemic nature of environmental crime and harm, thereby also directing more explicit attention to nonhuman suffering and negative impacts (White 2002).

Although criminological engagement with environmental issues is starting to make its imprint on the discipline as a whole, in the grand scheme of things it is still a relatively minor subject area. Lynch and Stretesky (2014), in view of this, argue that in order for contemporary criminology to engage its subject matter (crime, harm, and justice) in a comprehensive and relevant manner, it is essential to take the *environment* as the point of departure. In contrast, thus far criminological theory and analysis has built on human-centred frames of reference in which the environment enters at most as a secondary consideration, or worse still, as little more than an externality. These human-centred frames, it is argued, ignore a crucial point. This is that ultimately, "the environment defines the maximum scope of human possibilities" *and* imposes boundaries on the limits of human forms of organization (Lynch and Stretesky 2014: 40–41). Hence, the authors argue that criminology should radically rethink the ways in which it understands and analyses crime and harm, and that this necessitates a green frame of reference.

Within a green frame of reference, critical green criminology can take various forms. Of particular relevance here is the eco-global perspective advanced by White (2011). White (2011) directs attention to the cultural, political, and economic arrangements that give rise to the generation of social and environmental harm and conflict, and the transference of such harm and conflict to the Global South, whose human populations and natural environments are differentially targeted and victimized. The social and environmental harms of palm oil production that this study is concerned with, moreover exemplify what White refers to as "paradoxical harm". Paradoxical harm occurs when proposed solutions to harm generate new forms of harm. As argued:

> Such harm is paradoxical precisely because the harms stem from the pursuit of sectional social interests that inevitably fashion responses to, rather than resolution of, the key contradictions of the present age (namely, the preservation of the capitalist growth economy versus transformation towards sustainable ecology). Paradoxical harm is not the same as unintended consequences. In many instances the harms are known, and the acts leading to the generation of the harms are intentional. (White 2011: 45)

Both the "agrofuels solution" (as a green alternative to fossil fuels) and the palm oil industry more broadly (as a way to mitigate rural poverty and stimulate "sustainable development") can be seen as sources of paradoxical harm that further compound existing environmental and social harm. In a green frame of reference, this study advances a harm perspective that critically interrogates the power dynamics that invest the discourses and practices of harm that as such infuse the production of palm oil in the south Pacific coast region of Colombia.

Book Outline

Embedded in a discussion of how considerations of harm and power figure implicitly or explicitly in existing critical criminological work, in Chap. 2 the theoretical framework that underpins this research will be set out. I expand on how green criminological perspectives extend and deepen the critical criminological tradition, review in more detail the harm debate within critical criminology and suggest to redirect this debate, and subsequently present the contours of an explanatory framework for the play of power in the "politics of harm" in the context of palm oil production in Colombia's Pacific coast region. Thereby my point of departure is the theoretical basis of critical, green criminological studies of environmental harm and crime related to resource extraction, which generally draw on Marxist political economy analysis. I argue that while such works offer crucial insights into the subject matter at hand, they do not arrive at a thorough theorization of the power–harm–legality dynamic and complexities.

Important in this regard is that critical accounts of the impacts provoked by the palm oil industry and other large-scale economic activity in Colombia, confront us with images of violent dispossession and forced displacement, and of territories "cleansed" of their human inhabitants, nonhuman and natural diversity (Tenthoff and Eventon 2013; Mingorance 2006). While this violent reality continues unabated in many parts of Colombia, there is a risk that exclusive emphasis on the coercive and violent dimensions of agroindustry establishment and expansion, as well as rigid assumptions about the capital–nature antagonism, is insufficiently attentive to the nonviolent forms of imposition and more subtle workings of power that inscribe contexts as these. The growing involvement of small growers in oil palm cultivation, the forging of social and environmental compromises, the different realities of harm lived and perceived by small growers on the one hand and local palm oil critics on the other hand, and the granting of collective land titles to Afro-Colombian and indigenous communities are all aspects that ask for a more refined analysis of the power dynamics at play in this context.

Chap. 3 provides the necessary legal, political, demographic, social, and ecological background to prepare the presentation and analysis of the primary data in Chaps. 4–6.

In Chap. 4, I analyse the broader frame within which to interrogate the politics of harm in the Colombian Pacific region, drawing attention to the fact that Colombia's contested grounds are at once (i) socionatural spaces where human and nonhuman lives interweave, (ii) sites of capitalist industrial development, and (iii) sites of armed conflict and illicit economic activity. In view of this, the chapter takes stock of the multiple interests that in this convergence of factors, actors, and dynamics coexist, compete, and interact.

Chap. 5 is organized around the analysis of the ways in which the ground has been and is prepared for palm oil production in Tumaco. I discuss the establishment and expansion of the palm oil industry, related conceptions of the land, and attendant perceptions of harm from the perspectives of corporate actors, industry representatives,[18] public officials, members of NGOs, local palm oil critics, and small growers of oil palm. Considerations of coercion and consent are central to the discussions in this chapter.

In Chap. 6, the focus shifts to the alleged social and environmental harms incurred, or brought about, during the phases of oil palm cultivation and the palm oil production process. I thereby contrast perspectives that insist on the social and ecologically beneficent character of oil palm cultivation, with the socioecological, cultural, and economic rationalities adhered to by those communities within the local population that continue to object to such agroindustrial developments. In addition, specific attention goes out to the fact that it is increasingly difficult for communities to withstand the corresponding pressures to put their lands "to productive use" in accordance with neoliberal dictates of development and capitalist criteria of productivity. I also address the small grower experience and the tensions that accordingly exist within the local population.

In the concluding chapter, I recap the foregoing and expand on the conclusions that thus can be drawn regarding the appropriate object of criminological study. To aid this discussion, I draw on several concepts that, although not introduced as part of this study's conceptual and theoretical framework in Chap. 2, nonetheless carry relevance for the discussion and, as critical afterthoughts, should be read as an invitation to take the debate on the fundamental matters addressed in this book further.[19] I close with suggestions for future research directions.

Notes

1. A note on terminology: "Oil palm" refers to the oil palm tree and its fruits; "palm oil", on the other hand, is the vegetable oil that is extracted from the fruits of the oil palm tree.
2. The kernel of the oil palm fruit moreover consists of oil cake or palm kernel cake, which is mainly used for animal feed.
3. It is important to note that these targets are pursued in an overall framework that fails to question contemporary patterns of production

and consumption, projected levels of economic growth, and a continuously growing transport sector (Dauvergne and Neville 2009; Levidow and Paul 2010; Franco et al. 2010).

4. Understood as a metaphor referring to entrenched geopolitical power imbalances, it "references an entire history of colonialism, neo-imperialism, and differential economic and social change through which large inequalities in living standards, life expectancy, and access to resources are maintained" (Dados and Connell 2012: 13; see also Carrington et al. 2016).
5. This leaves untouched the effects of agroindustry-related emissions of methane (CH_4) and nitrous oxide (N_2O). These are two greenhouse gases with a much higher global warming potential than CO_2: the global warming potential of methane is said to be 25 times larger than that of carbon dioxide, whereas in the case of nitrous oxide it is almost 300 times larger (Smolker et al. 2008: 63; Don et al. 2012: 374).
6. As mulch, for instance. Mulch is a protective layer applied to the soil to enhance moisture retention or improve the fertility of a soil.
7. The concept of "food regime" should be understood, in the words of McMichael (2009a: 281), as "not about food per se, but about the relations within which food is produced, and through which capitalism is produced and reproduced".
8. Henceforth, for purposes of consistency, I use the term "biofuels" only with reference to policy and industry discourse.
9. The others being mining, transport, innovation, and housing.
10. Notably, of the produce in Colombia's western palm oil production zone—by and large constituted by Tumaco, the main focus of this study—69.4% was exported in 2013 (Fedepalma 2014).
11. Plan Colombia is a United States' counternarcotics and counterinsurgency aid package that entered into force in 2000. Under the pretext of combatting drug trafficking, to which terrorism was added later on, it consists primarily of military assistance and funding. For a critical account, see Stokes (2005).
12. Rather than a method, ethnography is a methodological approach followed towards obtaining an in-depth understanding of micro-level interactions, practices, perceptions, and meanings, *situating these in their broader context*—i.e. viewed against the broader structures of power and control in which they are embedded—and hence adding to empirical and theoretical understanding (Zaitch et al. 2010).

13. The Colombian palm oil industry is (as of yet) not a prime target of foreign direct investment, but still mostly controlled by domestic corporations.
14. For a comprehensive analysis of the continuities and changes over time regarding the dynamics of extractivist modes of accumulation, including reflection on the "neo-extractivism" of some supposedly more progressive post-neoliberalist Latin American governments, see Veltmeyer and Petras (2014b), Seoane (2012), Acosta (2013), and Grigera and Álvarez (2013).
15. Unless stated otherwise, throughout this book, all translations are mine.
16. The article originally appeared in *Issues in Criminology* in 1970.
17. To an extent this argument has been invoked to insist on the wider relevance of a green perspective for mainstream criminology, i.e. even where environmental harm *as such* does not constitute a crime, such harm can be a contributory factor in the genesis of "real" crime and thus carries importance also for more conventional, mainstream, or orthodox criminology (Potter 2014).
18. E.g. working for organizations like Fedepalma, Cenipalma, and Cordeagropaz.
19. Most notably, these concepts include clearance, ecocide, cultural genocide, and—after brief initial mention in Chap. 6—neoliberal multiculturalism.

References

Acosta, A. (2013). Extractivism and neoextractivism: Two sides of the same curse. In M. Lang & D. Mokrani (Eds.), *Beyond development: Alternative visions from Latin America* (pp. 61–86). Amsterdam: Transnational Institute and Rosa Luxemburg Foundation.

Alimonda, H. (2011). La colonialidad de la naturaleza. Una aproximación a la Ecología Política Latinoamericana. In H. Alimonda (Ed.), *La Naturaleza colonizada. Ecología política y minería en América Latina* (pp. 21–58). Buenos Aires: CLASCO.

Altieri, M. (2009). Green desserts: Monocultures and their impact on biodiversity. In M. S. Emanuelli, J. Jonsén, & S. Monsalve Suárez, (Eds.), *Red sugar, green deserts. Latin American report on monocultures and violations of the human rights to adequate food and housing, to water, to land and to territory* (pp. 67–76). Halmstad: FIAN International.

Borras, S. M., Jr., & Franco, J. C. (2012). Global land grabbing and trajectories of agrarian change: A preliminary analysis. *Journal of Agrarian Change, 12*(1), 34–59.

Carrere, R. (Ed.). (2001). *The bitter fruit of oil palm: Dispossession and deforestation*. London: World Rainforest Movement.

Carrington, K., Hogg, R., & Sozzo, M. (2016). Southern criminology. *British Journal of Criminology, 56*(1), 1–20.

Castiblanco, C., Etter, A., & Ramirez, A. (2015a). Impacts of oil palm expansion in Colombia: What do socioeconomic indicators show? *Land Use Policy, 44,* 31–43.

Castiblanco, C., Moreno, A., & Etter, A. (2015b). Impact of policies and subsidies in agribusiness: The case of oil palm and biofuels in Colombia. *Energy Economics, 49,* 676–686.

Cazaux, G. (1999). Beauty and the beast: Animal abuse from a non-speciesist criminological perspective. *Crime, Law and Social Change, 31*(2), 105–126.

Cerdas Vega, G. (2009). Monocultures and agrofuels: Key elements for debate. In M. S. Emanuelli, J. Jonsén, & S. Monsalve Suárez, (Eds.), *Red sugar, green deserts. Latin American report on monocultures and violations of the human rights to adequate food and housing, to water, to land and to territory* (pp. 49–65). Halmstad: FIAN International.

Dados, N., & Connell, R. (2012). The global south. *Contexts, 11*(1), 12–13.

Dangond Lacouture, L. F. (2014). Palma de aceite: compromiso con el progreso y la convivencia. *Revista Palmas, 35*(3), 129–133.

Danielsen, F., Beukema, H., Burgess, N. D., Parish, F., Brühl, C. A., Donald, P. F., et al. (2009). Biofuel plantations on forested lands: Double jeopardy for biodiversity and climate. *Conservation Biology, 23*(2), 348–358.

Dauvergne, P., & Neville, K. J. (2009). The changing North-South and South-South political economy of biofuels. *Third World Quarterly, 30*(6), 1087–1102.

Dauvergne, P., & Neville, K. J. (2010). Forests, food, and fuel in the tropics: The uneven social and ecological consequences of the emerging political economy of biofuels. *The Journal of Peasant Studies, 37*(4), 631–660.

Departamento Nacional de Planeación (DNP). (2008). *Lineamientos de política para promover la producción sostenible de biocombustibles en Colombia. Documento Conpes 3510*. Bogotá: DNP.

Departamento Nacional de Planeación (DNP). (2011). *Plan Nacional de Desarrollo 2010–2014: Prosperidad para todos*. Tomo 1. Bogotá: DNP.

Don, A., Osborne, B., Hastings, A., Skiba, U., Carter, M. S., Drewer, J., et al. (2012). Land-use change to bioenergy production in Europe: Implications for the greenhouse gas balance and soil carbon. *Global Change Biology Bioenergy, 4,* 372–391.

Donnermeyer, J. F., & DeKeseredy, W. S. (2014). *Rural criminology*. Abingdon: Routledge.

Escobar, A. (2008). *Territories of difference: Place, movements, life, redes*. Durham, NC: Duke University Press.

European Commission (EC). (2009). *Directive 2009/28/EC on the promotion of the use of energy from renewable sources*. European Parliament and the Council of the European Union.

Fedepalma. (2000). Visión de la palmicultura colombiana al 2020. *Revista Palmas, 21*(2), 3–6.

Fedepalma. (2002). *The oil palm agroindustry in Colombia* [CD ROM, promotional video]. Ríos, O. dir. Bogotá: Fedepalma.

Fedepalma. (2005). *Anuario Estadístico 2005/Statistical yearbook 2005. La agroindustria de la palma de aceite en Colombia y en el mundo/The oil palm agroindustry in Colombia and the world, 2000–2004*. Bogotá: Fedepalma.

Fedepalma. (2006). *La Agroindustria de la Palma de Aceite en Colombia*. Bogotá: Fedepalma.

Fedepalma. (2014). *Anuario Estadístico 2014/Statistical yearbook 2014. La agroindustria de la palma de aceite en Colombia y en el mundo/The oil palm agroindustry in Colombia and the world, 2009–2013*. Bogotá: Fedepalma.

Fitzherbert, E. B., Struebig, M. J., Morel, A., Danielsen, F., Brühl, C. A., Donald, P. F., et al. (2008). How will oil palm expansion affect biodiversity? *Trends in Ecology & Evolution, 23*(10), 538–545.

Franco, J., Levidow, L., Fig, D., Goldfarb, L., Hönicke, M., & Mendonça, M. L. (2010). Assumptions in the European Union biofuels policy: Frictions with experiences in Germany, Brazil and Mozambique. *The Journal of Peasant Studies, 37*(4), 661–698.

Giarracca, N., & Teubal, M. (2014). Argentina: Extractivist dynamics of soy production and open-pit mining. In H. Veltmeyer & J. Petras (Eds.), *The new extractivism: A post-neoliberal development model or imperialism of the twenty-first century?* (pp. 47–79). London: Zed Books.

Gerasimchuk, I., & Koh, P. Y. (2013). *The EU biofuel policy and palm oil: Cutting subsidies or cutting rainforests?* Winnipeg: The International Institute for Sustainable Development (IISD).
Gibbs, H. K., Johnston, M., Foley, J. A., Holloway, T., Monfreda, C., Ramankutty, N., et al. (2008). Carbon payback times for crop-based biofuel expansion in the tropics: The effects of changing yield and technology. *Environmental Research Letters, 3,* 1–10.
Godnick, W., & Klein, D. (2009). *The challenges of supporting 'alternative' economic opportunities for peacebuilding—Perspectives from Colombia.* London: International Alert.
Grigera, J., & Álvarez, L. (2013). Extractivismo y acumulación por desposesión. Un análisis de las explicaciones sobre agronegocios, megaminería y territorio en la Argentina de la postconvertibilidad. *Theomai, 27–28,* 80–97.
Gutiérrez-Gómez, L. (2017). Mining in Colombia: Tracing the harm of neoliberal policies and practices. In D. R. Goyes, H. Mol, A. Brisman, & N. South (Eds.), *Environmental crime in Latin America: The theft of nature and the poisoning of the land.* London: Palgrave Macmillan.
Halsey, M. (1997). Environmental crime: Towards an eco-human rights approach. *Current Issues in Criminal Justice, 8*(3), 217–242.
Halsey, M., & White, R. (1998). Crime, ecophilosophy and environmental harm. *Theoretical Criminology, 2*(3), 345–371.
Harvey, D. (2003). *The new imperialism.* Oxford: Oxford University Press.
Hazlewood, J. A. (2010). Más allá de la crisis económica: CO_2lonialismo y geografías de esperanza. *Íconos. Revista de Ciencias Sociales, 36*(enero), 81–95.
Hillyard, P., Pantazis, C., Tombs, S., & Gordon, D. (Eds.). (2004). *Beyond criminology. Taking harm seriously.* London: Pluto Press.
Lederer, E. M. (2007, October 27). Production of biofuels 'is a crime'. *The Independent* [Online], (Environment). Available from: http://www.independent.co.uk [Accessed 3 February 2015].
Levidow, L., & Paul, H. (2010). Global agrofuel crops as contested sustainability, Part I: Sustaining what development? *Capitalism Nature Socialism, 21*(2), 64–86.
Lynch, M. J., & Stretesky, P. B. (2014). *Exploring green criminology. Towards a green criminological revolution.* Farnham: Ashgate.
McCarthy, J., & Zen, Z. (2010). Regulating the oil palm boom: Assessing the effectiveness of environmental governance approaches to agro-industrial pollution in Indonesia. *Law & Policy, 32*(1), 153–179.

McClanahan, B. (2014). Green and grey: Water justice. *Criminalization and Resistance. Critical Criminology, 22*(3), 403–418.
McMichael, P. (2009). A food regime analysis of the 'world food crisis'. *Agriculture and Human Values, 26*(4), 281–295.
McMichael, P. (2010). Agrofuels in the food regime. *The Journal of Peasant Studies, 37*(4), 609–629.
Mesa Dishington, J. (2014). Palabras del Presidente Ejecutivo de Fedepalma, Jens Mesa Dishington, en la apertura del XLII Congreso Nacional de Cultivadores de Palma de Aceite. *Revista Palmas, 35*(3), 57–64.
Mingorance, F. (2006). *The flow of palm oil Colombia-Belgium/Europe. A study from a human rights perspective.* Brussels: Human Rights Everywhere/Coordination Belge Pour La Colombie.
Mondaca, E. (2017). The Archipelago of Chiloé and the uncertain contours of its future: Coloniality, new extractivism and political-social re-vindication of existence. In D. R. Goyes, H. Mol, A. Brisman, & N. South (Eds.), *Environmental crime in Latin America: The theft of nature and the poisoning of the land.* London: Palgrave Macmillan.
Moore, J. W. (2000). Environmental crises and the metabolic rift in world-historical perspective. *Organization & Environment, 13*(2), 123–158.
Nestlé. (2013). *Progress Report Palm Oil.* Available from: http://www.nestle.com/asset-library/documents/creating-shared-value/responsible-sourcing/progress-report-palm-oil-autumn-2013.pdf [Accessed 27 January 2015].
Oosterveer, P. (2014). Promoting sustainable palm oil: Viewed from a global networks and flows perspective. *Journal of Cleaner Production,* http://dx.doi.org/10.1016/j.jclepro.2014.01.019 [ahead of print].
Oslender, U. (2007). Revisiting the hidden transcript: Oral tradition and black cultural politics in the Colombian Pacific coast region. *Environment and Planning D: Society and Space, 25*(6), 1103–1129.
Ospina Bozzi, M. L. (2007). *Los rostros de la palma.* Bogotá: Fedepalma.
Passas, N., & Goodwin, N. (2004). Introduction: A crime by any other name. In N. Passas & N. Goodwin (Eds.), *It's legal but it ain't right: Harmful social consequences of legal industries* (pp. 1–27). Ann Arbor, MI: University of Michigan Press.
Pirker, J., Mosnier, A., Kraxner, F., Havlík, P., & Obersteiner, M. (2016). What are the limits to oil palm expansion? *Global Environmental Change, 40,* 73–81.
Potter, G. R. (2014). The criminogenic effects of environmental harm: Bringing a 'green' perspective to mainstream criminology. In T. Spapens, R. White, & M. Kluin (Eds.), *Environmental crime and its victims: Perspectives within green criminology* (pp. 7–21). Farnham: Ashgate.

Rist, L., Feintrenie, L., & Levang, P. (2010). The livelihood impacts of oil palm: Smallholders in Indonesia. *Biodiversity and Conservation, 19*(4), 1009–1024.

Rival, A., & Levang, P. (2015). The oil palm (*Elaeis guineensis*): Research challenges beyond controversies. *Palms, 59*(1), 33–49.

Rojas-Páez, G. (2017). Understanding environmental harm and justice claims in the global south: Crimes of the powerful and peoples' resistance. In D. R. Goyes, H. Mol, A. Brisman, & N. South (Eds.), *Environmental crime in Latin America: The theft of nature and the poisoning of the land.* London: Palgrave Macmillan.

RSPO. (2013). *Why palm oil matters in your everyday life.* Kuala Lumpur: RSPO Secretariat.

Santos, J. M. (2014). Mensaje del Excelentísimo Señor Presidente de la República, Dr. Juan Manuel Santos Calderón a la comunidad palmera. *Revista Palmas, 35*(3), 134–135.

Sayer, J., Ghazoul, J., Nelson, P., & Boedhihartono, A. K. (2012). Oil palm expansion transforms tropical landscapes and livelihoods. *Global Food Security, 1*(2), 114–119.

Seeboldt, S. (2010). Palm oil in Colombia: Shifting power play? In S. Seeboldt & Y. Salinas Abdala (Eds.), *Responsibility and sustainability of the palm oil industry. Are the principles and criteria of the RSPO feasible in Colombia?* (pp. 15–39). The Hague: Oxfam Novib/Indepaz.

Seoane, J. (2012). Neoliberalismo y ofensiva extractivista: Actualidad de la acumulación por despojo, desafíos de Nuestra América. *Theomai, 26.*

Sellin, T. (1938). Culture conflict and crime. *The American Journal of Sociology, 44*(1), 97–103.

South, N. (1998). A green field for criminology? A proposal for a perspective. *Theoretical Criminology, 2*(2), 211–233.

Sutherland, E. H. (1940). White-collar criminality. *American Sociological Review, 5*(1), 1–12.

Szasz, A. (1986). Corporations, organized crime, and the disposal of hazardous waste: An examination of the making of a criminogenic regulatory structure. *Criminology, 24*(1), 1–27.

Tappan, P. W. (1947). Who is the criminal? *American Sociological Review, 12*(1), 96–102.

Tenthoff, M., & Eventon, R. (2013). *A 'veritable revolution': The land restitution law and the transformation of rural Colombia.* Amsterdam: Transnational Institute.

Vélez, I. (Ed.). (2010). *Misión internacional para la verificación del impacto de los agrocombustibles en 5 zonas afectadas por los monocultivos de palma aceitera y caña de azúcar en Colombia*. Bogotá: CENSAT Agua Viva.
Vélez, H., & Vélez, I. (2008). Los espejismos de los agrocombustibles. In I. Vélez (Ed.), *Agrocombustibles "Llenando tanques, vaciando territorios"* (pp. 15–58). Bogotá: CENSAT Agua Viva.
Veltmeyer, H., & Petras, J. (2014a). Introduction. In H. Veltmeyer & J. Petras (Eds.), *The new extractivism: A post-neoliberal development model or imperialism of the twenty-first century?* (pp. 1–20). London: Zed Books.
Veltmeyer, H., & Petras, J. (2014b). A new model or extractive imperialism? In H. Veltmeyer & J. Petras (Eds.), *The new extractivism: A post-neoliberal development model or imperialism of the twenty-first century?* (pp. 21–46). London: Zed Books.
Walters, R. (2010). Toxic atmospheres air pollution, trade and the politics of regulation. *Critical Criminology, 18*(4), 307–323.
Walters, R. (2011). *Eco Crime and Genetically Modified Food*. Abingdon: Routledge.
White, R. (2002). Environmental harm and the political economy of consumption. *Social Justice, 29*(1–2), 82–102.
White, R. (2008). *Crimes against nature. Environmental criminology and ecological justice*. Cullompton: Willan Publishing.
White, R. (2011). *Transnational environmental crime. Towards an eco-global criminology*. London: Routledge.
World Growth. (2011). *The economic benefit of palm oil to Indonesia*. Arlington: World Growth Palm Oil Green Development Campaign.
Reiman, J. (2007). *The rich get richer and the poor get prison: Ideology, class, and criminal justice* (8th ed.). Boston: Pearson/Allyn & Bacon.
Schwendinger, H., & Schwendinger, J. (1975). Defenders of order or guardians of human rights? In I. Taylor, P. Walton, & J. Young (Eds.), *Critical Criminology* (pp. 113–146). London: Routledge & Kegan Paul Ltd.
Smolker, R., Tokar, B., & Petermann, A. (2008). *The real cost of Agrofuels: Impacts on food, forests, peoples and the climate*. Global Forest Coalition.
Stokes, D. (2005). *America's other war: Terrorizing Colombia*. London: Zed Books Ltd.
Zaitch, D., Mortelmans, D., & Decorte, T. (2010). Participerende observatie in de criminologie. In T. Decorte & D. Zaitch (Eds.), *Kwalitative methoden en technieken in de criminologie* (2nd ed., pp. 262–314). Leuven: Acco.

2

The Play of Power in the Politics of Harm

Many of the adverse social and environmental impacts associated with the palm oil industry that were mentioned in the previous chapter exceed strictly legalistic definitions of crime. Criminological analysis of this context therefore asks for a broader concept of harm. The notion that strict adherence to a legalistic definition of crime excludes a whole range of serious and widespread harms from criminological analysis has led a growing number of criminologists to argue for a reconsideration of the focus of criminology towards a broader engagement with harm. Yet there is still a profound lack of consensus about the perceived theoretical and political validity of broader notions of harm as an appropriate object of criminological analysis, with ongoing debate over *how* to conceptualize a criminologically relevant notion of harm and *whether* such objectives and the corresponding types of analysis should even be pursued at all (e.g. Hillyard et al. 2004; Michalowski 2009; Potter 2013).

H. Mol, *The Politics of Palm Oil Harm*, Palgrave Studies in Green Criminology, DOI 10.1007/978-3-319-55378-8_2

To advance this debate, this study puts forward a theoretical and analytical approach to a criminologically relevant, critical engagement with harm that draws on and contributes to green criminological analyses of the extractive industries. In this chapter, I explicate what this approach entails, how it redirects the harm debate within criminology, and why criminology is in need of such redirection. Central to my argument is the notion that harm is contested and that this contestedness exists on two levels. Existing debate over the appropriate object of criminological analysis is principally centred on the *academic* contestedness of harm *within criminological theory and analysis*. Considerations of power are generally not absent from these works; at times implicit, at times more explicit, reference is made to the distribution of power and wealth to explain and critique what practices are dealt with as crime and which ones are not. Still, the argument put forward here is that, to enhance our understanding of the power relations and mechanisms that invest discourses and practices of harm and that draw the boundaries between the legal and the illegal, we should shift our criminological lenses to a second level of contestedness. That is, harm is also contested in the broader social field. Although the academic debate is not uninformed by the *on-the-ground* contestedness of harm, criminology has not granted this dimension the central attention it warrants.

In what follows, first the green criminological perspectives and concepts that carry relevance for the purposes of the harm approach here suggested will be addressed. Subsequently, following on from what was outlined by way of introduction in the previous chapter, the various positions on harm within critical criminology will be addressed in more detail. This then takes us to the crucial turning point in the chapter where I redirect the focus to the politics of harm. After this, the contours of an explanatory framework for the operation of power in the politics of harm in the context of Colombian palm oil production will be laid out. I thereby draw on the political economy framework of analysis that generally underpins critical, green criminological studies of crime and harm related to processes of natural resource exploitation (e.g. White 2011; Stretesky et al. 2014) and also point out the need for a more refined and integrated theorization of harm, power, and legality.

A Critical, Green Perspective on Harm

As noted by White (2013b), green criminology is not a unified field but has developed into a fairly broad area of scholarship wherein a diversity of substantive concerns, conceptual foci, theoretical positions, and political orientations finds common ground in the perceived need to grant more specific criminological attention to environmental issues. Below I expand on three key directions in which green criminology has sought to rethink crime and the criminological endeavour, specifying also how and to what extent these notions figure in this study.

Extending the Focus from the Human to the Nonhuman

Green perspectives extend the disciplinary reach of criminology beyond exclusively human-centred analysis towards a more encompassing concern with the impacts of environmental harm on humans, nonhumans, and the natural environment. Whether something comes to be defined as an environmental issue to be dealt with as crime, or whether it comes to be defined as an environmental issue at all, is dependent on philosophical principles, questions of power, and particular interests (White 2008: 4–5). Let us first consider some of the eco-philosophical principles that underpin our understanding of the human–environment nexus and societal and individual attitudes towards nature and that lend themselves to different conceptualizations of environmental harm and crime as a result (Halsey and White 1998). At the outset, I should state that there lies a world of subtleties, complexities, and significant overlap between different eco-philosophies (see, e.g., Halsey 1997) and that it is beyond the purposes of this study to elaborate on this. Most relevant here are critiques of the type of anthropocentric or human-centred attitudes towards nature that rest on purely instrumental views of the natural world and that reduce nonhuman nature to human property. From an anthropocentric stance, nature generally tends to be viewed and treated as an exterior realm that is open to human exploitation and appropriation, as "natural capital" at our disposal (Plumwood 1991; Halsey and White 1998). From such views, environmental harm is problematized only to the extent that it impedes human interests. It is thereby moreover *sectional* human interests that are often of decisive influence.

In contrast, an ecocentric or socioecological approach rests on the notion that there exists a substantial degree of continuity and interdependence between humans, animal and plant species, and the broader natural environment. Yet it *also* perceives a level of distance and distinctiveness that demands that human beings use, interact, and live with nature in sustainable ways in order to minimize or avoid generating adverse impacts (Halsey and White 1998; Plumwood 1991). Thus considered, humans are neither superior to nonhuman nature nor "just another" species but instead have specific responsibilities towards each other and towards nonhuman nature so as to sustain both current and future generations (Halsey 1997; South 2008). Even when an ecocentric perspective is adhered to, the focus regarding who or what is being victimized may vary. An ecocentric perspective or socioecological approach to a particular environmental problem is, for instance, not incompatible with a primary emphasis on how this affects certain *human populations*.

In regard to who or what is victimized, criminological engagement with environmental harm occurs along three intersecting, and potentially conflicting, lines of enquiry: (i) from the viewpoint of environmental justice, analysis is primarily centred on the human consequences of environmental issues; (ii) from the viewpoint of ecological justice, analysis centres on the adverse impacts of environmental crime and harm on the integrity of the natural environment at large; and (iii) from the viewpoint of species justice, the concern lies with the harms and crimes perpetrated against animal species, which may refer to individual cases of animal abuse, institutionalized abuse, as well as habitat destruction stemming from broadly accepted social and economic activities (White 2013a). Particular ideas of eco-justice (White 2013a) thereby underpin different conceptions of rights. Thus, from an environmental justice perspective, environmental rights are thought of as a necessary extension of human rights, considering that access to and the use of a healthy environment are crucial components of social justice. In view of the intrinsic worth of nonhuman nature on the other hand, ecological justice and species justice can be seen to entail the need to extend the reach of rights to the natural environment and animal species.

Ideas of eco-justice are also bound up with notions of power. Environmental justice—from which this study takes its cue—has been defined by White (2013a) as "the distribution of environments among peoples in terms of access to, and use of, specific natural resources in defined geographical areas" (White 2013a: 15). As a consequence of power differentials operating along lines of gender, class, ethnicity, race, geopolitical location, age, and so on (Stephens 1996; Wachholz 2007; Lynch and Stretesky 2003), environmental problems are often shifted onto, or disproportionately affect, particular human groups. Thus, environmental *injustice* is intricately linked to social systems of oppression and differentiation that lead to the differential victimization of certain human populations and individuals (Lynch and Stretesky 2003). It follows that justice, rights, harm, and power intertwine. However, understanding how harm comes about and persists requires an explicit focus on harm vis-à-vis power. It is from this angle that rights enter the analysis in Chap. 5 (centred on how the ground has been, and is being, prepared for palm oil production), Chap. 6 (which analyses the constructions, practices, and perceived and lived realities of harm in the context of cultivation and production processes of the palm oil industry), and the concluding chapter.

Extending and Deepening the Critical Criminological Tradition

As hinted at above, environmental issues can also be assessed in terms of the power relations that imbue environmental crime and harm. As I have argued elsewhere (Mol 2013), how power produces and operates through green issues is interlinked with the ordering of an array of social and socioecological relations. In the analysis of the social and environmental harms of palm oil, questions of power pertain to who or what is being harmed; where (geographically) such harm is experienced or transferred to; the causes or driving forces behind these harms; how alleged harms are conceptualized or denied; and so on.

Analysis of the multiple ways in which power operates through social differentiation based on class, race, ethnicity, gender, and persistent colonial patterns of domination and exploitation has increasingly been finding its way into critical criminological analysis. The critical criminological tradition arose in the late 1960s to advocate a praxis-oriented, structural analysis of power and an attendant critique of existing (inequitable) social arrangements in the study of crime and deviance. The founding principles of this critical project were perhaps best exemplified by, and for the first time thoroughly spelled out in, the landmark book "*The New Criminology*" by Taylor et al. (1973).

Later, the limitations of the initial concern with what was primarily the class character of crime, crime control, and criminal justice procedures began to be laid bare, realizing that class was but one component in a range of power relations that criminologists should focus their energies on. Progressively, considerations of race, patriarchy, gender, culture, and so on have thus gained a more significant place in criminological analysis.[1] Donnermeyer and DeKeseredy (2014: 37), for instance, in their exposition of a critical rural criminology, clearly articulate that it is crucial to take account of, *inter alia*, "the patriarchal and ethnic relations that also control our society", all the while being attentive to macro-forces as well as micro-relations.

Green criminology, too, embeds itself in, continues, and deepens the critical tradition by taking the analysis and the interrogation of power into the socioecological realm, extending it to human–nonhuman dualisms, and examining the systemic nature of environmental crime and harm. Premised on an attentiveness to "the ability of powerful groups to manipulate and use race, class, gender *and the environment* to preserve the basis of their power" (Lynch 1990: 1, emphasis added), the "greening of criminology" was first explicitly called for over two decades ago by Lynch (1990). More recently, a strand of green perspectives has once more taken up considerations of political economy in the analysis of environmental crime and harm (Lynch et al. 2013; Stretesky et al. 2014). Analysis and theorization along these lines centre primarily on global political and economic structures, processes, and relations that are being managed by standards of economic performance that fail to observe the environmental and social costs of production models, being geared instead to the accumulation of capital and economic-reductionist criteria of wealth (Ruggiero and South 2013). This is closely linked to ideologies that tie human welfare and societal progress to economic growth and likewise seek the "solutions" to environmental problems in market expansion, individualized forms of responsibilization, and technological innovation (White 2011; Stretesky et al. 2014). All too often existing harms are perpetuated or exacerbated in the process, or new forms of harm are generated.[2]

Stretesky et al. (2014) draw on Schnaiberg's theory of the "treadmill of production" to theorize the systemic nature of environmental harm. They argue that the expansionary logic of capitalism and the ecological additions and withdrawals central to capitalist production cause ecological disorganization.[3] Also, existing regulatory frameworks and the dynamics of law enforcement—in other words, the extent to which environmental crimes and harms can be and are officially dealt with—by and large reflect and reproduce the power configurations of contemporary capitalist society (Stretesky et al. 2014).

The present work is strongly committed to the type of structurally oriented analysis that seeks to theorize environmental crime and harm with an explicit view on power, conflict, and political economy. I will, however, also argue for the need for a more multiple view of power.

Transcending the Legal–Illegal Divide

Despite growing environmental awareness, as well as legislative and judicial gains in relation to environmental matters, there is still a substantial discrepancy between official definitions of environmental crime on the one hand, and *legal* (i.e. lawful) environmental harms endured by humans, plant and animal species, environments, and ecosystems on the other hand. Owing to this mismatch between acts legally designated as environmentally harmful or problematic, versus ecologically informed notions of harm (Halsey and White 1998; White 2011), a central endeavour of green criminology is to rethink and theorize "harm", and the legal–illegal divide, within criminology. As Halsey (2004) states:

> [C]riminology should not be constrained by a strictly delimited field of analysis. Indeed, the vitality of the discipline depends on its capacity to subject to critique events and processes which, when viewed through one lens or another, are apt to attract the label 'harm' or a closely associated term. Indeed, a key critical criminological task is to bring to light factors which function to divide criminal from so-called normal, routine or acceptable practice. (Halsey 2004: 837)

As touched upon previously, the routine character and broad societal acceptance of acts and processes that generate (or are conducive to) environmental harm must be viewed in terms of the economic and political dictates that inscribe global capitalism, and the construction of needs and corresponding patterns of production and consumption in late modern consumer culture (White 2002; Stretesky et al. 2014; O'Brien 2008; Brisman and South 2014). South (1998: 226) for that matter has noted that: "Late modern society is a consumption society but this also means it is a "throwaway", "discard and dispose" society, a society producing more and more desired goods but also more and more undesired "bads"—waste, effluent, toxins and so forth". Arguably, we can even go as far as to state that the "discard and dispose" logic signalled by South (1998) extends to whole groups of seemingly expendable human beings, nature, and nonhuman life (see, e.g., O'Brien 2008).

In their critique of narrow corporate constructions of environmental problems, Lynch and Stretesky (2003) elaborate on the contrast between environmental justice and corporate versions of "green". The latter version rests on a depoliticized view not only of environmental problems but also of environmental law, regulation, and enforcement; points at consumption and individual behaviour as sources of (and hence the key to solving) environmental harm; and frames as environmentally problematic only practices officially defined as illegal. Hence, its definitive feature is that it leaves untouched the structural arrangements and underlying power differentials that are at the basis of environmental victimization. In view of this, Lynch and Stretesky (2003, 2014) insist that a critical green criminology must take a firm political stance in analysing and confronting environmental issues.

Although I concur with the view that considerations of power should be central in the criminological analysis of environmental crime—and, by implication, *harm*—I differ on the view advanced by Lynch and Stretesky (2014) that it is essential that criminologists thereby strive to base their analyses on objective, scientifically grounded notions of harm. A central argument of this chapter (and book) is that it is much more insightful, and in fact crucial, to approach the conceptualization of harm, too, as an unequivocally political process. Before elaborating on this point, in order to situate the foregoing in wider perspective, I will first turn in more detail to the longstanding debate over (social) harm within criminology at large.

Beyond Crime: Criminological Concern with "Harm"

The origins of the debate over criminology's core organizing referents can be traced back to the time of Edwin Sutherland's presidential address to the American Sociological Society in 1939, where Sutherland (1940) directed attention to the crime-equivalent nature of the social harms perpetrated by "white collar criminals". The discussion thus instigated has lost none of its vigour or relevance over time. Yet the directions that have been taken since are manifold: from calls for a move "beyond criminology" (Hillyard et al. 2004), to expressions of concern that some harm perspectives appear to discard the potential for progress *within* criminology (Hughes 2006; Muncie 2005), to the resolute stance that criminologists are committing a conceptual and analytical error when blurring the categories of crime and harm (Green and Ward 2000; Lasslett 2010).

There is always the risk of oversimplification when trying to translate a longstanding debate into a categorization of its key conceptual premises. Nevertheless, in my view, it is possible to discern three main positions from which and between which the debate over the conceptualization and the criminological relevance of harm has developed. A first strand of works insists on the crime-equivalent character—in scope, severity, and nature—of a variety of social harms (Sutherland 1940; Schwendinger and Schwendinger 1975; Michalowski 2009). This strand of works rests on the notion that these legal harms can be legitimately incorporated into criminological analysis by broadening the definition of crime. Thereby the objective is not necessarily to criminalize the practices or relations in question, but to *analytically* deal with these as (equivalent to) crime. Diverging theoretical and political orientations notwithstanding, the common denominator in these works is the view that criminological analysis must address the variety of social harms that escape scrutiny for being outside official, legalistic definitions of crime. Such endeavours to broaden the definition of crime to the inclusion of a wider set of harms are subject to critique from two distinct and mutually exclusive camps.

On one end, social harm-oriented scholars question whether it is theoretically accurate and politically useful to maintain the conceptual distinction between crime and harm (Hillyard and Tombs 2004; Pemberton 2004). From their point of view, no matter how critical, a focus on crime maintains and reinstates the "myth of crime" and, by doing so, adds legitimacy to an inequitable and ineffective criminal justice system (Hillyard and Tombs 2004). This has led to calls for a shift away from crime to an all-encompassing focus on social harm and, in the long run, the altogether abandoning of criminology. While it has been suggested to refer to this field of study as "zemiology", this term does not enjoy broad acceptance (Hillyard et al. 2004: 276). Pemberton (2007) for instance has pointed out that "zemiology", as the study of *all* harms, is not the preferred term to refer to the study of *socially mediated* harm, which is what the political and theoretical project of a social harm approach is principally concerned with.

However, there is another line of critique that stands in sharp contrast to social harm perspectives in the way it takes issue with a broadening of the object of criminological study. For these scholars, however, their critique rests precisely on the argument that the concepts of crime and harm are distinct categories *that ought to be retained as such.* It is asserted that crime and harm cannot and should not be conflated, nor merged for analytical purposes (Ward 2004; Green and Ward 2000; Lasslett 2010). In any given historical and social context, particular sets of social relations and practices assume the form of "crime" and come to be enforced as such, while others—no matter how harmful—are tolerated and/or socially accepted (Matthews 2009; Lea 2009). It is therefore considered incoherent for criminologists to study social harm; notwithstanding the significance of harm as a sociological phenomenon, harm as such, it is argued, is not the sociological phenomenon that falls within the scope of *criminological* analysis.

Below, each of these three positions will be discussed in more detail. Subsequent to this outline, I suggest a distinct focus that redirects our criminological engagement with harm. In the concluding chapter, I reflect once more on the three positions here addressed in the light of the findings of this study and the discussions developed throughout the book.

Off with the Old Criminologies[4]: Broadening the Definition of Crime

It is reasonable to see in Sutherland's pioneering work on white-collar crime (1940, 1983) the early foundations of the debate over criminology's appropriate object of study. Directing long due attention to the crimes of the powerful, Sutherland argued that the social harms perpetrated by "persons of respectability and high socio-economic status in the course of their occupation" (1983: 7) are not categorically different from conventional crimes and *are* crimes indeed. This challenged conventional depictions of crime as disproportionately or all but completely concentrated in the lower classes. The core of Sutherland's argument rests on the view that what sets the crimes of the powerful apart from the crimes committed by persons of low socio-economic status is that they are *differentially dealt with*; rather than being dealt with through the criminal justice system, the crimes of the powerful are taken up by administrative and civil procedures and hence become neither perceived nor officially labelled as crime.

By rejecting exclusive adherence to definitions of crime that encompass only the perpetration of acts that are in violation of the criminal law and have been tried and penalized in criminal court accordingly (cf. Tappan 1947), Sutherland extended the reach of the definition of crime to any act legally defined as socially injurious and for which the legal provision of a penalty is in place, irrespective of the type of legal statute under consideration. This therefore included civil and administrative law. However, even if rejecting narrow, criminal law definitions of crime, Sutherland did not interrogate the power dynamics and structures at the very basis of prevailing constructions, and the functioning, of a particular concept of crime and the institutions bound up with it. On this point, critical criminologists such as Taylor et al. (1973) challenged Sutherland's work, lamenting the lack of "examination of the ways in which white-collar infractions were (and are) functional to industrial-capitalist societies at points in their development" (Taylor et al. 1973: 274).

Where Sutherland failed to truly challenge the legal and ethical boundaries set by the State (Schwendinger and Schwendinger 1975), the Schwendingers went further, claiming that the legal definition of crime in capitalist society reflects and operates in the service of a bourgeois morality that functions to reproduce a repressive and exploitative class system (1977). To avoid complicity in the reproduction of the existing social order via acceptance of the legal definition of crime handed down by the State, the Schwendingers put forward a human rights-based concept of crime, consistent with which the criminal character of social systems and practices follows from the latter's violation of basic human rights. Imperialism, racism, sexism, and poverty are thus considered crimes that demand criminological analysis (Schwendinger and Schwendinger 1975).

But where would Schwendinger and Schwendinger draw the line as regards the criminal status of human rights violations? Are all violations criminal, and as such the legitimate object of criminological scrutiny? Stan Cohen (1993) considered this aspect of the Schwendingers' position problematic. Hence, while in principle urging criminologists to pursue a more thorough consideration of the violation of human rights in their analyses of the crimes of the powerful, Cohen insisted that criminologists should restrict themselves to the study of evidently criminal violations of human rights. According to Cohen, the Schwendingers had failed to establish the criminal character of human rights violations, which led him to denounce their unqualified, overly broad reliance on human rights rhetoric as a "moral crusade" (1993: 98).

One sees a focus on the "evidently criminal" also reflected in a more general reluctance in criminological work on crimes of the powerful to stray too far from existing legal frameworks. As pointed out by Michalowski (2009), the majority of criminologists dedicated to the study of corporate, political, and state crime continue to hold on to some form of "legal formalism". That is to say, they study acts that are formally prohibited by law, albeit in a legal framework that transcends domestic criminal law, from a broader and complementary focus on international law (e.g. Kauzlarich 1995; Rothe and Friedrichs 2006). On a pragmatic level, it is argued that such adherence to the legal framework adds legitimacy to criminological analysis, which may enhance the acceptance of such work at the institutional level and by the general public, as well as increasing the chances of assimilation of this type of analysis into the mainstream of criminology (Kauzlarich 1995). However, as Michalowski (2009) rightfully observes:

> The problem, as I see it, is that limiting criminological analyses to only those harmful actions that have been prohibited through the workings of hegemonic power structures inherent in law formation renders criminological inquiry constitutive of the dominant social order rather than analyses of that order. (Michalowski 2009: 307)

Michalowski therefore questions the reliance on existing legal frameworks, international ones included, as "epistemological warrants" for criminological analysis. According to Michalowski, there are certain acts and processes that, although crime-equivalent in scope and severity, in the light of geopolitical interests and global power imbalances are unlikely to be critically examined under existing legal provisions.[5] Michalowski (2009) has put forward the concept of "analogous social injury" for the criminological analysis of the social relations, political and economic structures, and cultural framework that underpin these crime-equivalent harms. His notion that "studying the non-creation and non-enforcement of laws in the face of significant social injuries is as central to the sociological study of crime as studying the origin and enforcement of established laws" (2009: 320) parallels the assertion by Kramer et al. (2002: 266) that "it is in the differences between crime and not-crime that the underlying dynamics of making law and practicing "justice" are revealed". Within green criminology, a similar argument has been made by Halsey (2004), which I presented earlier. These crucial reflections arguably allow for a more productive engagement with the legal–illegal construct than tendencies to dismiss the concept of crime altogether, as some social harm scholars (see below) suggest. I will return to this later.

Hence, overall, the works that have been addressed in this section problematize strict legalistic definitions of crime and as such challenge the official discourse of crime. However, all make reference to, or retain, *some* concept of crime. In contrast, it is the very discourse and category of crime that is rejected by social harm scholars.

Thinking Harm Outside the Box: Abandoning Criminology?

From the view that a differentiation between criminal and noncriminal harm is theoretically incoherent (Hillyard and Tombs 2004), attempts to decentre the category of "crime" are central to social harm approaches. Insistence on the argument that the designation of certain acts as "crime" and others as "not-crime" is not supported by any intrinsic quality held by the first category, while absent from the latter, draws significantly on Hulsman's (1986) critique of critical criminology and the concept of crime. Hulsman insisted that crime lacks ontological reality and argued that although critical criminologists analyse crime and crime control in view of inequitable power configurations and existing political and economic structures, they do not debunk the concept of crime *as such* (Hulsman 1986).

Social harm scholars, as well as critical criminologists more generally, argue that the image of crime as ontologically real is socially constructed and perpetually reproduced through legislative, judicial, and political processes within national as well as supranational frameworks and discourses of criminal justice (Hillyard et al. 2004; Michalowski 2009). This is claimed to divert attention from other—not infrequently more serious—forms of suffering, and the role of governments, corporations, intergovernmental organizations, and financial institutions in the production and/or persistence of such suffering. The difference between

Michalowski's (2009) notion of "analogous social injury" and Hillyard et al.'s (2004) concept of social harm consists in the open-ended nature of social harm versus the *crime-equivalent* character of analogous social injury (Michalowski 2009), meaning that the latter draws on a certain parallel with acts officially designated as illegal. In contrast, social harm, as a concept and analytical approach, resists analogies with legal definitions of crime. Michalowski's "analogous social injury" thus appears to sit more comfortably with efforts to broaden the concept of crime (see the previous section) than with the social harm perspectives discussed in this section.

Advocates of a focus on social harm question the "theoretical rationale and political utility of retaining a commitment to the analysis of crime, (criminal) law and the criminal justice system" (Hillyard et al. 2004: 1). Both criminological reliance upon existing legal frameworks *and* critical criminological efforts to bring about a broadening of the definition of crime are in this light deemed problematic from the viewpoint that this perpetuates the "myth of crime" and as such reinforces hegemonic, misguided notions of the true nature and extent of harm that people endure throughout their lives (Hillyard and Tombs 2004; Pemberton 2004). Pemberton, even if not denying the political utility of drawing upon existing legal norms and principles to lay bare "the inconsistencies inherent in the 'law and order' project" (2004: 71), problematizes the recourse to legal discourses of harm from the view that this ultimately fails to challenge dominant tendencies to perceive the most serious harms predominantly in terms of criminal justice notions of "crime". He sees this as applying to the normative framework of human rights as a definer of criminal harm, too.

Mainstream criminology *and* critical criminology are thus targeted as ill-positioned to break away from the hegemonic imagery and institutional arsenal built up around the legal category of crime. Criminology's proximity to the state and its apparatus of criminal justice—focused on the intentional actions and moral agency of the individual actor—is held to preclude adequate engagement with the *social* forces that are at the basis of a wide range of wholly preventable harms (Hillyard and Tombs 2004; Gordon 2004; Pemberton 2007). There is as such a strong emphasis on the need for criminologists to engage the systemic character of the social harms that inhere in the social, political, and economic organization of contemporary societies (Tombs and Hillyard 2004).

However, in response to such criticisms it has been argued—in my view rightly so—that "a reconsideration of the parameters of criminology" is already well under way (Muncie 2005; Hughes 2006). One can think for instance of critical criminological studies of crimes of globalization[6] that thoroughly engage the cultural, political, and economic forces conducive to harm (intended or not) and the ways in which these harms are perceived and dealt with (or not) by governments and/or suprastate bodies. As one example of such work, take the in-depth analysis by Rothe et al. (2006) of the sinking of the Senegalese state-owned Le Joola ferry in 2002. There, Rothe et al. analyse the criminogenic contexts that result from the convergence of legacies of colonialism, the dictates of global capital, and structural adjustment and austerity measures imposed by the World Bank and IMF; factors which conditioned expenditure on transportation and infrastructure by the Senegalese State, which ultimately led to the sinking of the Le Joola ferry and the consequent death of 1863 persons. Criminological attention for crimes of omission as one dimension of a "complicity continuum of state crime" (Kauzlarich et al. 2003) likewise moves criminological analysis away from traditional concerns with intent. In addition, major examples can also be found within the field of green criminology; for example, Halsey (1997) on oil as the "life-blood" of the global economic system, and the social and environmental consequences of this taken-for-granted addiction; Boekhout van Solinge (2010) on the local–global dynamics that connect processes of deforestation in the Amazon rainforest to patterns of unmaintainable meat consumption in the west; Zaitch et al. (2014) on natural resource exploitation and the nature and effects of consequent land use change in Latin America; and, for an edited volume on environmental crime and social conflict, Brisman et al. (2015). All such work reflects the potential for critical analysis *within* criminology while at the same time upholding *some* discourse of crime. And perhaps this is precisely the strength of such analyses. I come back to this in the concluding chapter.

Crime Matters: Back to the Core

A third strand of perspectives is critical of both the type of criminological work that broadens the definition of crime *and* of social harm approaches that seek to dissolve the very category of crime and the discourses and institutions bound up with it. These scholars take issue with the shift from the analysis of crime to broader notions of harm, and urge criminologists to revive the study of crime and criminalization. Zedner (2011) for that matter claims that "crime needs to be put firmly back onto the criminological agenda" (p. 272). She emphasizes that acceptance of "crime" as a legal category and as criminology's core organizing referent does not impede asking critical questions regarding "the whys and wherefores of criminalization" and crime control. Against the argument that a social harm approach is better positioned to challenge power, Zedner states (2011: 275):

> To the extent that the problem lies outside the legal category of crime and in the realm of power politics, it is unclear that moving "beyond criminology" would liberate new conceptions of harm from the hierarchical political relations and interest group politics that have bedevilled it thus far. That crime has been mobilized to serve sectional interests, that it takes particular forms, and targets particular social and ethnic groups does not mean that it is incapable of reform. Nor does it mean that any alternative concept would be free from the effects of these embedded structural inequalities. If powerful constituencies mobilize crime for their own political ends, what reason have we to think that social harm, or indeed any other conceptual category (dispute or conflict, for example), would be immune?

Of course, *no* conceptual category, nor any aspect of social life, exists outside of or is immune to power, let alone that it could be liberated from it. The argument put forward by social harm proponents, to be fair, rather seems to revolve around the point that "harm" does not come with the institutional and ideological baggage that to a large extent *is* indeed bound up with "crime"; hence, the notion that, at least in principle, analyses centred on social harm may be better positioned to challenge existing power configurations and structural inequalities.

Other perspectives that seek to reinstate crime as the object of criminological study more explicitly address the relation between crime and harm. This has led to claims that, while overlapping, crime and harm are distinct concepts (Green and Ward 2000; Ward 2004; Lasslett 2010). To expand on the type of constructionist thinking that tends to underpin the attendant view of crime as a social relationship that is not without objective reality, it is instructive to draw on Matthews (2009). From a critical realist position, Matthews insists that crime, as a construct embedded in social structures, is not a mere act or transgression but the historical product of a complex interplay between action and reaction. Crime is not something simply construed into existence but a social relationship embedded in a set of material conditions, structures, and ideologies by which it obtains its concrete quality (Matthews 2009, 2014). In keeping with this version of social constructionism, it is acknowledged that a phenomenon does not have an essence *in and of itself* that inscribes it with a criminal status, but that it is the larger totality of relations and processes in which phenomena are embedded that inscribe these phenomena with definite characteristics (Lasslett 2010). Thus considered, Lasslett posits that:

> Hillyard and Tombs are quite correct to assert that there is nothing "intrinsic" in an act which makes it criminal, nevertheless, acts can certainly acquire this characteristic as a result of the social complex in which they are situated, and may thus be said to have an ontological reality. (Lasslett 2010: 3)

Lasslett (2010) explicitly decouples crime and harm, whose relationship, he argues, is at most contingent. Thereby crime is the outcome of processes of social contradiction and struggle by which a certain social audience succeeds in labelling an act as deviant. It follows that not all harmful acts will acquire the characteristic of criminality, just as not all acts that are assigned a deviant status will be necessarily harmful (Lasslett 2010). This conception coincides with, and draws significantly on, the view adhered to by Green and Ward (2000), which rests (i) on a commitment to a conceptual link between crime and deviance, and (ii) the argument that, although closely related, harm and deviance are distinct areas of study. What results for Green and Ward (2000) is a definition of crime that encompasses a set of human rights violations that are at once "objectively illegitimate" and "subjectively deviant". Accordingly, to focus on human rights violations per se—i.e. without specifying what defines the criminal status of a human rights violation (cf. Schwendinger and Schwendinger 1975)—is believed to stretch the concept of crime too far if criminology is to retain its coherence as a field of study distinct to that of the study of social harm. Criminology, thus perceived, is the study of deviant behaviour; although there can be overlap between crime and harm, the undifferentiated study of social harm is not considered the domain of criminology in this view (Green and Ward 2000; Ward 2004).

The Contestedness of Harm

The above-outlined positions argue, respectively, for (i) a broadening of the definition of crime in order to include the analysis of crime-equivalent harms that fall outside strict legalistic definitions of crime; (ii) the analysis of social harm, based on the view that there are neither theoretical nor political grounds to maintain the differentiation between categories of crime and legal forms of harm; and (iii) maintaining a clear differentiation between crime and harm, reinstating the concept of crime as the object of criminological analysis. Clearly then, the concept of harm—both its conceptualization and whether or not it is an appropriate object of criminological analysis—is contested within criminology. But notions of harm are contested not only within criminological theory and debate; harm is also contested in the broader social field, where it is the object of conflict and struggle and differently constructed by the various actors involved. There is, as such, *a second level of contestedness* that is pushed from view when criminologists preoccupy themselves primarily with adopting a particular position on (or against) harm, within or outside criminology. When criminologists are mostly concerned to resolve the academic contestation around "harm", the bigger picture of harm's contestedness *on-the-ground*, and, crucially, what can be learned from this dimension, moves to the background. The argument advanced here is that to advance the criminological debate on harm, this on-the-ground dimension of contestedness is in need of critical interrogation, and it is in this vein that this study engages (and theorizes) the social and environmental harms associated with palm oil production in the Colombian Pacific coast region. In what follows, I will explicate this book's consequent focus on the politics of harm. In the concluding chapter, I return to the three above-outlined positions on harm.

The Politics of Harm

Harm is contested, but this contestation is not limited to the academic realm. As a normative concept, the notion of harm has an unequivocal political dimension: to speak of harm is to challenge, to dispute, or to make a claim to something, the assertion of a right, a demand for change, and so on. The politics that as such inhere in "harm" manifest themselves in two forms. One way is via the denunciations voiced by those who endure alleged harms, and those who represent or support the former in their struggles. Furthermore, politics also inhere in the *production* of harm: bringing about a degree of harm may be crucial to secure, facilitate, or reproduce particular political and economic interests, privileges and arrangements, and the broader cultural framework in which these are embedded. No less crucial, in turn, are the ways in which these alleged harms are discursively framed, denied, justified, relegated to external factors and processes, and so on.

As such, I argue that a politics of harm consists of two dimensions: (i) a discursive dimension, which refers to how a concept of harm is articulated, understood, constructed, denied, reconfigured, or used strategically, and (ii) a practical dimension—i.e. "the actual" or that what actually happens—in this case referring to the operations of the palm oil industry and the dynamics revolving around it, which includes struggle(s) over the practices, social relations, and human–environment interactions thereby implied. Thus, this study's focus is on the on-the-ground practices, discourses, and relations in the context of palm oil production in

Colombia's Pacific coast region, analysed against the broader structures of power and control in which these are embedded, as well as the different perceptions and meanings ascribed to these practices and relations by local subjects and wider stakeholders. The perspectives that are thereby attended to are those of (a) palm oil industry representatives, (b) corporate executives, (c) public officials, (d) local, small-scale agriculturalists dedicated to oil palm cultivation, (e) local community members critical of the perceived imposition of palm oil production onto the region, and (f) agroindustry-critical civil society organizations. Through this focus, this study aims to arrive at a more encompassing understanding of the lived and perceived realities of harm in the context of palm oil production, along with the interrogation of the power relations and mechanisms thereby at work.

The production of harm, the "validity" accorded to some conceptualizations of harm versus the discursive displacement or disqualification of others, the classification of harm as legal or illegal, and the ways in which the latter category of harms is dealt with (or not!) by a state's criminal justice apparatus or regulatory entities are all intimately bound up with the operation of power in a given context. It is worthwhile drawing on Foucault (1991) here, and his reflections on the shifting "space of tolerance" granted to given sets of illegalities—shifts that tend to accompany transitions in the social, economic, and political organization of a society. Important to emphasize in this regard is that power not only differentiates harm into legal harm and illegal harm but also distributes the harms that belong to the latter category along an "economy of illegalities" that reflects the values and precepts useful for a society's political and economic functioning. Hence, it can be explained that, in keeping with a bourgeois legality, a gradual redistribution of illegalities took place with the historical transition to capitalism (see Foucault 1991: 76–89, 272–292). Think also of the dehumanizing practices committed against colonial subjects, and the violence and inferior treatment that indigenous peoples and Afro-descendants in the Americas (similar experiences apply elsewhere) have been subjected to from the time of the Conquest, and still *are* to this very day. In view of such injustices, Rojas-Paéz (2017), drawing on de Sousa Santos (2007), explains: "the categories of 'crime', 'legal', and 'illegal', fell short in describing the socio-legal reality of the colonial world, in which other forms of legality existed and differed widely as regards the treatment of human beings and the exploitation of nature" (2017: 66).

A Multiple View of Power

In view of the above, this study examines the politics of harm as spanning from legal harm to tolerated illegal harm and nontolerated illegal harm. Considering that differential systems of legality say something about the order of power in any particular society—the international frame of reference included—it is task to investigate the power dynamics that draw and keep in place such boundaries and the hegemonic notions and practices of legality that reproduce corresponding realities of harm. This will be guided by a multiple view of power. Ekers and Loftus (2008) note that, other than a singular view of power, how it is exercised and what it does, one can also take a multiple view of power that draws on both relational and more realist understandings of power; that thinks of power as consolidated in social structures and institutions but as also operating at the level of the subject; as something held and deployed, as well as an effect; and sometimes more consensual whereas at other times more coercive. In addition, it is necessary to remain open to interacting and overlapping oppressions linked to social differentiation along, *inter alia*, class, race, ethnic, and colonial lines of power, and the human–nonhuman or human–environment nexus. Rather than assuming the existence of a single determining principle of articulation—for instance class, under which race, ethnicity and so on are then subsumed—this study is open to the possibility of the structuring force of social relations other than those corresponding to a capitalist logic of power, i.e. the structuring force of social relations, practices, cultural forms and meanings that do not necessarily bear a one-on-one relationship to a society's economic foundations (Hall 1996). Alongside capitalist social relations, there are other social relations and cultural practices and meanings to take account of. These may articulate with, but not necessarily, let alone principally, be determined by class struggle or the capitalist mode of production (Jessop 1990; Moore 1996). Regarding the merits and limitations of a macro-structural political economy framework for the analysis of land and resource-related conflict, Moore (1996: 126) has noted that:

> Global capitalism, from this [macro-structural] perspective, not only shapes but also exactly determines heterogeneous local histories, cultures, and societies. Cultural practices and beliefs usually enter this discussion derivatively, as exotic trappings to the nuts and bolts of "underlying" structures. Although it would be wrong to minimize the force of political economy, too much emphasis on structural determination elides other factors shaping conflicts over Third World environmental resources [...] Macro-structural accounts miss also local differentiation among resource users; particularly those mediated by class, gender, ethnicity, and age.

An explanatory framework of the play of power in the politics of harm in the context of palm oil production must therefore simultaneously include and go beyond the dictates and dynamics of the political economy of global capitalism.

A sometimes rigid emphasis on the capital–nature antagonism and on capital's inherent tendency to expand destructively, to impose, coerce, and obliterate, thereby also warrants to be qualified, considering that capital may (selectively) protect and conserve some natures and environments (see Cárdenas 2012), make concessions, and forge environmental and social compromises. A Gramscian perspective—for the more autonomous role it grants to ideology, culture, and politics—may carry relevance here and has the potential to counter somewhat mechanical understandings of the link between the economic infrastructure and environmental harm and crime (see, e.g., Levy and Egan 2003; Moore 1996).[7]

In addition, in keeping with the above, it must be stressed that it is vital to be attentive to culture and meaning. The politics of harm in connection to palm oil is a cultural politics, too: as noted by Moore (1996: 127–128), "struggles over land and environmental resources are simultaneously struggles over cultural meaning [and practices]". Recent endeavours to work towards a green cultural criminology (Brisman and South 2014) and considerations of "the rural" from a green cultural criminological perspective (Brisman et al. 2014) have started to integrate such notions more expressly into green criminology by calling attention to "the intersection of the rural, the cultural and the ecological", which includes taking account of the contestation of space and constructions of environmental crime and harm. Brisman et al. (2014) thereby also go some way in pointing out the need to challenge stereotypical and monolithic depictions and understandings of rural life and livelihoods, and the ways in which "the rural" is either impacted by, or impacts on, environmental degradation.

It is with these notions in mind, that this study addresses the constructions, practices, lived and perceived realities of harm, as well as the meanings ascribed to land use change to oil palm cultivation by local subjects and wider actors that have a stake in the politics of palm oil harm—i.e. small growers, (local) palm oil critics, and industry protagonists. The aim in the remainder of this chapter is to fuse the aforementioned considerations regarding harm, power, and legality into an explanatory framework for the play of power in the politics of palm oil harm, to refine green criminology's analysis and theorization of extractivist dynamics and impacts.

Towards an Explanatory Framework of Power in the Politics of Palm Oil Harm

As briefly mentioned earlier in this chapter, critical green criminological perspectives insist that the form and pace of the transformation and degradation of nature cannot be understood in isolation from the dynamics and the expansionary logic of the capitalist mode of production (White 2002; Stretesky et al. 2014). Hence, the overriding theoretical framework deployed in green criminological analyses of natural resource extraction draws principally on Marxist-inspired political economy perspectives. Below, some of the work that to this end has been developed within green criminology and in the broader academic literature will be expanded on first.

Green Criminology and Political Economy Analyses of Environmental Harm

Insistence on the continued relevance of political economy is central not just to critical green criminological perspectives (Stretesky et al. 2014; White 2013b) but has been reiterated in scholarship in the field of crimes of the powerful as well (Tombs and Whyte 2002). As stated by Tombs and Whyte:

> The labour theory of value and the theory of surplus value, the necessarily antagonistic relationship between classes, the inherent tendency of capitalism to expand, destructively, whilst at the same time reproducing the contradictions upon which it is founded, all seem to be crucial tools for understanding and engaging with the trajectories of the world. (Tombs and Whyte 2002: 222)

Green criminology specifically extends this analysis of power in structural terms to questions related to environmental harm and crime. The dynamics that inhere in the capitalist mode of production and the concomitant social, economic, and political configurations, globally and nationally, entail growing pressures on the natural world (White 2002, 2011; Stretesky et al. 2014). How this constant drive to accumulate and generate more profits results inevitably in the production of social and environmental harm is approached from different angles.

Within green criminology, Stretesky et al. (2014) have drawn on Schnaiberg's treadmill of production theory as a theoretical basis for the analysis of environmental harm. Treadmill of production theory explains how the extraction of raw materials, and the conversion of these raw materials into commodities, causes ecological disorganization, damaging or destroying ecosystems to such extent that the conditions to sustain human and nonhuman life are severely disrupted, sometimes irreversibly. This occurs through ecological withdrawal and ecological additions. Harms of withdrawal are brought about directly by the technologies and processes of extraction and harvesting. Harms of addition stem from production-related waste streams and the contamination of soil, water, and air. Due to the expansionary drive of capital, this is a continuous process that leads to ever more intensive, widespread, and accelerated ecological disorganization (Stretesky et al. 2014; Lynch and Stretesky 2014).

Outside of criminology, a strand of relevant work takes its cues from Marx's writings on the "metabolic rift" (Moore 2000; McMichael 2009b; Schneider and McMichael 2010); a concept that revolves around the notion that the push towards ever more capital-, energy-, and technology-intensive forms of agriculture exacerbates the separation of agriculture from its biological base—and of humans from nature more generally—and disrupts the natural nutrient cycle to unprecedented extents (see also Crook and Short 2014). Reworked,[8] the concept explains the rapid exhaustion of soil and ecological conditions as agriculture comes to be subordinated to the logic of capital and the capitalist division of labour (Schneider and McMichael 2010). Moore (2000), through a discussion of the successive metabolic rifts that are cause and consequence of global capitalist development, substantiates the claim that capitalism *inevitably* destroys the ecological basis of its production conditions. The capitalist logic of productivity cannot but depend on large-scale industrially farmed monocultures that exhaust soil, water sources, and ecological conditions that sustain life. Through the concept of "metabolic rift", it is possible to arrive at enhanced insight into the dynamics and implications of the "subordination of agriculture to capitalist production relations" (McMichael 2009b: 827). In Chap. 6 of this book, in the discussion of the social and environmental harms linked to oil palm cultivation as a consequence of the displacement of traditional models of production and subsistence in the process of the neoliberal capitalist restructuring of agriculture, the relevance and explanatory power of the concept of the metabolic for the theorization of agroindustry-related environmental harm in green criminology are demonstrated.

Harvey's (2003) notion of "accumulation by dispossession", too, carries relevance for the green criminological analysis of the social and environmental harms that result from global patterns of production and consumption.[9] Bearing in mind that the extended reproduction of the capitalist system necessitates constant expansion, this entails that if the production of surplus value can no longer be realized within existing production settings,[10] new frontiers for capital accumulation must be opened up. Revisiting Marx's notion of primitive accumulation, Harvey (2003: 144) has noted "the continuous role and persistence of the predatory practices of 'primitive' or 'original' accumulation". As such, in order to sustain economic growth, capitalist penetration and processes of commodification reach into all but every corner of the world and aspect of human and nonhuman life, to open up "non-capitalist territories"[11] to capitalist accumulation. Agribusiness is one such driver of dispossession, undermining smallholder agriculture, subsistence economies and the cultural and socioecological dynamics of locally embedded forms of life and coexistence, and disrupting ecological processes (McMichael 2009a).

On the whole, the importance of macro-structural engagement with political economy as a framework of analysis of the social and environmental harms of palm oil production is indisputable. But the on-the-ground dynamics of the politics of palm oil harm simultaneously ask for closer reflection on the day-to-day struggles over access to, control, and use of land; the cultural meanings and practices that invest the respective territories; and the multiplicity of power relations and mechanisms at work in this context. Consider for instance that although the presentation of the primary research data in Chaps. 4–6 in many ways bears witness to processes of "accumulation by dispossession", I will also demonstrate that this notion cannot fully comprehend the ways in which the Colombian palm oil industry operates and expands. Moreover, local communities do not share a single reality of lived and perceived harm; instead, it is crucial to attend to the different *realities* of harm in connection with the palm oil industry. This indicates a manifest need for theoretical refinement of green criminological engagement with harm and crime linked to natural resource extraction. Such refinement must also account for colonialist practices and attitudes, which often figure prominently in extractivist patterns of accumulation (Mondaca 2017; Rojas-Paéz 2017). The case of Colombian palm oil forms no exception to this, as the discussion below elucidates.

Peripheral Natures and Peoples: The Centrality of a Persistent Coloniality

In making the case for an eco-global criminological perspective, White (2011) takes up the theoretical and methodological implications of the spatial dimensions, transnational character, and local–global dynamics of environmental issues for criminology. In addition to a focus on the transference of harm, he thereby also calls attention to the fact that the world is viewed and perceived differently through different eyes and from different localities, histories, and subjectivities. The "local", on such accounts, is not a mere physical construct or geographical marker, but refers just as much to one's social and epistemological location and ontological being (White 2011). The colonial character of many a case of environmental victimization, the transference of harm, as well as the production of knowledge regarding such harm, is certainly acknowledged within green criminology (in addition to White 2011, see also South 2007; Walters 2011). At the same time though, colonial patterns of power in the analysis of social and environmental harm arguably merit a more central place in green criminological analysis, without thereby *reducing* a colonial logic of power to a capitalist one, notwithstanding their intricate relation. In what follows, I outline some of the works that confirm the relevance of such a focus in connection with the operations of the palm oil industry in the Colombian Pacific.

Colombia's Pacific coast region, to reiterate, is a region predominantly inhabited by Afro-Colombian and indigenous communities. The heterogeneity that characterizes this region's cultural and ethnic diversity, its "disorderly" nature, and forms of sociocultural organization and local ways of relating to the region's natural environments have come under growing pressure from the homogenizing mechanisms of dominant models of development (Escobar 2008). The push for the agroindustrial capitalist development of Afro-Colombian and indigenous territories by sectors such as the palm oil industry, according to Escobar (2008), entails the subjugation of local relations, practices, cultural beliefs, and ways of being and knowing. Denunciations of the palm oil industry are in this regard closely linked to the displacement of local social relations and conceptions of the land and historically and culturally specific systems of production and subsistence by projects that supposedly bring progress, development, and sustainability (Ramírez Vidal 2007).

Colombia's Pacific coast is an example of a region that, in keeping with an imaginary geographical and racial hierarchy known as "andinocentrism", is still significantly portrayed as backward, its inhabitants ranked as racially and culturally inferior (Oslender 2007; Arocha Rodríguez and Moreno Tovar 2007). The agroindustrial production of palm oil is considered exemplary of the imposition of this andinocentric, or "Euro-Andean" (Escobar 2008), model of development. Such processes are moreover to a large extent sustained and enabled by the "armed machinery" that operates in the region (see Chap. 4) and which is claimed to have subjected many inhabitants of the Pacific to a new diaspora (Arocha Rodríguez and Moreno Tovar 2007).

With reference to the enduring forms of colonial domination of non-Western cultures, Quijano (2007) has coined the concept of "coloniality" to emphasize the continuity of a colonial technology of power, notwithstanding the end of colonial administrations (Castro-Gómez 2002). The disqualification of "alternative" ways of knowing, seeing, and being, as well as the broader devaluation of human and nonhuman life in regions construed as Colombia's Other (Serje 2007) draw attention to the persistence of a colonial imaginary that divides social reality into distinct albeit interrelated realms.[12] Boaventura de Sousa Santos (2007) speaks of such divisions in terms of "this side of the line" and "the other side of the line", whereby the latter is constitutive or forms the condition of possibility of the former (see also Oslender 2007). This logic applies as much to global North–South divides as to centre–periphery relations within regions of the Global South. An assigned peripheral status thereby sustains a view of the environments and human inhabitants of the Global South or peripheral regions as instrumental, manipulable, and expendable in the process of implanting dominant models of development and industries primarily geared to support the lifestyles of those in the North or centre.

Escobar (2007, 2008) has extended the notion of coloniality to include the ecological, arguing that "it is in the nature of coloniality to enact a coloniality of nature" (2008: 120). A coloniality of nature is thereby discernible in the subordination and exploitation of biophysical nature as well as through the subalternization of local models of nature, "particularly those that enact a continuity between the natural, human, and supernatural worlds" (ibid.: 121). As Alimonda (2011) has argued more broadly:

> A persistent coloniality impacts on Latin American nature. The latter, both as biophysical reality (its flora, fauna, human inhabitants, the biodiversity of its ecosystems) and its territorial configuration (the

> sociocultural dynamic that significantly articulates these ecosystems and landscapes) is depicted, in global hegemonic thought and by local elites, as a subaltern space open to exploitation, devastation, and reconfiguration according to the demands of current regimes of accumulation. (Alimonda 2011: 22)

Ramírez Vidal (2007), looking back upon research carried out in Tumaco in the late 1990s, recalls how palm oil companies in the region "had become the new symbol of mestizo and white cultural penetration". Consequently, "the control that Afro-Colombian groups had come to take of their environments, was being seriously threatened and undergoing profound socioeconomic and cultural transformation" (Ramírez Vidal 2007: 410). Thus, critics stress how the palm oil industry is "infused with colonial overtones" (Escobar 2008: 70), which manifests itself in an imposed alteration of local land uses that reinvigorates exploitative configurations of human–environment relations (Ramírez Vidal 2007; Escobar 2008; Cárdenas 2012: 330).

However, notwithstanding the above, the palm oil industry is not being unequivocally and unanimously opposed in Colombia's zones of palm oil production. In order to bring into view the full range of dynamics of agroindustry expansion, alongside coercive forms of domination and exploitation, it is therefore necessary to be attentive to more consensual dynamics that are at play in the exercise of power in these contexts, too.

Between Coercion and Consent: Small Growers in the Midst of Opposition

Where the smooth incursion of agroindustries and wider projects of economic restructuring are obstructed by dissenting populations that oppose the imposition of such logics onto their territories, in Colombia the answer often assumes the form of a "politics of terror" and violent persecution of local communities (Oslender 2008). However, somewhat disparate from well-documented cases that link the establishment and expansion of the Colombian palm oil industry to violent and coercive processes of dispossession (Mingorance 2006; Grajales 2013; Maher 2015), in many of Colombia's palm oil production zones, palm oil is not so much, *or at least no longer,* the mere product of violent imposition and dispossession. In the introductory chapter I noted how, during my initial encounters with the palm oil industry in Tumaco, I was confronted with the involvement of a substantial number of small growers in the cultivation of oil palm (see also, Leech 2009; Cárdenas 2012). What is it that drives smallholders to opt for the cultivation of oil palm on their lands? If local populations "opt" for palm oil, then what does this say about the dynamics of land use change or land grabs? Borras Jr. and Franco (2012) have cautioned against the imprecise and uncritical use of the "catch-all phrase" of land grab, arguing that such tendencies risk obscuring the complexity and multidimensional character of the nature, mechanisms, objectives, and directions of land use change. It should as such not be assumed that mechanisms of land use change always depend on violence and coercion. Alongside the forced imposition and the resort to coercive mechanisms of land use change, there are also more consensual processes by which local subjects are incorporated into projects of agroindustrial capitalist development (Cárdenas 2012). If power works in coercive and violent as well as in noncoercive ways, it follows that it is crucial to analyse how coercion and consent figure in the play of power in the politics of harm, and how, or to what extent, these two dimensions may articulate.

Also of relevance in this regard is that, since 1991, an expanded legal framework (see Chap. 3) seeks to include historically excluded segments of the population, among them Colombia's ethnic minorities. But, as Lemaitre Ripoll (2009) notes, parallel to the respective constitutional and legal changes, increases have occurred in the violent persecution of these groups. Rural communities are especially hard-hit in this regard. Notwithstanding advances in the legal recognition and protection of Colombia's ethnic and cultural diversity, it is still the case that when neoliberal development models run up against the legal limits set by the collective land titles granted to Afro-Colombian and indigenous peoples, such "obstacles" are often sought to be violently overcome:

> There is a general opinion in Colombia that an error of historic proportions was committed when the government handed over 25% of the nation's territory in the form of *resguardos* to [indigenous] communities, in effect placing these lands beyond the scope of the market and of all possibility of investment and development. Evidently, the corrective to this has been to put into practice a covert program of extermination, hidden behind the veil of the country's armed conflict. The rate of violence in indigenous zones is 100% greater than the national mean. (Serje 2007: 46)

For a more thorough understanding of the conditions that enable and/or constrain opposition to palm oil, and the effective space opened up to alternative notions of legality, it is crucial to reflect on the embeddedness of Colombia's expanded legal framework—in relation to the territorial and cultural rights of ethnic minorities—in the wider configuration of social, cultural, political, and economic relations and processes. With the legal recognition of ethnic and cultural diversity and the allocation of collective land titles, to what extent can alternative social, cultural, and ecological rationalities effectively be enacted?

It is crucial to take up this set of questions, too, to reflect on the actual degree of autonomy that Afro-Colombian and indigenous communities are allowed to exercise in the cultural, territorial, and economic sphere; and on the implications of Colombia's expanding legal order and the corresponding set of legal practices for the lived experience and contestedness of harm. Informed by the analytical approach and theoretical contours of the framework set out over the course of this chapter, in Chaps. 4–6 the fieldwork data of this research will be analysed and discussed. To this end, the next chapter provides some further detail on the ecology, demographics, and social turmoil in the region under analysis and more generally places Colombia's palm oil industry in its national and regional context.

Notes

1. For an overview and discussion of directions in critical criminology that have emerged since the 1970s, see DeKeseredy (2011).
2. I mentioned in the introductory chapter that White (2011: 45) refers to this as "paradoxical harm".
3. I expand on this point later on in this chapter, when engaging in a more detailed discussion of the Marxist analytical framework initially envisioned by Lynch (1990)—and later followed by others (e.g. White 2002; Stretesky et al. 2014)—as the terrain from which to pursue the greening of criminology.
4. "Off with the old criminologies, on with the new orientations, the new horizons!" was Tappan's (1947: 96) reproach to attempts to extend the criminological scope beyond the mere study of offenders convicted by the state for violations of the state's criminal law.
5. Recent withdrawals by several African nations from the International Criminal Court (The Guardian 2016) are signal events worth taking serious in this respect. Accusing the ICC of a racist bias in its selection of cases to investigate and prosecute, it is claimed that western nations are led off the hook despite having committed "heinous war crimes" (think, e.g., of the 2003 Iraq invasion).
6. A term first coined by Friedrichs and Friedrichs in (2002), and most recently extensively dealt with in Rothe and Friedrichs (2015).
7. Chapter 5 and the concluding chapter take these ideas further.
8. Reworked in the sense of shifting the emphasis from a principal concern with the *organization* of labour to the *practice* of labour; i.e. looking more meticulously at agricultural practice under capitalism (Schneider and McMichael 2010).
9. See also Gutiérrez-Gómez (2017) for the application of this concept to state-corporate harm in the context of gold mining in Colombia.
10. That is, within the limits of, for instance, existing manufacturing, agricultural, or extractive activities.
11. These are territories where a noncapitalist logic of production and subsistence prevails, even if not wholly external to the capitalist economy.

12. Based on a false dichotomy, there is a prevailing notion that there are two separate Colombias: the prosperous Andean zone which is seen as the centre of development, modernization, order, stability, and legality, versus a Colombia characterized by absence, lack, and disorder, onto which is projected an imagery of backwardness, marginality, and violence (Serje 2007, 2012).

References

Alimonda, H. (2011). La colonialidad de la naturaleza. Una aproximación a la Ecología Política Latinoamericana. In H. Alimonda (Ed.), *La Naturaleza colonizada. Ecología política y minería en América Latina* (pp. 21–58). Buenos Aires: CLASCO.

Arocha Rodríguez, J., & Moreno Tovar, L. del M. (2007). Andinocentrismo, salvajismo y afro-reparaciones. In C. Mosquera Rosero-Labbé & C. L. Barcelos (Eds.), *Afro-reparaciones: Memorias de la Esclavitud y Justicia Reparativa para negros, afrocolombianos y raizales* (pp. 587–614). Bogotá: Universidad Nacional de Colombia.

Boekhout van Solinge, T. (2010). Deforestation crimes and conflicts in the Amazon. *Critical Criminology, 18*(4), 263–277.

Borras, S. M., Jr., & Franco, J. C. (2012). Global land grabbing and trajectories of agrarian change: A preliminary analysis. *Journal of Agrarian Change, 12*(1), 34–59.

Brisman, A., & South, N. (2014). *Green cultural criminology: Constructions of environmental harm, consumerism, and resistance to ecocide.* Abingdon: Routledge.

Brisman, A., McClanahan, B., & South, N. (2014). Towards a green-cultural criminology of "the rural". *Critical Criminology, 22*(4), 479–494.

Brisman, A., South, N., & White, R. (Eds.). (2015). *Environmental crime and social conflict: Contemporary and emerging issues.* Farnham: Ashgate.

Cárdenas, R. (2012). Green multiculturalism: Articulations of ethnic and environmental politics in a Colombian 'black community'. *The Journal of Peasant Studies, 39*(2), 309–333.

Castro-Gómez, S. (2002). The social aciences, epistemic violence, and the problem of the "invention of the other". *Nepantla: Views from the South, 3*(2), 269–285.

Cohen, S. (1993). Human rights and crimes of the state: The culture of denial. *Australian and New Zealand Journal of Criminology, 26*(2), 97–115.

Crook, M., & Short, D. (2014). Marx, Lemkin and the genocide-ecocide nexus. *The International Journal of Human Rights, 18*(3), 298–319.

DeKeseredy, W. S. (2011). *Contemporary critical criminology*. Abingdon: Routledge.

Donnermeyer, J. F., & DeKeseredy, W. S. (2014). *Rural criminology*. Abingdon: Routledge.

Ekers, M., & Loftus, A. (2008). The power of water: Developing dialogues between Foucault and Gramsci. *Environment and Planning D: Society and Space, 26*(4), 698–718.

Escobar, A. (2007). Worlds and knowledges otherwise: The Latin American modernity/coloniality research program. *Cultural Studies, 21*(2–3), 179–210.

Escobar, A. (2008). *Territories of difference: Place, movements, life, redes*. Durham, NC: Duke University Press.

Foucault, M. (1991). *Discipline and punish: The birth of the prison*. London: Penguin Books.

Friedrichs, D. O., & Friedrichs, J. (2002). The World Bank and crimes of globalization: A case study. *Social Justice, 29*(1–2), 1–12.

Gordon, D. (2004). Poverty, death and disease. In P. Hillyard, C. Pantazis, S. Tombs, & D. Gordon (Eds.), *Beyond criminology: Taking harm seriously* (pp. 251–266). London: Pluto Press.

Grajales, J. (2013). State involvement, land grabbing and counter-insurgency in Colombia. *Development and Change, 44*(2), 211–232.

Green, P., & Ward, T. (2000). State crime, human rights, and the limits of criminology. *Social Justice, 27*(1), 101–115.

Gutiérrez-Gómez, L. (2017). Mining in Colombia: Tracing the harm of neoliberal policies and practices. In D. R. Goyes, H. Mol, A. Brisman, & N. South (Eds.), *Environmental crime in Latin America: The theft of nature and the poisoning of the land*. London: Palgrave Macmillan.

Hall, S. (1996). Gramsci's relevance for the study of race and ethnicity. In D. Morley & K. Chen (Eds.), *Stuart Hall: Critical dialogues in cultural studies* (pp. 411–441). New York: Routledge.

Halsey, M. (1997). Environmental crime: Towards an eco-human rights approach. *Current Issues in Criminal Justice, 8*(3), 217–242.

Halsey, M. (2004). Against 'green' criminology. *British Journal of Criminology, 44*(6), 833–853.

Halsey, M., & White, R. (1998). Crime, ecophilosophy and environmental harm. *Theoretical Criminology, 2*(3), 345–371.

Harvey, D. (2003). *The new imperialism*. Oxford: Oxford University Press.

Hillyard, P., & Tombs, S. (2004). Beyond criminology? In P. Hillyard, C. Pantazis, S. Tombs, & D. Gordon (Eds.). *Beyond criminology: Taking harm seriously* (pp. 10–29). London: Pluto Press.
Hillyard, P., Pantazis, C., Tombs, S., & Gordon, D. (Eds.). (2004). *Beyond criminology. Taking harm seriously*. London: Pluto Press.
Hughes, G. (2006). Review of "beyond criminology: Taking harm seriously", by P. Hillyard, C. Pantazis, S. Tombs, & D. Gordon, Eds. *Social and legal studies, 15*(1), 157–159.
Hulsman, L. H. C. (1986). Critical criminology and the concept of crime. *Contemporary Crises, 10*(1), 63–80.
Jessop, B. (1990). Poulantzas and Foucault on power and strategy. In B. Jessop (Ed.), *State theory: Putting the capitalist state in its place* (pp. 220–246). Cambridge: Polity Press.
Kauzlarich, D. (1995). A criminology of the nuclear state. *Humanity & Society, 19*(3), 37–57.
Kauzlarich, D., Mullins, C. W., & Matthews, R. A. (2003). A complicity continuum of state crime. *Contemporary Justice Review, 6*(3), 241–254.
Kramer, R. C., Michalowski, R. J., & Kauzlarich, D. (2002). The origins and development of the concept and theory of state-corporate crime. *Crime & Delinquency, 48*(2), 263–282.
Lasslett, K. (2010). Crime or social harm? A dialectical perspective. *Crime, Law and Social Change, 51*(1), 1–19.
Lea, J. (2009). *Marx and Engels as criminologists* [Online]. Writings on criminology. Available from: http://www.bunker8.pwp.blueyonder.co.uk/ [Accessed 09 February 2015].
Leech, G. (2009). The oil palm industry: A blight of Afro-Colombia. *NACLA Report on the Americas, 42*(4), 30–34.
Lemaitre Ripoll, J. (2009). *El derecho como conjuro: fetichismo legal, violencia y movimientos sociales*. Bogotá: Siglo del Hombre Editores y Universidad de los Andes.
Levy, D. L., & Egan, D. (2003). A neo-gramscian approach to corporate political strategy: Conflict and accommodation in the climate change negotiations. *Journal of Management Studies, 40*(4), 803–829.
Lynch, M. (1990). The greening of criminology: A perspective on the 1990s. *Critical Criminologist, 2*(3), 1–4, 11–12.
Lynch, M. J., Long, M. A., Barrett, K. L., & Stretesky, P. B. (2013). Is it a crime to produce ecological disorganization? Why green criminology and

political economy matter in the analysis of global ecological harm. *British Journal of Criminology, 53*(6), 997–1016.
Lynch, M. J., & Stretesky, P. B. (2003). The meaning of green: Contrasting criminological perspectives. *Theoretical Criminology, 7*(2), 217–238.
Lynch, M. J., & Stretesky, P. B. (2014). *Exploring green criminology. Towards a green criminological revolution.* Farnham: Ashgate.
Maher, D. (2015). Rooted in violence: Civil war, international trade and the expansion of palm oil in Colombia. *New Political Economy, 20*(2), 299–330.
Matthews, R. (2009). Beyond 'so what?' criminology: Rediscovering realism. *Theoretical Criminology, 13*(3), 341–362.
Matthews, R. (2014). Cultural realism? *Crime, Media, Culture, 10*(3), 203–214.
McMichael, P. (2009a). A food regime analysis of the 'world food crisis'. *Agriculture and Human Values, 26*(4), 281–295.
McMichael, P. (2009b). The agrofuels project at large. *Critical Sociology, 35*(6), 825–839.
Michalowski, R. (2009). Power, crime and criminology in the new imperial age. *Crime, Law and Social Change, 51*(3–4), 303–325.
Mingorance, F. (2006). *The flow of palm oil Colombia-Belgium/Europe. A study from a human rights perspective.* Brussels: Human Rights Everywhere/ Coordination Belge pour la Colombie.
Mol, H. (2013). 'A gift from the tropics to the world': Power, harm, and palm oil. In R. Walters, D. Westerhuis, & T. Wyatt (Eds.), *Emerging issues in green criminology: Exploring power, justice and harm* (pp. 242–260). Basingstoke: Palgrave Macmillan.
Mondaca, E. (2017). The Archipelago of Chiloé and the uncertain contours of its future: Coloniality, new extractivism and political-social re-vindication of existence. In D. R. Goyes, H. Mol, A. Brisman, & N. South (Eds.), *Environmental crime in Latin America: The theft of nature and the poisoning of the land.* London: Palgrave Macmillan.
Moore, D. S. (1996). Marxism, culture, and political ecology: Environmental struggles in Zimbabwe's Eastern Highlands. In R. Peet & M. Watts (Eds.), *Liberation ecologies. Environment, development, social movements* (pp. 125–147). London: Routledge.
Moore, J. W. (2000). Environmental crises and the metabolic rift in world-historical perspective. *Organization & Environment, 13*(2), 123–158.
Muncie, J. (2005). Review of "beyond criminology: Taking harm seriously", by P. Hillyard, C. Pantazis, S. Tombs, & D. Gordon, Eds. *Crime, Law and Social Change, 43*(2), 199–201.

O'Brien, M. (2008). Criminal degradations of consumer culture. In R. Sollund (Ed.), *Global harms: Ecological crime and speciesism* (pp. 35–50). New York: Nova Science Publishers.
Oslender, U. (2007). Revisiting the hidden transcript: Oral tradition and black cultural politics in the Colombian Pacific coast region. *Environment and Planning D: Society and Space, 25*(6), 1103–1129.
Oslender, U. (2008). Another history of violence: The production of "geographies of terror" in Colombia's Pacific coast region. *Latin American Perspectives, 35*(5), 77–102.
Pemberton, S. (2004). A theory of moral indifference: Understanding the production of harm by capitalist society. In P. Hillyard, C. Pantazis, S. Tombs, & D. Gordon (Eds.), *Beyond criminology: Taking harm seriously* (pp. 67–83). London: Pluto Press.
Pemberton, S. (2007). Social harm future(s): Exploring the potential of the social harm approach. *Crime, Law and Social Change, 48*(1), 27–41.
Plumwood, V. (1991). Nature, self, and gender: Feminism, environmental philosophy, and the critique of rationalism. *Hypatia, 6*(1), 3–27.
Potter, G. R. (2013). Justifying 'green' criminology: Values and 'taking sides' in an ecologically informed social science. In M. Cowburn, M. Duggan, A. Robinson, & P. Senior (Eds.), *Values in criminology and community justice* (pp. 125–141). Bristol: The Policy Press.
Quijano, A. (2007). Coloniality and modernity/rationality. *Cultural Studies, 21* (2–3), 168–178.
Ramírez Vidal, L. A. (2007). Afro-reparaciones en tierras de comunidades negras: Vuelta de Candelilla, Tumaco. In C. Mosquera Rosero-Labbé & C. L. Barcelos (Eds.), *Afro-reparaciones: Memorias de la Esclavitud y Justicia Reparativa para negros, afrocolombianos y raizales* (pp. 405–421). Bogotá: Universidad Nacional de Colombia.
Rojas-Páez, G. (2017). Understanding environmental harm and justice claims in the global south: Crimes of the powerful and peoples' resistance. In D. R. Goyes, H. Mol, A. Brisman, & N. South (Eds.), *Environmental crime in Latin America: The theft of nature and the poisoning of the land.* London: Palgrave Macmillan.
Rothe, D., & Friedrichs, D. O. (2006). The state of the criminology of crimes of the State. *Social Justice, 33*(1), 147–161.
Rothe, D., & Friedrichs, D. O. (2015). *Crimes of globalization.* Abingdon: Routledge.
Rothe, D., Muzzatti, S., & Mullins, C. W. (2006). Crime on the high seas: Crimes of globalization and the sinking of the Senegalese Ferry Le Joola. *Critical Criminology, 14*(2), 159–180.

Ruggiero, V., & South, N. (2013). Green criminology and crimes of the economy: Theory, research and praxis. *Critical Criminology, 21*(3), 359–373.
Santos, B. de Sousa (2007). Beyond abyssal thinking: From global lines to ecologies of knowledge. *Review, 30*(1), 45–89.
Schneider, M., & McMichael, P. (2010). Deepening, and repairing, the metabolic rift. *The Journal of Peasant Studies, 37*(3), 461–484.
Schwendinger, H., & Schwendinger, J. (1975). Defenders of order or guardians of human rights? In I. Taylor, P. Walton, & J. Young (Eds.), *Critical criminology* (pp. 113–146). London: Routledge & Kegan Paul.
Schwendinger, H., & Schwendinger, J. (1977). Social class and the definition of crime. *Crime and Social Justice, 7,* 4–13.
Serje, M. (2007). Iron maiden landscapes: The geopolitics of Colombia's territorial conquest. *South Central Review, 24*(1), 37–55.
Serje, M. (2012). El mito de la ausencia del Estado: la incorporación económica de las "zonas de frontera" en Colombia. *Cahiers des Ameriques Latines, 71,* 95–117.
South, N. (1998). A green field for criminology? A proposal for a perspective. *Theoretical Criminology, 2*(2), 211–233.
South, N. (2007). The 'corporate colonisation of nature': Bio-prospecting, bio-piracy and the development of green criminology. In P. Beirne & N. South (Eds.) *Issues in Green Criminology. Confronting harms against environments, humanity and other animals* (pp. 230–247). Cullompton: Willan Publishing.
South, N. (2008). Nature, difference, and the rejection of harm: Expanding the agenda for green criminology. In R. Sollund (Ed.), *Global harms: Ecological crime and speciesism* (pp. 187–200). New York: Nova Science Publishers.
Stephens, S. (1996). Reflections on environmental justice: Children as victims and actors. *Social Justice, 23*(4), 62–86.
Stretesky, P. B., Long, M. A., & Lynch, M. J. (2014). *The treadmill of crime: Political economy and green criminology.* Abingdon: Routledge.
Sutherland, E. H. (1940). White-collar criminality. *American Sociological Review, 5*(1), 1–12.
Sutherland, E. H. (1983). *White collar crime: The uncut version.* New Haven, CT: Yale University Press.
Tappan, P. W. (1947). Who is the criminal? *American Sociological Review, 12*(1), 96–102.
Taylor, I., Walton, P., & Young, J. (1973). *The new criminology: For a social theory of deviance.* London: Routledge.

The Guardian. (2016, October 26). Gambia is latest African nation to quit international criminal court [Online], (World). Available from: https://www.theguardian.com [Accessed 1 November 2016].

Tombs, S., & Hillyard, P. (2004). Towards a political economy of harm: States, corporations and the production of Inequality. In P. Hillyard, C. Pantazis, S. Tombs, & D. Gordon (Eds.), *Beyond criminology: Taking harm seriously* (pp. 30–54). London: Pluto Press.

Tombs, S., & Whyte, D. (2002). Unmasking the crimes of the powerful. *Critical Criminology, 11*(3), 217–236.

Wachholz, S. (2007). 'At risk': Climate change and its bearing on women's vulnerability to male violence. In P. Beirne & N. South (Eds.), *Issues in green criminology. Confronting harms against environments, humanity and other animals* (pp. 161–185). Cullompton: Willan Publishing.

Walters, R. (2011). *Eco Crime and Genetically Modified Food.* Abingdon: Routledge.

Ward, T. (2004). State harms. In P. Hillyard, C. Pantazis, S. Tombs, & D. Gordon (Eds.), *Beyond criminology: Taking harm seriously* (pp. 84–100). London: Pluto Press.

White, R. (2002). Environmental harm and the political economy of consumption. *Social Justice, 29*(1–2), 82–102.

White, R. (2008). *Crimes against nature. Environmental criminology and ecological justice*. Cullompton: Willan Publishing.

White, R. (2011). *Transnational environmental crime. Towards an eco-global criminology*. London: Routledge.

White, R. (2013a). *Environmental harm: An eco-justice perspective*. Bristol: Policy Press.

White, R. (2013b). The conceptual contours of green criminology. In R. Walters, D. Westerhuis, & T. Wyatt (Eds.), *Emerging issues in green criminology: Exploring power, justice and harm* (pp. 17–33). Basingstoke: Palgrave Macmillan.

Zaitch, D., Boekhout van Solinge, T., & Müller, G. (2014). Harms, crimes and natural resource exploitation: A green criminological and human rights perspective on land-use change. In M. Bavinck, L. Pellegrini, & E. Mostert (Eds.), *Conflicts over natural resources in the global south—Conceptual approaches* (pp. 91–108). London: Taylor & Francis Group.

Zedner, L. (2011). Putting crime back on the criminological agenda. In M. Bosworth & C. Hoyle (Eds.), *What is criminology?* (pp. 271–285). Oxford: Oxford University Press.

3

Palm Oil in Colombia: National and Local Context

As mentioned previously, the principal focus of this study lies on the social and environmental harms associated with the operations of the palm oil industry in the Pacific coast region of Colombia. This region constitutes the most western part of Colombia, comprising the Chocó department in the north and the coastal municipalities of the departments of Valle de Cauca, Cauca, and Nariño to the south. It forms part of the *Biogeographic Chocó*; a humid ecoregion of rivers, forests, mangroves, swamps, and floodplains,[1] encompassing the lowlands west of the Andes and stretching from the mountain ranges that form the border between Colombia and Panama in the north all the way down to the northwest of Ecuador. With rainfalls up to 12,000 mm in the central zone and 3000–4000 mm in the northern and southern extremes, the Colombian Pacific is one of the rainiest regions of the Americas (Pintaud et al. 2008). One of the main reasons the region is so humid and experiences such abundant rainfall is due to being positioned in the Intertropical Convergence Zone[2] and located between the Pacific Ocean on the west and the Andes mountain range to the east (Delgado et al. 2007: 46–47). As noted by Restrepo:

H. Mol, *The Politics of Palm Oil Harm*, Palgrave Studies in Green Criminology, DOI 10.1007/978-3-319-55378-8_3

> The Colombian Pacific is not only one of the most humid places of the world; the density and variety of its vegetation and fauna also define it as one of the most biodiverse regions of the planet. (Restrepo 2002: 37)

Demographically, the majority of the region is Afro-Colombian, followed by a smaller presence of mestizo population, and indigenous peoples belonging to various ethnic groups.[3] Escobar (2008) offers a rich analysis of the resultant heterogeneity of the social relations and practices, production and subsistence patterns, and local ways of relating to the region's biodiverse forest and aquatic environments. According to Escobar, incursions of the palm oil industry into the region form part of a broader push towards the "reconfiguration of the biophysical and cultural landscapes of the Pacific" (2008: 64), which, as mentioned in the previous chapter, is increasingly displacing the economic, cultural, and ecological difference that marks the ways of being of the region's Afro-Colombian and indigenous communities. It is important to note that a region's biophysical properties—in terms of its vegetation, soil conditions, biodiversity, precipitation regimes, humidity, and so on—are key factors to consider in the analysis of the specific environmental, social, and cultural impacts of land cover and land use change to agroindustrial models of production, which adds weight to the claim that criminology ought to adopt an environmental frame of reference (Lynch and Stretesky 2014). In what follows, I outline the extent to which Colombia's legal and political framework accommodates concern for the ways in which changes in land use, and the pressures of agroindustry, affect environmental well-being and the ability to enact ethnic and cultural difference. In addition, I briefly address the presence of illegal armed groups in the municipality of Tumaco, Nariño—the regional focus of this study—and the different modalities of oil palm cultivation in this zone.

Colombia: A "Pluri-Ethnic and Multicultural Nation"

Constitutional reform in 1991 marked momentous change in Colombia's political and legal framework in the domain of ethnic and cultural diversity. From an assimilationist discourse and politics that had its ideological basis in views of indigenous peoples and Afro-descendants as backward, undeveloped, and racially inferior, a shift toward the recognition and protection of Colombia's ethnic diversity was formally instituted (Arocha 1998; Semper 2006). Colombia in this regard forms no exception to a wider trend of constitutional reform in Latin America (see Van Cott 2000). Demands for constitutional reform in Colombia were primarily driven by the view that the violence that was tearing Colombia apart was a product of persistent social and political exclusion of the poor, working classes, women, ethnic minorities, LGBTs, and so on (Lemaitre Ripoll 2009). As Lemaitre sums it up:

> The Constitution would put an end to the violence because it would end with two of its principal sources: the exclusion of minority groups from political participation and the readiness of the partisan State to take up arms against its enemies. (2009: 128)

This ideal of greater political participation and inclusion has found expression, amongst others, in the recognition and protection of ethnic and cultural diversity, granting specific cultural and territorial rights to indigenous and Afro-Colombian communities. Accordingly, Colombia has been reimagined as a "pluri-ethnic and multicultural" nation. Below I reflect on the space that such reform has opened up to halt, and potentially reverse, the dispossession of land and of ways of being inscribed in the land.

Colombia's Multiculturalist Turn and the Titling of Collective Land

Since 1991, constitutional safeguards, related legal provisions, and a favourable interpretation thereof in the jurisprudence of Colombia's Constitutional Court (see, e.g., Lemaitre Ripoll 2009: 330–331) are important instruments in indigenous and Afro-Colombian struggles to defend land, life, and livelihoods. This is not to say that there are no forerunners whatsoever of this kind. The juridical figure of the indigenous *resguardo*, for instance, is not a recent invention but has its origins in colonial times, created to designate areas where indigenous groups were to settle

(Semper 2006).[4] However, at that time, the corresponding "recognition" had its motivation and logic in the depiction of indigenous peoples as savages that were to be treated differently so as to enable their transition or integration into "civilized life" (Arocha 1998; Semper 2006). In contrast, with Colombia's constitutional change in 1991, the space opened up for expressions of ethnic and cultural diversity rests on a view of plurality as (in principle) something positive (Lemaitre Ripoll 2009). This recognition moreover extends to Afro-Colombian communities, whose existence as a distinct ethnic group was finally recognized with the adoption of Law 70 in 1993, after a centuries-long history of invisibilization and dehumanization (Arocha 1998). One of the decisive factors that led a growing number of Afro-Colombian organizations and communities to mobilize and articulate demands for such recognition and attendant territorial and cultural rights was the growing threat of dispossession posed by encroaching extractive industries. With utmost disregard for the lives of the populations thus affected, the impacts of concessions granted by the Colombian State to timber, mining, and agroindustrial companies began to grow unbearable from the 1980s onwards (Restrepo 2004a; Pardo 2002).

Although Afro-Colombian organizations did not have their own representative in the Constituent Assembly, primarily via indigenous delegates in the Assembly they achieved that Transitory Article 55 (AT 55) was ultimately included in the Constitution.[5] AT 55 ordered the formation of a commission that was to draft a law to deal specifically with the collective land rights of (rural) Afro-Colombian communities. In 1993, Law 70 was adopted as a result. Decree 1745 of 1995 laid down the terms and procedures that must be complied with in order to obtain a collective land title (Arocha 1998; Pardo 2002; Restrepo 2004a).

Two decades later, by 2012, Afro-Colombian communities in the Pacific coast region held approximately 5,275,145 ha of collective territory, in what corresponds to 169 titles (UAEGRTD 2013). Nationwide, the area of indigenous resguardos at that juncture reached approximately 30 million ha (UAEGRTD 2013). In both cases, allocated land titles are inalienable, imprescriptible, and inembargable (República de Colombia 1991: Art. 63). What this means is that the rights exercised over these lands are nontransferable, not subject to prescription (i.e. it is a right that lasts and that does not expire in case a land is not used or claimed not to be used), and the land is not subject to seizure (the land can, for instance, not be mortgaged and consequently expropriated due to an inability to pay off debts).

If their Constitutional rights are violated or threatened by the Colombian State or any public entity in particular—whether actively or by omission—Colombians have access to the action of the *tutela*, a writ that can be directed "without the aid of a lawyer, to any judge with jurisdiction over the dispute" (Delaney 2008: 54). A ruling must follow within 10 days, which may order that the action in question is halted immediately or that protective measures in order to prevent further harm are taken (Cepeda-Espinosa 2006). With the ratification of Convention 169 of the International Labour Organization via Law 21 of 1991, Colombia's indigenous and Afro-descendant communities are furthermore endowed with the right to prior consultation whenever projects of natural resource exploitation, and legislative or administrative measures, may affect the lives and territories of these communities (Amparo Rodríguez 2014). The requirement of prior consultation is a fundamental right to protect the exercise of *effective* control and autonomy over land and livelihoods, and ensure the cultural, social, and economic integrity of indigenous and Afro-Colombian populations and hence these populations' existence as a people (Amparo Rodríguez 2014; Semper 2006).

However, regardless of a range of legal protections and the allocation of collective land titles, Afro-Colombian and indigenous communities are still being forced off their lands or, if not dispossessed of their lands as such, suffer the consequences of extractive operations on or around their lands. An alarming 5,185,406 persons have been officially registered as internally displaced in Colombia from 1997 to 2013. Afro-Colombians and indigenous peoples are disproportionately represented in this number (UNHCR 2015). But, as Oslender (2008) notes, these figures fail to grasp the experiences of those that are resisting *in place*, i.e. those that stay put on their lands and continue to withstand the pressures related to the presence and operations of extractive industries and armed actors within or near their territories. Either way, it is evident that critical analysis will have to reflect on the *effective* reach of formal recognition and protection of ethnic and cultural diversity in Colombia.

A Green Constitution Without an Environmental Politics

Colombia's constitutional reform and relevant case law of the Constitutional Court, in addition to advancements in the recognition of ethnic and cultural diversity, also led to a normative reappraisal of the human–environment relation. The significance granted to environmental protection, such that environmental provisions are incorporated into the constitutional framework, is explained not only with reference to the notion that the natural environment in itself merits protection, but, above all, from the view that a healthy environment is a prerequisite for the meaningful preservation and permanence of human life; the existence and dignity of the present and future generations depend on having access to healthy environments (Corte Constitucional 2010: 35.) In view of the constitutional safeguards put in place accordingly, Colombia's Constitution has even been classified as "green" or "ecological" (ibid: 36). But the proclaimed environmental spirit of Colombia's Constitution may have to be qualified in several ways. I mention two here.

First, Colombia is often criticized for being "*a país leguleyo*"", a term that seeks to draw attention to the fact that Colombia is a country replete of laws and lawyers, a country where recourse to the law and legal procedure is the norm, but that ultimately falls short in terms of law enforcement and compliance. In fact, it has even been argued that Colombia experiences a "legislative inflation". On this view, the existence of an ever greater amount of laws and legal provisions, in a logic similar to monetary inflation, simultaneously brings about the devaluation of the juridical system, thus as it were hollowing out its perceived credibility (González 2011).

But, more than anything, it is important to point out that a progressive legal framework that works in an overall context devoid of a sustainable *politics* sorts limited effect. This brings me to the second reservation that I wish to make, for which it is instructive to draw upon the environmental drama that unfolded in Casanare, located in central east Colombia. In the first half of 2014, months of severe drought caused the death of thousands of animals in Casanare, including capybara, cows, and turtles (Correa 2014). Human populations were also seriously affected by the experienced water scarcity. After months of inaction, a specialist unit of the Attorney

General, charged with the criminal investigation of environmental issues and natural resource-related activity, travelled to the area to clarify what factors had led up to this situation. The ex-Minister of the Environment, Manuel Rodríguez Becerra, got to the hearth of the matter when stating: "It is madness to see that the Environmental Crime Unit of the Attorney General's Office is involved in this. This is a stance of "let's find the culprit". What is to blame is a badly oriented development politics" (Rodríguez Becerra, quoted in Correa 2014).

Rather than reducible to the actions or omissions of a single entity within a narrowly delimited time frame, the situation in Casanare is the outcome of an economic model whereby, for several decades already, the savannahs of Casanare have been converted into one of Colombia's main areas of oil extraction, large-scale cattle ranching, rice fields, and vast plantations of oil palm. It must be reiterated that no matter how "green" a Constitution and legal framework appear to be, such frameworks generally reflect, and exist in parallel with, deeply engrained conceptions of nature as "capital" at our disposal, open to human exploitation and appropriation (White 2002). This is by no means to deny the importance of environmental legislation and regulatory measures, but so long as these provisions are subservient to the prevalent view that natural resources can be put to sustainable use on the capitalist path to progress, ultimately the green credentials of such frameworks are empty.

In relation to the palm oil industry, it is of similar importance to bear in mind the notion that a progressive legal framework must be accompanied by, or function within, a sustainable environmental *politics*. Having outlined some key aspects against which Colombia's legal and constitutional framework ought to be assessed, the remainder of this chapter will provide more background regarding the palm oil industry and the region that is the main focus of this study.

The Palm Oil Industry in Tumaco

There are four main regions in Colombia where the palm oil industry has a presence, referred to as the northern, central, eastern, and western zones of palm oil production. The western production zone is almost completely constituted by Tumaco—although Guapi (located north of Tumaco, Nariño, in the Cauca department) is seen as a potential site of oil palm cultivation, so far its share in the produce of the western zone is negligible.[6]

Tumaco forms the most southern municipality of the Colombian Pacific coast region. Its inhabitants proudly refer to Tumaco as "the Pearl of the Pacific", variously explained by reference the zone's natural beauty, its fertile and productive lands, or the immense pearl that supposedly once was found on its shores (Velandia Cruz 2012). But, on a less positive note, it is also the case that the social and economic deprivation experienced in Tumaco is alarming: 84% of the population lives in poverty, compared to 50% for Colombia at large (of course *both* figures are disturbing); the level of Unsatisfied Basic Needs is 48%, compared to a national average of 27%; sewerage service exists for 5% of the population, where this is 73% for the country as a whole; and over 60% of the population has no access to water supply utilities (Diócesis de Tumaco; 2012; Alcaldía de Tumaco & Gobernación de Nariño 2014). For many of Tumaco's inhabitants, the conditions to subsist are dire, and especially in the rural areas the provision of basic services falls short.

Powerful economic and political interests have furthermore turned the "Pearl of the Pacific" into a whirlpool of threats and adversities. Along with the state-corporate push for the capitalist development of the region's territories, or, arguably, *intertwined* with the pressures placed on the land and existing land uses by agribusiness and other industries, since the late 1990s armed conflict and illicit economies have brought a wave of terror upon Tumaco's population and environments (Diócesis de Tumaco 2012). With its dense (although reduced) forest cover, traversed by an extensive river network, bordering with Ecuador to the south and having quick access to the Pacific Ocean to the west, the region is of great geostrategic and economic interest for groups involved in narco-business and contraband activity. Various paramilitary groups, guerrilla forces (FARC, ELN), and "Bacrim" currently have the region in its grip (Verdad-Abierta.com 2014; Human Rights Watch 2014; Corte Constitucional 2014).

The formal trajectory of paramilitary groups leads back to the 1960s, when the Colombian State laid the legal foundations for the creation of civil defence groups as part of its strategy to combat leftist guerrillas (Richani 2007). In the 1990s, these as well as other paramilitary groups—created to defend the economic and political interests of cattle ranchers, large landowners, agribusiness, and drug traffickers—became centrally organized under the command of the AUC (*Autodefensas Unidas de Colombia*, the United Self-Defence Forces of Colombia). Ballvé (2012: 603) refers to paramilitary groups as "an outgrowth of a complex alliance between narcos (drug traffickers) and agrarian elites, [that] simultaneously act as drug-trafficking private militias and counter-insurgent battalions, while using land appropriation and agribusiness as favored conduits for money laundering and illicit profit". In contrast to the antagonistic relationship of leftist insurgencies towards the Colombian State and the prevailing socioeconomic order, paramilitary groups have developed close links with corporate and institutional structures and the political establishment. Despite their formal demobilization since 2003, there is widespread agreement that paramilitary structures have not been dissolved and that new groups—such as the Rastrojos, Urabeños, and Águilas Negras—have emerged (Richani 2007; Ballvé 2012; Grajales 2013). The FARC, *las Fuerzas Armadas Revolucionarias de Colombia*, is a left-wing guerrilla group that has its genesis in the peasant self-defence groups that emerged in the 1920s and 30s in the struggle for land reform. In 1964, the Marquetalia massacre was the final push to give birth to this guerrilla group, which 2 years later named itself FARC. The ELN, *Ejército de Liberación Nacional*, created around the same time, differed from the FARC in that it was principally influenced by Che Guevara's revolutionary doctrine of the "foco"; several of its founders studied and received training in Cuba (Kirk 2003). "Bacrim" is a Spanish acronym for *bandas criminales*, criminal gangs, although in critical circles the term is viewed as a misleading euphemism that distracts from what are effectively "demobilized" paramilitaries (Diócesis de Tumaco 2011).

The presence and actions of these actors dramatically interfere with the territorial and cultural rights of indigenous and Afro-Colombian communities (Pardo 2002; Restrepo 2004a; Lemaitre Ripoll 2009). Considering that the palm oil industry in Tumaco operates within this broader context, integrated with the analysis of the harms associated with palm oil production there the various ways in which these different factors and forces converge, interact, and coexist will be addressed.

In terms of Tumaco's demographic composition, the following can be observed. Around 45% of Tumaco's 187,084 inhabitants live in the rural zone. In addition to the existence of individual land titles, most of the land of rural indigenous and Afro-Colombian communities is collectively titled. Of Tumaco's total of 360,238 ha, collectively titled Afro-Colombian territory comprises 173,632 ha and indigenous resguardos amount to 65,780 ha (Alcaldía de Tumaco & Gobernación de Nariño 2014). Article 5 of Law 70 requires that Afro-Colombian communities organize into community councils in order to be considered for the adjudication of a collective land title. In total, 15 Afro-Colombian community councils have thus been formed in Tumaco. The two community councils that are most affected by the palm oil industry are *Alto Mira y Frontera* and *Bajo Mira y Frontera*, respectively located on the higher (alto) and lower (bajo) parts of the Mira River. The community council Alto Mira y Frontera was formed in 1996 and obtained its collective title in 2005, which after amplification in 2006 covers 24,790 ha; Bajo Mira y Frontera obtained its title in 2003, which covers 46,481 ha (Diócesis de Tumaco 2012). Both community councils are located south of the road that leads from Tumaco to Pasto. There are 15 indigenous Awá resguardos in Tumaco and one of indigenous Eperara Siapidara (Diócesis de Tumaco 2012). Regarding indigenous resguardos directly affected by the presence and operations of the palm oil industry, this study addresses the situation of two Awá resguardos located north of the road that leads from Tumaco to Pasto; La Brava and Peña La Alegría. In 2000, Awá of La Brava obtained a collective title over 983 ha of land; Peña La Alegría obtained a collective land title in 2010, to an area that by then had been reduced to 30 ha.

Whereas La Brava and Peña La Alegría are impacted by the establishment of vast, corporate-owned oil palm plantations around *what is now left of* Awá territory, in the case of the Afro-Colombian community councils of Bajo Mira y Frontera and Alto Mira y Frontera the oil palm is not only encircling, traversing, and breaking up collective territory, but established *on* collective land, too. It traverses collective territory due to corporate occupation of these areas *before* Law 70 of 1993 was implemented, which led to the resultant exclusion of these areas from the collective title; oil palm cultivation within the boundaries of the collective title is a result of small grower involvement in the industry. There are, as such, different modalities of oil palm cultivation. Below, in the final section of this chapter, the main modalities of oil palm cultivation in Tumaco will be addressed, which will be followed by brief reflection on the extent to which these were made the focus of the site visits carried out during the fieldwork period.

Modalities of Palm Oil Production

The first oil palm plantations in Tumaco began to be established in the late 1950s, initially an endeavour coordinated by the Institute for Cotton Development[7] driven by government policy geared towards import substitution and the diversification of oleaginous crops. Soon this was followed by private sector investment and the consequent rapid expansion of the area cultivated with oil palm (Ospina Bozzi and Ochoa Jaramillo 1998: 47–54; Ospina Bozzi 2001: 21–59). Since then, the total extension of oil palm cultivation in Tumaco has grown to reach—at its height[8]—an estimated 35,000–36,000 ha.

In Colombia and globally, the two principal modalities of oil palm cultivation correspond to the vast plantations of big palm oil corporations and smaller-scale cultivation by smallholders that enter into partnership with the private sector. In 2010, 9% of Colombian palm oil production came from such Productive Alliances, or Strategic Alliances, of on average 12 ha (Rodríguez Raga et al. 2010). In Tumaco, before the bud rot epidemic destroyed most oil palms, small growers accounted for close to 40% of local palm oil production (Cárdenas 2012).

McCarthy (2010), writing on small grower cultivation of oil palm in Indonesia, notes that the integration of small growers into corporate-driven, agroindustrial value chains either tends to be presented as a viable strategy of poverty reduction and form of rural development, or, in contrast, critiqued for subjecting small growers to relations of dependency that reproduce or exacerbate social and economic inequalities.

To nuance this somewhat dualistic narrative, McCarthy demonstrates that in between these two extremes lie different degrees of a more or less beneficial through to a mostly adverse inclusion of smallholders. Whether and to what extent palm oil works for or against the poor depends on the terms on which small growers are incorporated into the oil palm economy (McCarthy 2010).

According to Cárdenas (2012: 317), small growers of oil palm in Tumaco "occupy an ambiguous position that straddles the divide between landless proletariats and willing (and truly advantageously positioned) stakeholders" (2012: 317). Although cultivation of oil palm by small growers has existed in Tumaco since the early stages of the sector's establishment (Ospina Bozzi 2001: 29–31, 59–61), the terms of small grower incorporation into the oil palm economy in Tumaco assumed a more formalized and entrepreneurial character with the creation of Cordeagropaz in 1999. Cordeagropaz was established to strengthen agribusiness-led development and smallholder economic activity in Tumaco, as a joint initiative of Tumaco's municipal administration and the private palm oil sector, backed by international cooperation and public funding (Cordeagropaz 2015). In view of the high levels of poverty and social vulnerability experienced by Tumaco's population and with an eye on mounting pressures on the area as a consequence of armed conflict and coca cultivation, fomenting small grower cultivation of oil palm was seen as a productive alternative that could contribute to peace and social and economic stability.[9] Cordeagropaz promotes, directs, and coordinates the entrance of smallholders into Strategic Alliances with palm oil companies; under its direction, growers that are organized into associations can get access to loans, technical assistance, and sell their oil palm fruits to the palm oil company that owns the extraction plant.

It is important to emphasize that the type of small grower cultivation promoted and supported through Strategic Alliances conforms to the agroindustrial logic of production, i.e. we are dealing with cultivation in monocultures, rows of oil palms planted at fixed distances from each other, the external input of fertilizers, the use of agrochemicals, and so on, all to maximize yields, efficiency, and profitability. In addition to the agroindustrial modalities, a third modality exists in Tumaco. In this modality, the oil palms are integrated into a nonindustrial, diversified system of traditional agriculture and, as such, are cultivated interspersed with other crops and vegetation (Restrepo 2004b; Cárdenas 2012).

This study centres on the two agroindustrial modalities of oil palm cultivation, since it is these that have grown most prominent and that are at the heart of palm oil-related tension and conflict in Tumaco. To this end, in addition to conducting semi-structured interviews (38 in total, see Appendix), and the site visits made to the Alto Mira y Frontera and Bajo Mira y Frontera community councils as well as indigenous Awá resguardos La Brava and Peña La Alegría, several small grower oil palm plantations along the road that leads from Tumaco to Pasto were visited. In Guapi, too, I was able to see several small grower projects. In Chaps. 5 and 6, I reflect on the divergent perspectives of small growers of oil palm on the one hand and local palm oil critics on the other; the extent to which involvement in the palm oil industry can be considered a viable social and economic activity for smallholders; and the dynamics of industry expansion in the light of Strategic Alliances. The next chapter has as its primary focus the fact that the palm oil industry in Tumaco operates in a conflict-ridden region where, as briefly alluded to, a variety of forces and interests converge. I reflect more closely on what this entails for practices and discourses of palm oil-related harm.

Notes

1. Floodplains are lands adjacent to rivers, lakes, and oceans that are prone to periodic flooding.
2. A belt of low-pressure moist air masses.
3. Respectively, these groups make up approximately 90 and 5% of the population in this region.
4. The *resguardo* is the juridical form under which indigenous land is collectively owned by the members of an indigenous community. For an outline of the invention and subsequent stages of the dissolution and the restoration of the *resguardo*, see Semper (2006).
5. Restrepo (2002, 2004a) notes that AT 55 was simultaneously an *outcome* of the mobilization and organization around an Afro-Colombian ethnic and cultural identity, and a factor in *strengthening* and *reproducing* that identity.

6. At the time of this research, primarily due to logistic problems small growers in Guapi were cultivating some 500 ha of oil palm, much less than aimed for.
7. *Instituto de Fomento Algodonero*, IFA.
8. "At its height" relates to the fact that, between 2005 and 2009, a bud rot epidemic led to the death of nearly all oil palm in Tumaco (see Chap. 6).
9. Hence the suffix *paz* (meaning peace) in Cordeagropaz.

References

Alcaldía de Tumaco & Gobernación de Nariño. (2014). *Bases para la construcción del plan especial de recuperación social y económica del municipio de Tumaco: 2014–2018*. Tumaco: República de Colombia, Departamento de Nariño and Municipio de Tumaco.

Amparo Rodríguez, G. (2014). *De la consulta previa al consentamiento libre, previo e informado a pueblos indígenas en Colombia*. Bogotá: Grupo Editorial Ibañez S.A.S.

Arocha, J. (1998). Inclusion of Afro-Colombians: Unreachable national goal? *Latin American Perspectives, 25*(3), 70–89.

Ballvé, T. (2012). Everyday state formation: Territory, decentralization, and the narco landgrab in Colombia. *Environment and Planning D: Society and Space, 30*(4), 603–622.

Cárdenas, R. (2012). Green multiculturalism: Articulations of ethnic and environmental politics in a Colombian 'black community'. *The Journal of Peasant Studies, 39*(2), 309–333.

Cepeda-Espinosa, J. M. (2006). How far may Colombia's constitutional court go to protect IDP rights? *Forced Migration Review*. Special issue, December 2006: 21–23.

Cordeagropaz. (2015). *Nuestra Empresa* [Online]. Available from: http://www.cordeagropaz.com [Accessed 8 April 2015].

Correa, P. (2014, March 29). Tragedias ambientales en un país de leguleyos. *El Espectador* [Online], (Medio Ambiente). Available from: http://www.elespectador.com [Accessed 11 March 2015].

Corte Constitucional. (2010). *Sentencia C-595. Demanda de inconstitucionalidad contra el parágrafo del artículo 1º y el parágrafo 1º del artículo 5º de la Ley 1333 de 2009*. Bogotá: República de Colombia.

Corte Constitucional. (2014). *Auto 073 de 2014. Medidas de prevención, protección y atención de las comunidades afrodescendientes de la región pacífica del departamento de Nariño en riesgo y víctimas de desplazamiento forzado.* Bogotá: República de Colombia.

Delaney, P. (2008). Legislating for equality in Colombia: Constitutional jurisprudence, Tutelas, and social reform. *The Equal Rights Review, 1,* 50–59.

Delgado, A., Ruiz, S., Arévalo, L., Castillo, G., Viles, N., Calderón, J., et al. (Eds.). (2007). *Plan de Acción en Biodiversidad del Departamento de Nariño 2006–2030 – Propuesta Técnica.* Pasto: Corponariño, Gobernación de Nariño (Secretaría de Agricultura), IAvH, UAESPNN, Universidad de Nariño, Universidad Mariana y Asociación para el Desarrollo Campesino.

Diócesis de Tumaco. (2011). *¡Que nadie diga que no pasa nada! Una mirada desde la Región del Pacífico Nariñense. Balance no. 2.* Tumaco: Diócesis de Tumaco.

Diócesis de Tumaco. (2012). *¡Que nadie diga que no pasa nada! Una mirada desde la Región del Pacífico Nariñense. Balance no. 3.* Tumaco: Diócesis de Tumaco.

Escobar, A. (2008). *Territories of difference: Place, movements, life, redes.* Durham, NC: Duke University Press.

González, A. (2011, August 26). ¿Cómo solucionar la "inflación legislativa"? *El Nuevo Siglo Bogotá* [Online]. Available from: http://www.elnuevosiglo.com.co [Accessed 5 March 2014].

Grajales, J. (2013). State involvement, land grabbing and counter-insurgency in Colombia. *Development and Change, 44*(2), 211–232.

Human Rights Watch. (2014, July 30). *Colombia: FARC Battering Afro-Ccolombian Areas. Atrocities by Guerrillas, Criminal Groups Go Unpunished.* Available from: http://www.hrw.org [Accessed 1 August 2014].

Kirk, R. (2003). *More terrible than death: Massacres, drugs, and America's war in Colombia.* New York: PublicAffairs.

Lemaitre Ripoll, J. (2009). *El derecho como conjuro: fetichismo legal, violencia y movimientos sociales.* Bogotá: Siglo del Hombre Editores y Universidad de los Andes.

Lynch, M. J., & Stretesky, P. B. (2014). *Exploring green criminology. Towards a green criminological revolution.* Farnham: Ashgate.

McCarthy, J. F. (2010). Processes of inclusion and adverse incorporation: Oil palm and agrarian change in Sumatra, Indonesia. *The Journal of Peasant Studies, 37*(4), 821–850.

Oslender, U. (2008). Another history of violence: The production of "Geographies of Terror" in Colombia's Pacific coast region. *Latin American Perspectives, 35*(5), 77–102.
Ospina Bozzi, M. L. (2001). *La palma africana en Colombia: Apuntes y memorias, Volumen 2* (2nd ed.). Bogotá: Fedepalma.
Ospina Bozzi, M. L., & Ochoa Jaramillo, D. (1998). *La palma Africana en Colombia: Apuntes y memorias, Volumen 1*. Bogotá: Fedepalma.
Pardo, M. (2002). Entre la autonomía y la institucionalización: Dilemas del movimiento negro colombiano. *The Journal of Latin American Anthropology, 7*(2), 60–85.
Pintaud, J-C., Galeano, G., Balslev, H., Bernal, R., Borchsenius, F., Ferreira, E. et al. (2008). Las Palmeras de América del Sur: diversidad, distribución e historia evolutiva. *Revista Peruana de Biología, 15*(Suppl.1), 5–27.
República de Colombia. (1991). *Constitución Política de Colombia 1991*. Bogotá: Presidencia de la República.
Restrepo, E. (2002). Políticas de la alteridad: Etnización de "comunidad negra" en el Pacífico sur colombiano. *The Journal of Latin American Anthropology, 7*(2), 34–59.
Restrepo, E. (2004a). Biopolítica y alteridad: dilemas de la etnización de las colombias negras. In E. Restrepo, & A. Rojas, (Eds.), *Conflicto e (in) visibilidad. Retos en los estudios de la gente negra de Colombia* (pp. 271–300). Popayán: Editorial Universidad del Cauca.
Restrepo, E. (2004b). Un océano verde para extraer aceite. Hacia una etnografía del cultivo de la palma africana en Tumaco. *Universitas Humanistica, 58*, 72–87.
Richani, N. (2007). Caudillos and the crisis of the colombian state: Fragmented sovereignty, the war system and the privatisation of counterinsurgency in Colombia. *Third World Quarterly, 28*(2), 403–417.
Rodríguez Raga, M. C., Carrizosa Umaña, A., Bonell, C., & Rengifo, S. (2010). *De Las Alianzas Productivas a los Negocios Inclusivos. Guía de Mejores Prácticas para la implementación de Negocios Inclusivos en palma de aceite*. Bogotá: SNV-Cecodes, Fedepalma, USAID/Programa MIDAS.
Semper, F. (2006). Los derechos de los pueblos indígenas de Colombia en la jurisprudencia de la Corte constitucional. In J. Woischnik (Ed.), *Anuario de Derecho Constitucional Latinoamericano – Tomo II* (pp. 761–787). Berlin: Konrad-Adenauer-Stiftung.
Unidad Administrativa Especial de Gestión de Restitución de Tierras Despojadas (UAEGRTD). (2013). *La Política Pública para la Protección y*

Restitución de los Derechos Territoriales de los Grupos Étnicos: Antecedentes, Acciones y Perspectivas en el Escenario de los Decretos con Fuerza de Ley para Grupos Étnicos (4633 y 4635 de 2011). Bogotá: República de Colombia.

UNHCR. (2015). Colombia. Available from: http://www.acnur.org/donde-trabaja/america/colombia/ [Accessed 12 March 2015].

Van Cott, D. L. (2000). *The friendly liquidation of the past: The politics of diversity in Latin America.* Pittsburgh: University of Pittsburgh Press.

Velandia Cruz, Á. I. (2012). Sobre el cacao y la Perla del Pacífico. In E. Chavarro Pinzón, S. C. Torres López, & H. F. Santos Duarte (Eds.), *Sostenibilidad y Legalidad: Buenas prácticas ambientales en los programas de desarrollo alternativo* (pp. 42–53). Bogotá: UACT and UNODC.

VerdadAbierta.com. (2014, March 2). Cómo reparar los daños de la guerra en el pacífico nariñense. [Online], (Justicia y Paz). Available from: http://www.verdadabierta.com [Accessed 2 March 2014].

White, R. (2002). Environmental harm and the political economy of consumption. *Social Justice, 29*(1–2), 82–102.

4

Colombia's Contested Grounds

If anything has generated an impact prior *to its arrival, it has been this, it has been palm*
(ONIC consultant).
60% of the inhabitants of the Pacific are displaced. And the few people that resist are under pressure from all sides; the air force constantly bombards them under the pretext of fighting the guerrilla, the guerrilla on the other hand to win followers, and the paramilitaries in turn are the ones that represent the Colombian bourgeoisie. Because unfortunately, we stand alone in all of this; the only thing, which isn't all that clear-cut either, is the little that the international community does and which of course is very much subject to government policy. I'm not saying that they [international cooperation] are malicious, they are fulfilling their mission. But this mission is not directed towards the Colombian people but to the Colombian government, and between these there lies an immense difference
(Afrodes activist).

Towards the end of August 2016, a peace agreement between the government of President Santos and the FARC was reached but when put to the Colombian people for approval in a referendum held on October 2, 2016, the agreement was rejected with a slight majority of votes. Similar to other parts of the country that are amongst the most impacted by the violence and repression linked to more than 5 decades of armed conflict, the result of the referendum left communities in Tumaco in a state of disbelief, distress, and uncertainty (Sánchez 2016). Up until the time of the referendum, the ceasefire that had been decreed unilaterally by the

H. Mol, *The Politics of Palm Oil Harm*, Palgrave Studies in Green Criminology, DOI 10.1007/978-3-319-55378-8_4

FARC in June 2015, and bilaterally since August 2016, had led to some overall improvements in the ability of communities to move through their territories, and FARC fighters had started to withdraw towards a specified demobilization zone. After the referendum, however, a reverse move of FARC fighters back to their bases was witnessed (Sánchez 2016), once more giving way to a prevailing sense of uncertainty and concern about how the situation would evolve.[1]

But the FARC is not the only threat faced by the local population; recently, for instance, various pamphlets have been circulating: one announcing a campaign of "social cleansing" by the self-named Organization of Assassins of the Pacific (*Organización Sicarial del Pacífico*); another, signed by the AUC (a supposedly demobilized paramilitary group), threatens to "finish off" collaborators of the FARC; and yet another, by the People of Order (*Gente de Orden*), prohibits citizens to collaborate with persons that via extortion, robberies, forced displacement, and assassinations seek to damage or spoil the image of Tumaco and its people (Espejo 2016). Salgar Antolínez (2016), for that matter, highlights that there are multiple factors that violate and threaten the territorial autonomy of Afro-Colombian (and indigenous) communities in the region, amongst which are drug trafficking, the expansion of the palm oil industry, paramilitary groups, and the FARC.

This "complex panorama" (Espejo 2016) is not something recent though. At the time of this research, a similar image emerged. Hence, in this chapter I discuss the various factors, actors, and dynamics that interact, compete, or exist alongside each other in zones where the palm oil industry operates. Thereby the principal aim is to disentangle the complex and varied linkages that exist in practice and in discourse between the harms and crimes endured by local populations and environments, the operations of the palm oil industry, and the presence of legal and illegal armed actors and illicit economic activity in the region. The main argument that will be thus put forward is that the existence in the Colombian Pacific of a variety of factors and dynamics unrelated or only remotely related to the palm oil industry allows for the type of discursive mechanisms by which substantive debate over alleged palm oil-related harm is diverted. In the discussion that as such unfolds, three observations assume centrality: (i) the situation whereby various factors compete, interact, or exist together in the same region allows for the *externalization* of harm by denying that the alleged crime or harm is palm oil related; (ii) Colombia's ongoing internal armed conflict allows for the delegitimization or undermining of allegations of harm by dismissing the latter as an expression of subversive sympathies and political ideology; and (iii) illegality is relegated to an exterior realm where the state is held to be absent, rather than accepting that this illegality exists *intertwined* with legal operations, economic development, and institutional structures.

I set this analysis up by outlining the emblematic case of Jiguamiandó and Curvaradó, in the northern part of the Colombian Pacific. Even though this region has not been the primary focus of the research carried out for this study, for mainly three reasons it is crucial to reflect on what took place there. First, the occurrences in the Lower Atrato region of the Chocó (where Jiguamiandó and Curvaradó are situated) are frequently taken as a reference point for the denunciations of the Colombian palm oil industry in reports by national and international civil society organizations (e.g. Mingorance et al. 2004; Mingorance 2006; Vélez 2008; World Rainforest Movement 2010), as well as in scholarly analysis (Grajales 2013; Ballvé 2013). The case significantly shapes the image of the Colombian palm oil industry, nationally and internationally, and was referred to in nearly all interviews conducted for this research.

Second, context-specific aspects notwithstanding, the occurrences in Jiguamiandó and Curvaradó raise some difficult questions on how to interpret the violent dynamics revolving around the establishment and expansion of palm oil operations in Colombia, and are of vital importance for the wider analysis of coercion–consent and legal–illegal dynamics in the politics of palm oil harm.

Third, the Chocó case was on several occasions brought up in *defence* of the palm oil industry. This applied to interviews with corporate executives, industry protagonists at the level of Fedepalma and local authorities, and small growers. Allegations regarding what took place in the Chocó were thereby invoked not as a problem *of*, but a problem *for*, the palm oil industry. A small grower, for instance, spoke about the difficulties experienced as a result of the rejection of palm oil by, above all, local community leaders. Such misguided opposition to palm oil, he argued, stems from the violent imposition of palm oil in the Chocó:

> The thing is that in Tumaco we are confronted with a situation that presented itself in... in the Chocó. What occurred there, travelled to Tumaco and other production zones of palm, in the sense that palm is said to be the number one enemy of the producer, of the country, and that people should not cultivate it. (Small grower and representative of Palmasur)

In this chapter and those that follow, I will demonstrate that allusion to the Chocó forms part of a broader set of discourses that seek to dissociate the "normal" operations and perceived virtues of the palm oil industry from allegations of palm oil-related crime and harm.

Violence, Conflict, and Palm Oil: Curvaradó and Jiguamiandó

As mentioned previously, the Curvaradó and Jiguamiandó river basins in the Lower Atrato region of Chocó are located in the most northern part of the Colombian Pacific. Situated at the Gulf of Urabá, this part of the Chocó department is also referred to as Urabá Chocoano or simply Urabá. Rather than a clearly delimited geographical area, Urabá is composed of parts of the Chocó (Urabá Chocoano) and Antioquia (Urabá Antioqueño).

Urabá Chocoano is inhabited principally by Afro-Colombian communities, followed by a smaller presence of indigenous Embera Dóvida, Embera Chamí, Embera Katio, Wounan, and Tule, and mestizo population (Mingorance et al. 2004). Generally, the latter are settlers (*colonos*) that began to arrive to the region in the 1970s and 1980s. They were either landless peasants or smallholders forced to leave the departments of Córdoba, Sucre, Atlántico, and Antioquia due to persecution by large landowners who were laying claim to the lands in those departments (CIJP 2005).[2]

To this day, significant parts of the Chocó are still little known. In addition to conditions relating to the climate and natural geography of the region, this is not least due to the prevailing andinocentric imaginary (see Chap. 2) that has construed these territories as backward and underdeveloped. The Chocó and, more broadly, the Colombian Pacific are said to have been historically neglected and invisibilized (Mingorance et al. 2004; Grajales 2013). In fact, as Mingorance et al. (2004: 88) put it, "the Chocó has been so utterly 'abandoned and forgotten' that even the war under which Colombia suffers, for a time seemed to have forgotten about these lands". But all of this changed rapidly from the mid-1990s, when the south-western part of Urabá began to experience levels of violence that for decades had almost exclusively affected the northern part of Urabá (Grajales 2013). Although the Lower Atrato had been a zone of FARC presence from the early 1980s on, counter-insurgency operations had been sporadic up to that time. But the convergence of geostrategic and economic interests linked to drug trafficking and contraband activity, as well as a growing awareness of the region's economic potential in view of its biodiversity and as a site of agroindustry, in the 1990s brought about a paramilitary influx and a surge in military actions against guerrilla groups (Grajales 2013). As a result, communities have come to endure repeated waves of forced displacement, harassment, violence, and brutal atrocities at the hands of paramilitary groups with the tacit or active complicity of military forces (CIDH 2003; Defensoría del Pueblo 2005).[3]

It is often alleged that the violence, land grab, and persecution of communities in the zone are the sole outcomes of territorial conflict between guerrilla and paramilitary groups and that military operations by Colombian State forces seek only to defeat or at least drive out the FARC. However, critics have pointed out that the means and methods resorted to cast doubt on the stated counter-insurgency objectives. Indiscriminate aerial bombardments have almost exclusively affected the civilian population and moreover been accompanied by massacres, selective assassinations, "disappearances", cases of torture, intimidation, and the plundering and burning down of villages (CIJP 2005; Grajales 2013). The close collaboration between Colombian State forces and paramilitary groups in these processes has been well established (Grajales 2013). Paramilitary movement and incursions into the region have been condoned, up to facilitated, by the public forces (CIJP 2005). In 1997, paramilitary groups actively joined forces with the military in Operation Genesis. This operation provoked the displacement of an estimated

15,000 inhabitants from the river basins of Cacarica, Curvaradó, Jiguamiandó, Domingodó, Truandó, and Salaquí (Defensoría del Pueblo 2005). Some sought refuge in the forests, others fled the region to other departments or across the border with Panamá (CIJP 2007a). With the appropriated lands emptied of their human inhabitants, and territorial control secured, from 2001 onwards oil palm plantations began to be established. Most of the more than 25,000 ha thus appropriated and occupied are located within collectively titled Afro-Colombian territory, to which the affected communities received land titles in 2000. Regardless of the existence of these legal title deeds, the grabbed lands became legalized (CIJP 2007a; Grajales 2011).[4]

In view of the above, in Urabá Chocoano, palm oil has grown synonymous with the systematic, violent persecution of local communities and individuals that stand in the way of the materialization of powerful political and economic interests. Palm oil there is viewed as at once an economic, political, and a (para)military project. Affected communities, and the NGOs that support them in their struggles to retrieve their lands, means of subsistence, and ways of life, have likened the planting of oil palm in Curvaradó and Jiguamiandó to the "implementation of death" (CIJP 2007a). In an interview, a member of Justicia y Paz insisted that throughout the process—from clearing the lands to the establishment and subsequent expansion of oil palm plantations—"*it wasn't the people who were protected but the very criminals that grabbed the lands*". He explained that the rejection of palm oil on the part of affected communities in Jiguamiandó and Curvaradó is due first and foremost to the criminal way in which this industry was able to establish its operations in the zone:

> The communities said, *say*: "This land is fertilized with the bodies of our loved ones". From 1996 to the present day, within the complete time frame of implementation of this project, more than 140 persons have been assassinated there. (Member of Justicia y Paz)

Moreover, as spaces of life were turned into spaces of terror, people's vital spaces of living became disintegrated. The transformation of the physical landscape of these territories also transformed the existential geography and the symbolism of the socionatural spaces targeted (CIJP 2007b: 19). Thus, processes of agroindustry establishment and expansion destroy and debilitate not only physical life but *ways* of life, too, as reiterated in the following quote:

> The foundations of people's lives are profoundly dislocated. It is brutal. In other words, people are not only affected because the palms were planted, no, people were uprooted. As if to say: there is no space for you here, what belongs here is *this*, in *this way*. And if you want to return it is to work *this*, and in *this way*. The prospects for a community to exercise autonomy are lost. (Member of Justicia y Paz)

The socionatural spaces that were thus targeted and appropriated are central to locally specific productive, social, and cultural dimensions of life (see also Chaps. 5 and 6). To depict palm oil as a legal alternative and productive opportunity capable of contributing to peace and rural development seems untenable in view of testimonies and accusations presented above. But such testimonies and accusations tend to be dismissed out of hand in corporate and official discourses on palm oil, as will be demonstrated below.

"Alternatives" in the Midst of Conflict

In response to accounts that link the palm oil industry to violence and dispossession, a study carried out by the Security and Democracy Foundation stated the following:

> [T]he African oil palm business has developed in a highly complex and sometimes critical context of rural insecurity that has conditioned, to a great extent, its projects and activities. But this insecurity is the result of various criminal factors, the most noteworthy of which are, for the effects of this paper, the following: drug trafficking; subversive, counter-insurgency and common criminal armed organizations; arms smuggling and trafficking; takeover of lands and displacement from properties. Given its complexity and extensiveness, this violence must be acknowledged and treated

> based on its particular conditions as a multi-variable phenomenon that includes various stages, inflection points, and recurrences. (Rangel et al. 2009: 61)[5]

In interviews and personal communication with corporate executives and representatives of the palm oil industry, too, repeated emphasis was placed on the fact that the sector operates in regions afflicted by a high degree of social turmoil and socioeconomic marginalization, but that this is due to variables external to the palm oil industry itself. The adverse variables that are at play in conflict-ridden zones are claimed to compound the operations and beneficent potential of the palm oil industry. While the industry is presented as an economic stimulus that contributes to social stability by offering alternative projects of life and giving a boost to local economies, it is emphasized that palm oil cannot work miracles in stabilizing conflict zones. It can, however, bring the agricultural modernization that is needed to overcome rural conditions that are conducive to conflict and illegality, palm oil proponents argue. In fact, palm oil is seen as one of the few actual counterweights to coca cultivation or the involvement in illegal armed groups, for generating employment and binding people to the formal economy.

Along the above lines, with regard to small grower involvement in palm, the Social and Business Coordinator of Cordeagropaz, for instance, stated: *"We have always seen palm as a productive, economic alternative, and really a crop in terms of which people, when dedicating themselves to its cultivation, are not thinking about any other activity, neither in illicit or illegal activities, or terrorist groups, or what have you; because this is an activity that you have to manage with an entrepreneurial spirit"*. Those that represent the industry insist on its capacity to maintain the regions where it operates in social and economic equilibrium by boosting and diversifying local business, around which then, gradually, a whole web of economic activities and social dynamics are held to develop. Rangel et al. (2009) in view of this have stated that analyses and denunciations that link the palm oil industry to forced displacement and the imposition of an economic model alleged to be detrimental to large segments of Colombia's rural population have their basis in anti-capitalist "ideological reductionism".

Considering that the onset and perpetuation of armed conflict, violence, and illegality in rural zones is viewed as the outcome of a lack of social investment in these regions, high rates of unemployment, and the absence of viable economic opportunities, opposition to the corporate sector is deemed problematic. One manager at a palm oil company put it like this: corporate entrepreneurs are the ones that invest in rural zones and that create the business opportunities without which these populations turn to illegality. Why oppose them? Colombia's violent conflict originates in the rural area, "*and why does warfare come from the rural area? Because the rural area has no business, there is nothing there that generates money. So people turn to either coca or warfare. One has to bring companies to the countryside so that... because this is not a country with business in the countryside*" (corporate manager).

The view that corporations play a decisive role in creating the social and economic infrastructure needed for a way out of the violence and conflict that has Colombia in its grips was widely shared among corporate executives, industry representatives, and public officials. As such they claimed that what rural zones need, in addition to a strong institutional state presence that goes beyond mere military presence, is industrial enterprise. Nuclei of agribusiness established by so-called "anchor" companies would then pave the way for smallholder economic activity to start forming around these nuclei. The conflict–development nexus is thus perceived such that (1) violent conflict impedes development (understood as economic growth and the spread of capitalist social and economic relations), and (2) development is a necessary step towards ending violent conflict (see Thomson 2011, for a critique of the accuracy of the "development in reverse" thesis vis-à-vis the Colombian context).

However, the perspectives that in the framework of this research were articulated by palm oil critics contrast sharply with views of agribusiness as central to bringing about social stability and reductions in the levels of violence and conflict. Consistent with Thomson's (2011) analysis, which builds on Marxist critiques of the coercive and violent character of the transition to capitalist accumulation that are particularly apropos in the context of Colombian agribusiness,[6] critics within local communities and civil society organizations claim that the palm oil industry *foments* violence and conflict or at any rate *benefits* from violence and conflict by exploiting the opportunities thus opened up for palm oil companies (Defensoría del Pueblo[7] 2005). The next sections offer a more in-depth discussion of the divergent perspectives on the coercive and violent character of land use change to industrial oil palm plantations in Colombia's Pacific coast region.

Dispossession and Displacement: Pacification or "To Fish in Troubled Waters"?[8]

In Colombia, the transformation of forests and diversified agricultural systems to monocrop oil palm plantations, in addition to being presented as rural and sustainable development, also forms part of "alternative development" programmes geared to crop substitution (e.g. of coca) and strategies of conflict resolution (Grajales 2013). Within this framework, the growth of the palm oil sector was perhaps pushed strongest under the two consecutive administrations of Álvaro Uribe (2002–2010), during whose Presidency palm oil came to be embedded in overt, confrontational strategies of "pacification".[9] Contrary to what the term "pacification" appears to suggest, in several interviews it was pointed out that pacification in this context does not entail a strategy aimed at reducing the spread and impacts of violent conflict. Quite the reverse, the strategy is more likely to draw the targeted territories and populations deeper into situations of conflict. Reflecting on the case of Curvaradó and Jiguamiandó, a member of Justicia y Paz remarked the following in terms of the perceived ends and impacts of "pacification":

> When speaking of "pacification" this means finishing off the guerrilla, this is the discourse. But those who endure the harms were the civil population. And the levels of harm caused to the guerrilla were minimal, because the guerrilla is mobile but the population is settled in place; the areas from which people were displaced *were their lands*. But the guerrilla on the other hand is mobile; in case of a military problem in one locale, they go to another. The people not, the people live in their territory. "Pacification" means to drive out the guerrilla, but in the course of driving out the guerrilla the objective is territorial control, physical as well as social. For this reason, people are displaced. After this, palm follows.

Also in other interviews, "pacification" was explained as a *politics of displacement* geared towards the implementation of projects of neoliberal development. Approached in this way, where trajectories of pacification involve agribusiness, the latter is embedded not only in a security strategy for territorial control but also in a political economy of capitalist development by dispossession. Displacement is then not an unfortunate by-product or unintended consequence of Colombia's internal armed conflict; much to the contrary, it is claimed that the conflict is *used* to displace the people and to dispossess them of their means of subsistence and ways of life. An activist from Afrodes stated the following on why people are deliberately targeted in their territories:

> They specifically *use* the war. Because we are not displaced as a consequence of the armed conflict. It is not that but quite the opposite; they use the war to displace us. And in this, everyone is involved, including the State; through the government on the one hand and the judicial system that doesn't fulfil its true role of protecting the public good on the other hand. In general terms, this is the problematic of palm, independently of whether what they call "development" arrives, but which by no means benefits the targeted communities.

As noted by Grajales (2011), forced displacement in Colombia is a phenomenon provoked by multiple, often intertwining factors, including military objectives, struggles for territorial control by illegal armed groups, and economic projects. As such, practices that on the face of it appear to have their basis in counter-insurgency objectives or coca crop eradication at times more likely emanate from an "underlying capitalist logic of displacement" (Oslender 2008: 97). This logic was also alluded to during a 3 day gathering for the campaign "Another Possible Pacific" (*Campaña Otro Pazífico Posible,* henceforth COPP), where the manifold problems experienced by Afro-descendant inhabitants of the Pacific coast (Colombia and Ecuador) were shared and discussed. On day two, an attendant took the floor and addressed the theme of coca crop eradication. He advanced the argument that the aerial fumigation of coca crops is not just aimed at the eradication of coca, but also functions as a means to "condition" the soils for the implementation (or rather, the perceived imposition) of agroindustrial projects. On another occasion, a consultant from the ONIC articulated the view that the presence of illegal armed actors and (alleged) cultivation of crops for illicit use are being instrumentalized for the depopulation and expropriation of lands that are highly valued as potential sites of lucrative business. On the matter of aerial coca fumigation, he stated:

> There was a time when in addition to the use of glyphosate they spoke of applying organic products. Supposedly they were after eradication. But behind all this is the depopulation of the territories in question as well, so that the next step is to come with all these proposals for the exploitation of all matter of resources: palm, mining, and others. I am stating a conjecture, because there are no studies of this. But it is *vox populi*. And what the people say that have felt the impact, who are there in the territories, who have been fumigated, who have been assassinated, displaced, what they feel is that with these crops for illicit use the aim is to get rid of the people and then with the design of palm allow them to return, but only as cheap labour power for these agroindustrial displays. There is not so much pacification, totally to the contrary. (ONIC consultant)

The presence of irregular armed actors and allegations of illicit crop cultivation on territories that Afro-Colombian and indigenous communities hold collective titles to, furthermore puts the legitimate character of ownership and use of these lands at risk. Under such conditions, the respective lands may come to be labelled as "*territorios de dudosa propiedad*", i.e. territories of questionable ownership (ONIC consultant). This may culminate in the annulment of the collective title deed (Mingorance et al. 2004: 146).[10] During this research, I did not encounter or hear of cases where this risk has materialized. However, the possibility that at some point such measures are taken adds another layer of concern to the already precarious situation of land tenure and land rights for the communities concerned. In view of this, it would seem that counter-narcotics and counter-insurgency practices and discourse pose a continued threat to the autonomy of rural communities, in the form of State interference, military intervention, and further exposure to economic models that do not spring from the communities themselves.

Allegations of Harm Externalized and Delegitimized

Against the above, in defence of the palm oil industry, *any* type of systematic or inherent link between forced displacement, violent dispossession, and palm oil tends to be denied. Thus, Curvaradó and Jiguamiandó, for instance, are considered "exceptional, isolated cases" that have been unduly generalized to the industry as a whole and that consequently have come to stigmatize and demonize the palm oil sector (Fedepalma's Director of Planning and Social Development). Palm oil proponents in various ways seek to debunk the alleged link between palm oil, illegalities, and violent conflict. It is imperative to delve deeper into these.

In the case of Curvaradó and Jiguamiandó, irregularities in the granting of land titles to palm oil companies, as well as the complicity of land registering authorities therein, have been officially acknowledged. However, it is firmly rejected by industry representatives that the communities in question have been displaced in order to enable oil palm cultivation or that the palm oil industry in a later stage has taken advantage of the situation so as to expand its operations. Instead, the case is explained (away) as an exercise of territorial control in a conflict zone. To quote at length from an interview with a director of Fedepalma:

> In the case of Urabá Chocoano, and Curvaradó and Jiguamiandó, in 1995 the guerrilla established several arms and drug trafficking routes between Colombia and Panama [...] and in this process the guerrilla organized several peasant marches by way of which these communities were expelled towards the populated centres of Apartadó, Carepa, Chigorodó, these zones. These communities were forced by the guerrilla to leave the zone so that they could operate this corridor. In 1997 initiates Operation Genesis, by the Colombian army, hand in hand with the paramilitaries. They cleansed the zone of guerrilla presence; the guerrilla withdrew towards the mountains, and so an exercise of paramilitary territorial control began. And it was at this point that these paramilitaries brought in investors to cultivate palm, to establish cattle ranging, to create licit activities as it were, to exercise territorial control. This is how the palm arrived. In 2002 the paras pulled out of the zone, due to Uribe's Democratic Security policy, and the communities that up to then had been in the populated

> centres returned. And they encountered their parcels planted with palm. So the palm ended up being as if these people were expelled in order to grow palm. But like I say, the construction goes a long way back. There was no palm when these people left and the people were not expelled in order to cultivate palm. So what was the idea coined at the time? That palm could be an alternative. If the palm was already planted, with the paras gone, and these people returning to their parcels, why not keep the productive product? And this is a matter that has led to much tension within the communities; between those that want palm, that are more pro paramilitary, and those who want nothing to do with palm, that are more pro guerrilla. And there is no middle ground or grey area to be found here, this is black or white, of this or that order. No agreement has been reached. (Director of Planning and Social Development at Fedepalma)

Several claims made by this industry representative are exemplary of how the prospects of substantive debate over perceptions and experiences of palm oil-related harm—its cultural, social, environmental, and economic impact—are being foreclosed through a variety of discursive mechanisms. One tendency, for instance, is to *externalize* harm by fully relegating the violence and dispossession in zones of palm oil production to the dynamics of Colombia's internal armed conflict and completely disconnect these from the subsequent planting of oil palm. Another tendency that can be observed is to *delegitimize* or *undermine* allegations of palm oil-related crime and harm by shifting the discussion to the position that those harmed take on the political spectrum, which is moreover reduced to paramilitary or guerrilla support.[11] As such, it is implied that palm oil critics do not reject palm oil *as such*, but that instead the issue revolves around whether people embrace (or reject) this or that actor in the armed conflict. In this regard, there is a persistent tendency among industry proponents to view opposition to palm oil—or *any* challenge to established political and economic interests for that matter—as an indicator of guerrilla sympathies, subversive motives, or a sign of guerrilla infiltration.

Another lengthy quote by a corporate executive more expressly exemplifies how opposition to palm oil is translated into "subversion" or ascribed to certain political ideologies:

> One cannot ignore the political concept here. Evidently these are zones of guerrilla presence, zones where a certain leftist ideology holds that the company is the enemy. Hence the discourse that 'such and such company arrives, and...' Overall, I can tell you that these companies – like the one I work for, like those of the Espinosa family, like Astorga – respect the law. There are others that don't. [...] But one cannot put the blame on the crop [...] [Y]es, in Urabá there were some paramilitaries that grew palm. What can one do? So palm took on this bad character, but in my view this is a crop that allows people to live a decent life in zones where the land is very bad. But there is a political element at play here. The other political element is that Uribe indeed actively promoted palm. But the reasons that the Uribe government chose palm was that there wasn't anything else. Palm is a crop that can be grown in regions of coca cultivation. So they said: "take out the coca, grow palm". But obviously, with Uribe, for those from the Left this is terrible. So palm took on this bad reputation. The strategy of Uribe was a strategy of... ehh... let's say, the guerrilla is coca, right? The guerrilla is a promoter of coca, they definitely are. So Uribe wanted to fight the coca. The strategy was to get rid of the coca and replace this with something else. I admit that it wasn't very successful. But it was the palm that ended up with a bad name. What happened in Urabá was very, very dreadful, very dreadful, because these *are* paras indeed. Everything indicates that indeed people were displaced at gunpoint and that they killed people and grew palm there. And so Uribe, palm, and paras became one and the same thing. The thing is that people point their energies at a particular sector – before it was the cattle ranchers – and then the whole sector is branded paramilitary. Well, everyone has cattle, that there are paras with cattle, yes, of course. (Corporate manager in palm oil company)

With opposition to palm oil explained as an undercurrent of political ideology, allegations of palm oil-related harm are being delegitimized out of hand. The occurrence and lived reality of such harm is disqualified well ahead of any possible discussion and thus, in effect, ruled out.

The two discursive strategies here addressed—the externalization of harm and the delegitimization of allegations of harm—give a radically different meaning to the claims put forward by palm oil critics. In addition to the above, a third observation can be made. When corporate executives, industry representatives, and public officials draw on territorial dispute, armed conflict, and subversion to deny that palm oil would be somehow linked to violence and land dispossession, the image often appealed to in the interviews is one of "statelessness". The regions where the palm oil industry operates are furthermore depicted as remote spaces that lag behind in social and economic development and where, as cause and consequence, illegality reigns. In order to more fully comprehend the legal and illegal dispossession of land (and specific land uses, see Chaps. 5, 6) in Colombia, it is necessary to probe deeper into the imaginaries and ideologies that inscribe the rationale and practices of taking control of these lands. Doing so, notions of the Other Colombia come into view again.

The "Absence of the State" in the Other Colombia

Although the excessive and overt display of violence in Curvaradó and Jiguamiandó appear to set the forces unleashed upon these territories and its inhabitants somewhat apart from the majority of *less evidently* illegal and antagonistic cases of land use change to oil palm, the dominant narratives and imaginaries that underpin and legitimize such violence are not so exceptional. To illustrate this, we have to delve into the cultural representations, the imagined geographical (and racial) hierarchies, and the political and economic interests that inscribe the dynamics of territorial seizure and control in Colombia, and accordingly lay bare what the palm oil project—or any large-scale economic project at that—ultimately represents.[12]

In Colombia, the push for land use change to large-scale industrial activity generally seeks its legitimization in narratives of modernization that call for the social and economic development of the marginalized peripheries that are construed as Colombia's Other (Serje 2007; Grajales 2013). The perception is that agricultural modernization aids the improvement of the underdeveloped, backward condition of these territories and populations. Agribusiness is one of the principal development pathways that in this way are envisioned to insert these peripheral regions into the global neoliberal order (Grajales 2013). Palm oil proponents insist that crime and violence perpetrated in these regions are disconnected from the operations of legal industries such as the palm oil sector. What is more, crime and violence are presented as destabilizing forces that preclude, or interfere with, the regular functioning of institutional structures and private sector investment.

As Serje (2007, 2012) has noted, the regions in Colombia's marginalized periphery are imagined as spaces beyond the sphere of legality and the order and control of state-governed developed, prosperous, "true" Colombia. Hence, the poverty, illegality, and violence that mark the territories of the "Other Colombia" are ascribed to an alleged state absence. Yet, rather than phenomena supposedly external to the regular functioning of the state, Grajales (2011) points out that crime and violence are often "constitutive of logics of competition, accumulation and economic development, ultimately, elements in the process of state formation" (p. 774). Ballvé (2012), too, argues against the narrow concept of the state in dominant discourses of state absence. An extended concept of the state allows one to recognize in the reconfiguration of territorial practices, social relations, and human interaction with the natural environment—irrespective of whether this reconfiguration is sought through legal or illegal processes and actors—the materialization of state structures, forms, and practices (Ballvé 2012). Crucially, Serje (2007, 2012) maintains that the very notion of state absence makes the intertwining of the legal and the illegal possible. The myth of the "absence of the state" according to Serje:

> ...performs a specific social function and, in effect, functions as a smoke screen that covers up a series of conditions experienced by these regions and their populations, at the same time as legitimizing and concealing a rather clear line of practices and interventions that seek to incorporate these territories into the circuits of the global capitalist economy. (2012: 99)[13]

In addition, the fluidity of the relationship between illegal armed groups and the Colombian State facilitates the resort to "techniques of obfuscation" (Jamieson and McEvoy 2005) that "other" the crimes in question all the more. Illegal armed groups in Colombia are not mere instruments of the political establishment but have a dynamic of their own. As Jamieson & McEvoy assert, the image that forces are "beyond the reach" of the state "is materially and symbolically convenient in the denial of state crime" (2005: 512). The agribusiness sector, too, in this sense can absolve itself of responsibility for the dispossession from which it would certainly appear to benefit quite significantly.

Meddling in Collective Territory: "As if It Were Some Dogs Living Here"

Notwithstanding what has been argued up to this point, it is important to direct attention to the fact that the physical, territorial, and cultural integrity of the communities inhabiting the Colombian Pacific, and the region's ecological health, are also trampled by a range of activities that are indeed unrelated (or only remotely related) to the operations of the palm oil industry. During the *Another Possible Pacific* gathering that took place in Tumaco late 2012, it was emphasized that the region is targeted *"from all sides"*: agribusiness (such as palm oil, sugar cane, and cattle farming), mining (legal and illegal), contraband activity (arms, munition, and combustibles), and the narco-business. Intertwined with these, as should by now be evident, communities endure the consequences of being situated in the midst of armed confrontations and territorial dispute between various illegal armed groups, as well as between the latter and Colombia's public armed forces.

Notwithstanding the connections that arguably exist between palm oil, violent conflict, and dispossession, it is also necessary to recognize that this presence of legal and illegal armed actors has a violent logic, raison d'être, and set of negative impacts of its own, which has the potential to severely threaten, dislocate, and destroy human lives and livelihoods and natural environments. In view of the focus and purposes of this study, the full scope of these dynamics and impacts will not be addressed (for an approximation, see Corte Constitucional 2014). Below I limit the discussion to two main themes that, although not directly related to the palm oil industry, are important to address not only in view of the severe impacts they produce in Tumaco, but also for the way they figured in the discursive dimension of the politics of palm oil harm in this context. One of these concerns the coca business, which was touched upon by all participants, although with the emphasis varyingly placed on either cultivation, trade, or aerial fumigation. Another theme concerns the presence, movement, and actions of illegal armed groups more generally.

Between Palm, Coca, and Armed Activity

From the year 2000 onwards, Tumaco began to experience sharp increases in the levels of armed conflict, mostly due to the displacement of crops for illicit use from the Putumayo to Nariño in the framework of Plan Colombia. According to the United Nations Office on Drugs and Crime, Tumaco "continues to remain the municipality with the highest number of coca crops within Colombia" (UNODC 2014: 17). As commented by a local official:

> Look, Tumaco at this moment, and this is not a secret to anyone but internationally known, is one of the municipalities where the conflict is most severe, due to the coca and illegal armed groups. When Cordeagropaz was created, one of the things said was that every single hectare cultivated with palm would be one hectare less for coca. [...] If there would have been a stronger politics, not just with palm but with other crops that could offer the zone alternative projects of life, surely coca would not have spread so much. (Mayoral advisor in Tumaco)

Apart from Tumaco's strategic location, assaults upon the region as a site for coca cultivation, processing, and commercialization are also facilitated by favourable soil characteristics and climate conditions. A former agronomic director of a palm oil company operating in Tumaco in this regard pointed to the "unfortunate situation" that oil palm and coca thrive in the same edaphoclimatic[14] zone, which in Tumaco has led to a situation wherein, around the palm, the existence of illicit crops generates problems of violence and insecurity. This, he argued, creates disincentives not only for the development of the palm oil industry, but for the very development of the country. Although the corporate interpretation of this situation—i.e. one in which oil palm and coca as it were compete for territory—diverges radically from that of palm oil critics within the local population, the impacts of the coca business are indeed hard felt in the zone. For many, these impacts come on top of the already experienced social, cultural, and environmental destruction generated by the palm oil industry:

> But this, too, the coca, another thing that is perhaps hard for you to imagine… What is going to become of us?? Many people that arrived from other parts of the country are interfering in our territories. They also finished off almost 10, almost 12 hectares of forest. There, others invaded to protect the people who cultivate their illicit crops. This is another major threat that we are faced with within our territories. In *all* the collective territories we are affected by these things. (Afro-Colombian community leader)

In order to gain access to the zones of the Alto Mira y Frontera community council where the presence of *colonos* and cultivation of coca is concentrated, in most cases permission from the illegal armed groups that control these parts of the collective territory is required; members of the community council are generally not excluded from this constraint. An inhabitant of Alto Mira y Frontera and former member of its junta (the community council's governing body) said about the presence of *colonos*: "*We understand that the colonos that arrived to our territories are not well off; they, too, come from conflict zones. There is this understanding. The problem exists in the crop they cultivate here*". This presence and the scale of devastation wrought by the operations revolving around the narco-economy severely affect the communities of Alto Mira y Frontera in their autonomy and territorial integrity. But within a context of armed conflict, and climate of fear, the leadership of the council runs extreme risks if denouncing these threats (legal advisor to Alto Mira y Frontera).

More generally, the movement of armed actors through the zone and their presence on Afro-Colombian and indigenous territories instil feelings of anxiety and distress in local inhabitants. To avoid putting their lives at stake, people respond to actual or perceived threats in different ways: "*many remain silent, many do not denounce, many do not denounce but move, others stay, but under the rules imposed on them*" (representative of the Alto Mira y Frontera community council). Whilst a threat to everyone in the territory, community leaders especially are at risk; over the years, many have received death threats, been displaced or have been assassinated for speaking and acting in defence of their lands and ways of life. However, in view of their responsibility in representing and protecting their communities, leaders are also forced to enter into dialogue with armed groups. On the necessity of dialogue, one community leader said:

> The armed actors are there, and at no point can you rise up as their enemy because, well, they will kill you. What must be understood is that there in the territory the armed actors are the law. As such, we cannot be their enemies. Rather, what you have to tell them is, "listen, as both of us are in the territory, this is my work; respect our work and we will respect yours". And our work is to orient and work with our communities. (Community leader Bajo Mira y Frontera)

But such dialogue then comes with the risk of, on the one hand, being accused of involvement with illegal actors by the public authorities, which may delegitimize communities' struggle for the effective recognition of their cultural autonomy and self-determination and corresponding territorial rights, and, on the other hand, being signalled as alleged "sympathizers" or "allies" of a given armed group, which may lead to repercussions from rivalling groups (Afro-Colombian activist from Tumaco; see also Corte Constitucional 2014: 22). The impunity with which such violence carries on, and people's lives, ways of life, and environments are constantly trampled upon, has left many locals feeling "*completely unprotected, isolated, and cornered*" (inhabitant of Bajo Mira y Frontera).

In recent years, practices of extortion in Tumaco have dramatically increased, affecting both the rural and urban zones, affecting the smallest street vendor of phone credits up to entire community councils; smallholder through to large companies; and so on. "*Many people, many campesinos are leaving out of fear because they are being extorted. 'Ah, you are selling cacao, you must give me this much of the deal'. It is no longer coca but with licit production that this is now happening*" (Social and Business

Coordinator of Cordeagropaz). It may not always be clear what group is behind such extortions, or perhaps, for fear of repercussions, it is simply better not to articulate this. During one of our conversations, one participant (for the purposes of this anecdote I will refer to him as Carlos) told me how his brother—who owned a lumber yard—was killed a year before, after refusing to pay the extortion imposed on him any longer. A while after, some men arrived at Carlos' door, saying that together with whatever information he had concerning the situation, they could help him find out who was behind the killing. But, to avoid more pain and violence being unleashed upon his family, Carlos decided to leave the matter untouched and therefore unresolved; having lived the transition of an unencumbered, peaceful Tumaco to its current context of violence, and based on his ample experience in the Afro-Colombian social movement, he suspected that rather than seeking to "help" him, most likely these men were inquiring into how much knowledge Carlos had about the situation, and as such whether he formed a threat to the perpetrators.

That the tranquillity that once characterized Tumaco has given way to a climate of fear, restricted mobility, forced displacements, assassinations, extortions, and the persecution of community leaders[15], was something expressed across the spectrum of perspectives addressed in this research (i.e. from palm oil critic, to small grower, to corporate executive). However, from the small grower, corporate, and official perspectives these issues tend to be primarily presented as the product of the "*matrimony between coca and illegal armed groups*" (Executive Director at Cordeagropaz), and as such these issues are sharply differentiated from "the licit". In contrast, from the critics' point of view, such differentiation belies the violent history of the imposition of palm oil and subsequent industry expansion in Tumaco (see the next chapter) and is moreover incongruent with allegations of an enduring link between illegal armed actors and legal industries in the region:

> It wasn't just the illicit crops that brought this violence. It was the palm that first brought the violence. Because when the first palm growers started to arrive there was no coca here. This was when the violence started, because many people resisted, either they sold their lands or they were

> killed. From this moment the violence arose. Later this is complemented with the theme of illicit crops; this from then on creates a stronger push [for violence]. (Community leader Bajo Mira y Frontera)

This differs sharply from the strict and seemingly clean separation between "the licit" and "the illicit" upheld by the small grower and representative of Palmasur quoted below, although this does not take away from the thus communicated severe impact that the context of violence, fear, and insecurity has on the daily lives of Tumaco's inhabitants:

> Speaking concretely about the Pacific coast of Nariño; this was a peaceful zone. People moved during the day, at night, through any part, through any village [*vereda*]. Today this is no longer possible due to the illicit, the difficulties that come with the illicit, the insecurity, people who in order to control *x* production do not hesitate to kill this or that person. Today all of us experience difficulties, not just with palm but all agriculturalists, because we are invested in the licit, not in the illicit. When we started dedicating ourselves to cultivate palm it was under these conditions: I have the illicit but the moment I establish the project I have to eliminate this crop and cultivate palm, or cacao, or plantain. And today we can say that the cultivation of illicit crops in the zone has significantly dropped. But as this zone became the [transit] hub for the narco trade [...], in the eagerness to control these borders, these exit and entry points, the agriculturalist becomes caught up in whatever disorder or conflict is generated between one force and another. We are caught up in this, it is detrimental to us. But not only the oil palm but all crops, in all daily activity the agriculturalist is immersed in this. And not only the agriculturalist, but the people from the city. Vendors, many vendors have left Tumaco for this very situation. The prevailing insecurity due to the process of narco-trafficking caused them to leave. And others, well, they go "on a trip" [*se van de viaje*], to the cemetery, this is the reality. So, we work, fortunately thus far we are still allowed to continue our work. But this, too, is more limited these days; where before we would work until four, today we have to head home already at two to be somewhat safer. But this has been detrimental to us, and it is of considerable detriment to us. (Small grower and representative of Palmasur)

Oslender (2008), with regard to the restrictions on everyday spatial mobility in the "contexts of terror" in the Colombian Pacific coast region, notes that these can be imposed explicitly but, also, that "they may be *implicit* restrictions imposed through fear that advises one not to move around in certain places" (p. 82). In either case, local testimonies are replete with mention of how daily routines are being affected, ways to cope with all the insecurity and violence around them, and of their youth being recruited by the various illegal armed groups that operate in the zone. Under such pressures, the social fabric of communities is disintegrating, and concerted efforts to mobilize against perceived harms and violations of rights are impeded. Territorial fragmentation and disconnection is moreover at the basis of the breakdown of existing kinship and community relations—for indigenous Awá a cross-border reality, as their social and family relationships extend to Awá communities across the border in Ecuador (members of UNIPA).

Meanwhile, the environmental harms provoked by coca cultivation and processing are enormous, as are the consequences that derive from aerial coca fumigation, which is having a destructive effect on local biodiversity, constitutes an additional source of contamination of water streams and rivers, and, given that the fumigations do not discriminate between crops for illicit use and subsistence crops, severely affect people's food security and sovereignty. A key concern of local communities in terms of the processing of coca leaves on the other hand, was the contamination of streams and rivers as a result of the illegal extraction of oil for use in coca laboratories (or, alternatively, to be sold), from the oil pipelines that traverse the region. Where oil spills are related to the illegal tapping into pipelines,[16] both valves and clandestine refineries are of a rudimentary character. The spilled or wasted hydrocarbon, every time it rains, washes into the nearest stream, and from there on flows into the nearest river (Diócesis de Tumaco 2012; Salgar Antolínez 2014). As stated by a local inhabitant:

> Now we have another problem in the Mira River: every day, oil is running downstream because it is not known where this comes from and they [the public authorities] cannot be bothered. This oil is harming our rivers, our ecosystem. And meanwhile they remain passive. And what are we going to

> do with this, when already the water is contaminated? This water is poisoning us, and yet they are calm, and no recognition. As if it were some dogs living here. This is yet another violation. This harms the environment, the fish, well, many things. Why isn't the government working on this? (Inhabitant of Bajo Mira y Frontera)

Hence, to reiterate, in view of what has been discussed above there are indeed a variety of harms and crimes that are external or only remotely linked to the presence and operations of the palm oil industry. However, it would be a mistake, as illustrated throughout this chapter, to conclude that these external factors hold no relevance for the analysis here, as, *discursively*, these do find their way into the politics of harm vis-à-vis palm oil. The actions of illegal armed groups, the narco-business, and government programmes of coca crop eradication assume a central place in the corporate constructions of harm that will be addressed in Chaps. 5 and 6. To anticipate the relationship that these constructions bear to perceptions of the "appropriate" uses of land, let me close with these words from a corporate executive:

> The thing these days is that many of these lands are occupied by narco-traffickers that are growing coca there, and the communities are in no position to face up to these narco-traffickers. In my view, communities were given a thing that they cannot handle. What they have been given is a situation wherein those who decide to persecute the narco-traffickers, in order to drive them out of there, will lose their life. [...] And even if they recover them, what are they going to do with these lands? That is to say, what is the future of these lands? (Managing director of palm oil company)

Discussion: Power, Legality, and the Contestedness of Harm

The central focus in this chapter has been on the convergence and coexistence of a variety of adverse factors and dynamics in zones of palm oil production in Colombia, some of which are alleged to be directly or indirectly related to the palm oil industry, while others are unrelated to the industry. Arguably, palm oil proponents mobilize and exploit the "messy" reality that is the result of this complexity.

First, to operate in the midst of conflict and a context characterized by a complex mix of factors and dynamics allows for a thoroughgoing externalization of harm and simultaneous affirmation of the virtues of palm oil production. Forced displacement and dispossession are ascribed to factors purportedly unrelated, as well as detrimental, to the operations and positive potential of the palm oil industry. Take, for that matter, the following response by the Executive Director of Cenipalma, when asked to comment on the acceptability of cultivating oil palm in a region where a significant part of the population experiences this industry as an imposition that clashes with their cultural and territorial integrity, relations, and practices:

> It is like with a house that has a living room, a kitchen, a bathroom, some vases organized like this, putting little plants there… a wholly diversified arrangement of the house scenery. In my view, Tumaco also reflected this kind of diversified management.[17] And one of the components has been palm, one of the components. And perhaps it has been the component that became what it is today, which is interesting because it generates money, but that is also at the centre of attention. What stands out is turned into something good, something bad, into everything, right? […] I do think that all these matters of diversity [of local culture] should be fomented. But the absence of this should not be blamed on palm. This is to look for a culprit among hundred suspects. I don't believe in this. I believe that palm is one more use of the land. And it is a good use. And it should not be blamed for the failures of Tumaco. The failures of Tumaco, ehm, it could be that there is an element of palm at play here; history cannot be denied. But it isn't palm that is responsible for Tumaco's current condition. I think it is good to protect these minorities, so that they do not lose their culture, so that life does not become even more wretched than it already is for them, but let's not say that everything else has caused this damage. *I would say that to centre on palm, is to miss the forest for the trees.* You are focussing on one tree and not the whole forest

> that lies behind. The palm is a tree, among the many trees here. And perhaps there is one bad tree that is also a palm. But among the millions of existing trees, there are a great many other bad things. (Executive Director of Cenipalma, emphasis added)

The tendency to conceptualize harm with reference to factors perceived to be external to the palm oil industry is not limited to the violence and violent dispossession that were at the centre of this chapter. As glimpsed in the above quote and illustrated in more detail in the following two chapters, it is a practice persistently resorted to in industry efforts to debunk and downplay the ways in which the social and environmental harms associated with palm oil are affecting local livelihoods.

In addition to this, allegations of palm oil harm are undermined and/or delegitimized by reference to political ideology and accusations of guerrilla sympathies. The practice of giving a subversive twist to expressions of opposition to palm oil through allegations of "third party interference" reduces palm oil critical members within affected communities to the passive pawns of subversive forces rather than active subjects whose conceptualizations, perceptions, and realities of harm ought to be accounted for (see also Chap. 6).

Thirdly, crime and violence are viewed as destabilizing practices that run counter to economic development and institutional structures, and as such are relegated to an exterior realm that lies beyond the reach of the state and the legal order, rather than being entangled with these. This binary differentiation between the legal and the illegal is also at play in discourses on illicit coca crop cultivation that frame the fundamental matter as one of enabling a transition from the damaging sphere of illegality to immersion in legal productive alternatives that, for being legal, are presented as inherently benign. This distracts from the inequalities and power imbalances bound up with issues of land access, use, and autonomy, as well as the harms and injustices that inhere in the social, socioecological, and economic relations, and broader cultural framework, in which the agroindustrial production model is embedded.

In this chapter, the focus has primarily been on violent and coercive manifestations of dispossession in regions of palm oil production. Violence and coercion, however, are but one way in which inequitable power relations are kept in place. In the next chapter, I will argue that such blatant manifestations of power have their counterpart in more persuasive and nonviolent exercises of power through which (alleged) social and environmental harms come about and persist. The violent and coercive dimensions of land conflict and land use change, as well as the complex mix of forces and interests that imbue Colombia's contested grounds, constitute the broader frame in which to understand the discussions that as such will be developed. This ultimately leads me to argue that there exists such *a thin line and dynamic interaction* between the illegal and the legal, coercion and consent, and violent and veiled imposition, and that an isolated treatment of only one side of each of these binaries is untenable. A corresponding focus on the continuum of legal harm, tolerated illegal harm, and nontolerated illegal harm allows for theorizing and comprehending more fully the structures, relations, and processes that underpin the social and environmental harms of palm oil; legalistic notions of crime are but one dimension of these harms.

Notes

1. An amended peace agreement was ratified in November 2016 and will gradually be implemented.
2. The referenced document ("La Tramoya") offers an in-depth, chronological description and narrative testimony of events in the Curvaradó and Jiguamiandó region. The term "tramoya" stands for a swindle or a scheme and in this case refers to the dirty business and entanglement of legal institutions and illegal forces in ways that seek to obscure the underlying relations and covert objectives of the forced displacement and persecution of affected communities.
3. There are few cases where the role of paramilitaries in land use change to palm oil production, and the exercise of power by paramilitary groups in regions of palm oil production more broadly, has been exposed to the extent of Curvaradó and Jiguamiandó (Ballvé 2013; Grajales 2013). But it should be noted that the paramilitary nexus with private corporations and institutional structures is complex, fluid, and different from one region to the other. Within the scope and primary focus of this study, it has not been possible to pursue a thorough analysis and exposition of this complex dimension.

4. See Ballvé (2012, 2013) and Grajales (2011, 2013) for in-depth analyses of the mechanisms and bureaucratic procedures through which such legalization is achieved.
5. It is worth mentioning that this study was carried out under the auspices of Fedepalma (Ocampo Valencia 2009: 175).
6. For the impact of capitalist patterns of accumulation and agrarian change on the dynamics of conflict and violence in the light of palm oil production, see Maher (2015).
7. Colombia's National Ombudsman for Human Rights.
8. *"Pescar en río revuelto"*, i.e. taking advantage of, or (indirectly) benefitting from, a given situation.
9. With terrains stripped of unwanted vegetation, rows of oil palm trees planted systematically at 9 m from each other, and traversed by a vast web of roads, smaller paths, and drainage canals, the design of oil palm monocultures is deemed particularly apt for the exercise of military control over a territory.
10. Article 33 of Decree 2664 of 1994, see also Flórez López and Millán Echeverría (2007: 141).
11. This offers a crude, simplistic representation of the social and cultural politics of those affected, and discards the fact that many of the communities affected reject *all kinds* of adverse interference in their territories, no matter the actor or entity involved.
12. That is, what follows should not be taken as exclusive of a particular economic sector or government administration.
13. Ballvé (2012: 611) likewise notes: "Although such accounts [of state absence] are not altogether inaccurate, the problem with them is that they reproduce superficial narratives of statelessness that obscure the mutually reciprocal and necessary relations between the state and paramilitaries".
14. Edaphology refers to the influence of soil characteristics and conditions on plants and cultivation practices.
15. For an enumeration of *known* cases, see Diócesis de Tumaco (2009, 2011, 2012).
16. Oil spills result also from attacks on pipelines by guerrilla forces; see Salgar Antolínez (2014). The most recent and thus far the socially and environmentally most dramatic oil spill in Tumaco occurred in June 2015 (El Espectador 2015), the consequences of which are felt to this day.

17. Use of the past tense refers to the fact that at the time of the interview the palm oil industry in Tumaco was restarting its operations after nearly all palm was destroyed by a bud rot epidemic, mentioned also in the introductory chapter and further discussed in Chap. 6.

References

Ballvé, T. (2012). Everyday state formation: Territory, decentralization, and the narco landgrab in Colombia. *Environment and Planning D: Society and Space, 30*(4), 603–622.

Ballvé, T. (2013). Grassroots masquerades: Development, paramilitaries, and land laundering in Colombia. *Geoforum, 50*, 62–75.

Comisión Intereclesial de Justicia y Paz (CIJP). (2005). *La Tramoya: Derechos Humanos y Palma Aceitera, Jiguamiandó y Curvaradó*. Bogotá: CINEP/Comisión Intereclesial de Justicia y Paz.

Comisión Intereclesial de Justicia y Paz (CIJP). (2007a). Palma, bendita que se hizo maldita. El caso de Curvaradó y Jiguamiandó. In *(Im)plantación de la Muerte: Violación de derechos e inseguridad (in)humana de comunidades en resistencia de Colombia* (pp. 37–46). Comisión Intereclesial de Justicia y Paz/Centro Tricontinental/PTM Mundubat.

Comisión Intereclesial de Justicia y Paz (CIJP). (2007b). Pueblos, comunidades y territorio. Entre la desterritorialización. In: *(Im)plantación de la Muerte: Violación de derechos e inseguridad (in)humana de comunidades en resistencia de Colombia* (pp. 12–21). Comisión Intereclesial de Justicia y Paz/Centro Tricontinental/PTM Mundubat.

Corte Constitucional. (2014). *Auto 073 de 2014. Medidas de prevención, protección y atención de las comunidades afrodescendientes de la región pacífica del departamento de Nariño en riesgo y víctimas de desplazamiento forzado.* Bogotá: República de Colombia.

Corte Interamericana de Derechos Humanos (CIDH). (2003). Medidas provisionales solicitadas por la Comisión interamericana de Derechos Humanos respecto de la República de Colombia, caso de las comunidades del jiguamiandó y Curvaradó. Resolución de la Corte Interamericana de Derechos Humanos de 6 de marzo de 2003.

Defensoría del Pueblo. (2005). *Resolución Defensorial No. 39, junio 2 de 2005. Violación de los derechos humanos por siembra de palma africana en territorios colectivos de jiguamiandó y Curvaradó – Chocó*. Bogotá: Defensoría del Pueblo.

Diócesis de Tumaco. (2009). *¡Que nadie diga que no pasa nada! Una mirada desde la Región del Pacífico Nariñense. Balance no. 1*. Tumaco: Diócesis de Tumaco.
Diócesis de Tumaco. (2011). *¡Que nadie diga que no pasa nada! Una mirada desde la Región del Pacífico Nariñense. Balance no. 2*. Tumaco: Diócesis de Tumaco.
Diócesis de Tumaco. (2012). *¡Que nadie diga que no pasa nada! Una mirada desde la Región del Pacífico Nariñense. Balance no. 3*. Tumaco: Diócesis de Tumaco.
El Espectador. (2015, July 2). ONU advierte de la crítica situación de 200 mil personas por ataques de Farc en Tumaco. *El Espectador* [Online], (Paz). Available from: http://www.elespectador.com [Accessed 22 November 2016].
Espejo, G. (2016, August 15). Tumaco, entre el crimen y el terror. *El Espectador* [Online], (Política). Available from: http://www.elespectador.com [Accessed 15 November 2016].
Flórez López, J. A., & Millán Echeverría, D. C. (2007). *Derecho a la alimentación y al territorio en el Pacífico Colombiano*. Tumaco: Diócesis.
Grajales, J. (2011). The rifle and the title: Paramilitary violence, land grab and land control in Colombia. *The Journal of Peasant Studies, 38*(4), 771–792.
Grajales, J. (2013). State involvement, land grabbing and counter-insurgency in Colombia. *Development and Change, 44*(2), 211–232.
Jamieson, R., & McEvoy, K. (2005). State crime by proxy and juridical othering. *British Journal of Criminology, 45*(4), 504–527.
Maher, D. (2015). Rooted in violence: Civil war, international trade and the expansion of palm oil in Colombia. *New Political Economy, 20*(2), 299–330.
Mingorance, F. (2006). *The flow of palm oil Colombia-Belgium/Europe. A study from a human rights perspective*. Brussels: Human Rights Everywhere/Coordination Belge pour la Colombie.
Mingorance, F., Minelli, F., & Le Du, H. (2004). *El Cultivo de la Palma Africana en el Chocó: Legalidad Ambiental, Territorial, y Derechos Humanos*. Colombia: Human Rights Everywhere.
Ocampo Valencia, S. (2009). Agroindustria y conflicto armado. El caso de la palma de aceite. *Colombia Internacional, 70,* 169–190.
Oslender, U. (2008). Another history of violence: The production of "Geographies of Terror" in Colombia's Pacific coast region. *Latin American Perspectives, 35*(5), 77–102.
Rangel, A., Ramírez, W., & Betancur, P. A. (2009). *Oil palm in Colombia: Conflict myths & realities*. Bogotá: Fundación Seguridad & Democracia.

Salgar Antolínez, D. (2014, June 5). La cultura es Resistencia en Tumaco. *El Espectador* [Online], (Nacional). Available from: http://www.elespectador.com [Accessed 13 June 2014].

Salgar Antolínez, D. (2016, June 8). Tumaco: voces de un conflicto ajeno. *El Espectador* [Online], (Territorio). Available from: http://colombia2020.elespectador.com [Accessed 15 November 2016].

Sánchez, N. A. (2016, October 9). Entre el miedo y la movilización: comunidades negras tras el plebiscito. *El Espectador* [Online], (Territorio). Available from: http://colombia2020.elespectador.com [Accessed 11 November 2016].

Serje, M. (2007). Iron maiden landscapes: The geopolitics of Colombia's territorial conquest. *South Central Review, 24*(1), 37–55.

Serje, M. (2012). El mito de la ausencia del Estado: la incorporación económica de las "zonas de frontera" en Colombia. *Cahiers des Ameriques Latines, 71*, 95–117.

Thomson, F. (2011). The agrarian question and violence in Colombia: Conflict and development. *Journal of Agrarian Change, 11*(3), 321–356.

UNODC. (2014). *Colombia. Coca cultivation survey 2013*. Bogotá: UNODC Colombia.

Vélez, I. (Ed.) (2008). *Agrocombustibles "Llenando tanques, vaciando territorios"*. Bogotá: CENSAT Agua Viva—PCN.

World Rainforest Movement. (2010). RSPO: The "greening" of the dark palm oil business. *WRM Briefing*. Available from http://wrm.org.uy/wp-content/uploads/2013/01/RSPO.pdf.

5

Preparing the Ground

In the previous chapter, I sketched the broader context within which to consider the operations of the palm oil industry, and the corresponding politics of harm, in the Colombian Pacific coast region. In this chapter, I delve into the practices through which in Tumaco the ground has been prepared for palm oil, as well as the discourses thereby deployed. I will draw attention to the fact that these practices and discourses seek to reconfigure existing social relations, ways of being, and human-environment interactions. Whereas some notions, practices, and relations become naturalized and, if need be, coercively enforced (i.e. those that are favourable to dominant social, cultural, political and economic arrangements); others are debilitated, disqualified, and ruled out (i.e. those that correspond to alternative economic, cultural, and ecological rationalities). The central aim of this chapter is to demonstrate that this occurs not just through violent and coercive imposition but, along with such practices, is achieved also through the manufacturing of consent and through more indirect forms of imposition. The ways in which thus, through illegal and legal practices, biodiverse forests and small-scale

---

Parts of this chapter appear also in Mol (2017).

H. Mol, *The Politics of Palm Oil Harm*, Palgrave Studies
in Green Criminology, DOI 10.1007/978-3-319-55378-8_5

diversified agricultural systems are converted into monocultures of oil palm, and the divergent views and experiences that at the local level are bound up with these practices and the impacts of these practices, are analysed and discussed. By doing so, the chapter demonstrates that a comprehensive empirical and theoretical understanding of the dynamics of palm oil industry establishment and expansion requires the type of analysis that moves beyond a sole focus on the violent, coercive, and illegal dimensions of land use change.

The Agricultural Frontier: Empty Forests, Underdevelopment, and Illegality

In the Colombian Pacific region, the opening up of new terrains to capitalist accumulation is driven significantly by private sector investment from the interior of Colombia, i.e. *domestic* external capital. Such is the case also for the business groups (and the wealthy families they originate in) that the palm oil companies operating in Tumaco belong to (Ospina Bozzi 2001). Incursions into the region moreover follow a common pattern regarding the discourses, cultural constructs, and legal categories deployed, and the political-economic processes that these in turn facilitate, legitimate, or are conducive to. Alongside ideological depictions of frontiers as untamed and lawless spaces—the "other" of civilization, order, and legality—frontier regions often also tend to be portrayed as devoid of (meaningful) human inhabitation (Hoefle 2006). Such constructions, with their evident colonial underpinnings, seek to legitimate the economic incursions made into these zones and the latter's incorporation into the modernizing logic of the centre (Serje 2012). Hence, Hoefle's (2006) claim that a political economy framework of analysis (centred on the dynamics of capital accumulation) must be combined with a radical critique of "the cultural construction of the frontier as an 'other' space" (p. 472) is important. The prevailing image that emerges from the interviews that for this study were conducted with corporate and industry actors confirms these notions, as will become increasingly evident as this chapter and the next unfold. For one thing, the developmentalist discourse adhered to by industry proponents generally upholds the view that the palm oil sector arrived to regions that to this very day remain unruly frontier zones where illegality reigns:

> There is no presence of the state in these frontier zones, in these remote zones, for the simple fact that the population grew and concentrated in the Andes, moving outwards very slowly. Ideally, people would not move towards the frontiers, in order to be able to conserve the natural resources. But at the same time the lack of state presence on the frontier is what allows illegality to take over, with coca and all that filth. (Executive Director at Cenipalma)

In addition, the image that prevails is that of "empty" forests and underdevelopment—empty in terms of physical presence as well as the alleged lack of potential offered by these forests. That there is a long history of human existence in these forests is given scant attention. Yet as I will begin to point out below, these forests were never empty. Arguably, the "marginality" that is claimed to be an inherent feature of the region is to a significant extent the product of an economic model which has reduced these lands to the status of mere supplier of raw materials that sustain only the continuous accumulation of capital and reproduction of existing consumption patterns outside of the region (Serje 2012; see also Chap. 2). It is the marginality that has *thus* been produced and that is continuously being reproduced that reinforces the very idea that it is necessary to bring alternatives to the region.

Baldíos, Forest Reserve Subtraction, and Palm Oil Concessions

Until 1991, when collective and individual land titles began to be allocated to Afro-Colombian and indigenous communities, the lands of the Pacific coast were referred to as *tierra baldía*: public lands belonging to the Colombian State. The juridical figure and discourse of the *baldío* discard the social and cultural history of the lands accordingly categorized (Serje 2012). It decontextualizes a given land, stripping it of its historical, cultural, and ecological values. Hence, the concept also fails to recognize the forests and territories of the Colombian Pacific as socioecological spaces of human and nonhuman presence. Restrepo (2004a) has asserted that the categorization and treatment as *baldíos* of the territories that stretch the Colombian Pacific coast is moreover indicative of the State's obliviousness to the populations of the region.

Although under Law 2 of 1959 the entire Pacific region was declared a forest reserve, from the 1960s on, and increasingly in the 1970s and 1980s, areas that were considered suitable for agriculture or livestock ventures were withdrawn from the forest reserve[1] so that concessions could be granted for the agroindustrial exploitation of these lands. A consultant from the National Indigenous Organization of Colombia in this regard noted that although on the surface it appeared that the idea behind drawing these *"baldíos"* into the forest reserve was to protect the forest, the protection granted to forest reserves is of a very particular kind. The real objective, the consultant stated, is to *"protect [the zone], but as a reserve, that is, to exploit it later"*. In addition, he said, politics responded to the economic potential of these zones by invisibilizing the native inhabitants of the region, which meant that local indigenous and Afro-Colombian groups began to be treated *"as settlers, as new arrivals, as strangers to these territories"* (ONIC consultant). And so, concessions for exploitation began to be granted to palm oil companies. Such was, for instance, the case with Astorga, a palm oil company owned by the Varela group in Cali (Valle de Cauca), which in the 1980s was granted authorization by the Colombian Institute of Agrarian Reform (Incora, later replaced by Incoder) to establish oil palm on Awá territory. As members of the UNIPA pointed out, *"Incora at that time was so to say "unaware" that there were indigenous Awá living in these forests. They told the companies, 'no, that is baldío, go, establish yourself there'"*.

The interviewed public officials, corporate actors, and industry representatives take a legalistic stance towards these concessions for agroindustrial exploitation and accompanying deforestation. Emphasis is placed on the legal character of industry establishment and forest reserve subtraction. A professional from Incoder insisted that the palm oil companies solicited and accordingly were granted the subtraction of these areas from the forest reserve, reiterating that, regardless of the environmental impacts that followed, all of this had taken place legally, "*through regular channels, through legal channels. Legally permitted, authorized subtraction. The law allows for this*" (Incoder professional).

Indeed, forest reserve subtraction is a phenomenon that stays within the bounds of the law.[2] Thus approached, the resulting social and environmental harms appear to reflect what Passas and Goodwin (2004) refer to as "lawful but awful" industrial activity. Effectively, the legal framework allows for the type of extreme disregard for the natural environment, and the human and nonhuman life dependent on it, via processes of deforestation and subsequent harmful practices (for the latter, see Chap. 6). Below, the conceptualizations of harm that against this background are ascribed to by palm oil proponents on the one hand versus local communities and allied actors and organizations critical of palm oil-related deforestation on the other hand are discussed.

Deforestation and Development: A Necessary Trade-off?

From the corporate perspective, as well as expressed by industry protagonists more broadly, the regions where the palm oil industry operates are viewed as underdeveloped. When asked about the social and environmental impacts of land use change to oil palm, without exception, the discussion would sooner or later be steered towards the perceived necessities of regions like the Colombian Pacific and attendant notions of "development". In their view, the productive potential of hitherto unproductive and underutilized ecosystems must be exploited—in essence equating human and environmental well-being to the capitalist development of these regions. Accordingly, a certain level of deforestation was deemed inevitable in Tumaco, and it was not uncommon that critical questions on the topic were answered with a hint of impatience; in one interview a sigh was followed by the claim that *"it took some deforestation and the planting of another tree"* (former agronomic director of palm oil company). The prevailing notion is that people cannot live off the forest; much less does the forest allow for the *development* of a people. In other words, the forest is viewed as an empty alternative that has to be put to use, and of course not just any use, but (see the next chapter) a use in keeping with capitalist criteria of productivity, profitability, and competition.

As such, corporate actors and industry representatives insisted that the only viable way to alleviate poverty and improve local standards of living is by putting in place agroindustrial projects. Thereby palm oil is claimed to be the only real alternative for the region, in view of its compatibility with soil and climatic conditions, and its guaranteed commerce and stable price. According to the Executive Director of Cenipalma, a trade-off ought to be made between the strengthening of local economies and protection of ecosystems. In asserting that poverty must be alleviated *and* the environment protected, he invoked Indonesia and Malaysia as examples to warn against an overly critical stance towards deforestation:

> Perhaps not everything should have been planted with palm, but neither do I want to take this to the other extreme and say that this wretched Indonesia destroyed the forest in order to cultivate this filthy palm. What were the options? Perhaps some of this was necessary because this was an ecosystem of only forest. Indonesia and Malaysia, all of this was forest. And if there are people there, what do they eat? Do we allow that the people die and the monkeys live? I think there is a trade-off to think through here. And in the case of Colombia, palm arrived to regions that had already been subject to intervention. (Executive Director at Cenipalma)

The last claim—that in Colombia the palm oil industry arrived to regions that had already been intervened—is part of a wider set of claims through which the industry's share in the total sum of deforestation in Colombia gets toned down, considering palm oil as neither the primary nor the most alarming cause of deforestation. In Tumaco for that matter, previous intervention into the forest is attributed amongst others to the timber industry which operated in the region from the 1950s to the mid-70s, arguing for instance that, effectively, the palm oil industry had "retaken these secondary forests" and "incorporated" them into the productive phase of palm (Social and Business Coordinator of Cordeagropaz).[3] Another factor that is frequently invoked as a major cause of deforestation and of destructive interference in the forest ecosystem is the coca trade. Commenting on this issue, one managing director of a palm oil company noted:

> The government allowed that 120,000 hectares were subtracted from the forest reserve of the municipality of Tumaco so that these could be cultivated with different crops. This was in the 1970s. Of these 120,000 that were taken out of the reserve, 35,000 were cultivated with oil palm. As such it follows that for these 35,000 hectares, they are blaming us for the loss of biodiversity in a municipality that must have in the order of 250,000 hectares or more. So it was these 35,000 hectares that *we* deforested that caused this loss of biodiversity? I think that more than 100,000 hectares have been deforested to cultivate coca. But the whole world leaves this topic unaddressed because who raises this issue dies.

Furthermore, the planting of oil palm is viewed as alleviating pressure on surrounding forest ecosystems by providing people with a viable economic alternative. Hence, rather than a harm in itself, any deforestation that has taken place so as to cultivate oil palm is framed as a *break* on environmental harm, preventing more enduring practices of environmentally destructive activity. In fact, it is claimed that, were there no such alternatives available, then the level of deforestation would have been much higher. The notion that people *will* intervene destructively in their environments if they have no viable economic alternatives is strongly emphasized. Not uncommonly, this "lack of alternatives" argument combines with critiques of local culture, reducing deforestation to a cultural trait that in the absence of other options would inevitably materialize. *"The culture of the coast in my view continues to do the same: where there is no palm, within forests with no control you will normally encounter a lot of deforestation"* (former agronomic director of palm oil company). Another corporate executive stated:

> One has to get rid of this ideology of the noble savage. No, for me, from my point of view, the key problem is that there are people who have no food, who have no work. When one doesn't have work, what does one do? Well, for instance indiscriminate hunting; we prohibited hunting on our

> premises, but our workers don't leave anything, nothing. They would see a rat: hunted. They would see a monkey: hunted. Because this is the culture of our peasantry. You know, this image that people have, well you noticed already that I am not a Marxist, but this Marxist view of the poor peasant, the peasant who takes care of everything… The peasant doesn't look after a thing, because he is hungry! Every living thing he sees he kills and eats. This is how things work. Slash and burn cultivation: the poor peasant. It so happens that people need to eat and the wheels of the economy must spin. (Manager at palm oil company)

To portray deforestation as an acceptable practice, *provided that there are appropriate reasons to do so,* suggests a parallel with Sykes and Matza's (1957) work on techniques of neutralization. The techniques appealed to in the addressed context are a denial of responsibility ("to cut a few trees is nothing like the true deforestation engaged in by other actors and industries") and a denial of injury ("this is in fact necessary to prevent greater, i.e. 'real', harm"). The historical and structural roots at the basis of the precarious conditions lived by affected communities, in contrast, remain unaddressed. Instead, the populations and regions in question are presented as "marginal", rather than *marginalized*; people are depicted as "lacking", rather than *deprived* of the social and ecological conditions upon which have once constructed their livelihoods.

Deforest to Develop?? "Before There was no Misery"

The proponents of agroindustrial palm oil production advocate a "development pathway" that rests on a notion of underdevelopment, ascribed to a perceived inability of local communities to create or exploit viable economic alternatives. Along such lines, ways of living and economic organization other than those pushed for are unconceivable. When such notions *are* allowed for, however, deforestation takes on a wholly different character; from a minimal infraction and necessary stage on the path towards social and economic progress, deforestation comes to be perceived as a harmful practice in itself:

> These forests were our subsistence. There was food; there was no misery back then, right? *There was no misery*. People lived content, earning very little. Economic resources were scarce indeed, but there in the forest people had their whole diet. (Community leader of Alto Mira y Frontera)

The responsibility of the palm oil industry in this, is thereby argued to extend much further than its proponents are willing to admit. Restrepo (2004b) has pointed out that 60% of the oil palm cultivated in Tumaco was planted at the expense of primary forest. From the interviews carried out for the present study, a similar image emerged. Corresponding conceptualizations of harm centre on various dimensions.

A first dimension centres on the destruction of natural habitats, as a result of which both individual animals and populations of animals have been displaced, killed, or condemned to death for being deprived of the vital conditions to live. One community leader, for instance, stated that, along the Mira River, *"the few animals that could save themselves fled, they left the zone. They… how to say? …emigration called upon them, too… the few remaining animals also emigrated from the region"*. A similar observation was made by an Afro-Colombian activist from the urban area of Tumaco, but who has long been involved in local struggles for the defence of land and culture: *"We saw the animals crossing the river, fleeing from the forest"*. Many indicated that oil palm destroyed and could not sustain the existing species diversity in the region. According to an indigenous Awá: *"The landscape and natural ecosystem were completely destroyed. Besides, what exists in palm? A monoculture, a single species, what lives in these palms? Rats. [Directs himself to one of his fellows:] one finds many rats in these plantations, right?"*.

In view of the high levels of endemic plant and animal species diversity in the *Chocó Biogeográfico* (Delgado et al. 2007: 183–187), processes of deforestation inevitably provoke animal death and suffering. This is, however, not to argue that oil palm plantations are always completely devoid of animal life. A fieldwork trip to Altamira (Casanare, in Colombia's eastern plains) gave some insight into this matter.[4] Photo material, as well as on-site animal traces there (footprints, faeces, etc.), suggested a reasonable species diversity of birds, reptiles, and mammals

Fig. 5.1 Jaguarundi within oil palm plantation, Altomira, Casanare (copyright Panthera/Manuelita)

existing around and within the plantation (see Fig. 5.1). But thereby it must be added that this oil palm plantation of roughly 4000 ha is embedded in an area of approximately 10,000 ha of seasonally flooded savannahs and swamps. This embeddedness in the broader landscape forms a protection buffer that to a significant extent allows to preserve the necessary conditions to sustain animal life. However, the biologists involved emphasized that the situation in Altamira would deteriorate dramatically if the company at some point would decide to drain the surrounding lands to cultivate these with oil palm as well, which to all likelihood will likely happen.

Another dimension concerns the disruption and degradation of local ecosystems and ecological processes. In addition to the intrinsic worth of these ecosystems and environments, the conceptualization of harm vis-à-vis the physical transformation and degradation of local ecosystems and environments centred mostly on the human consequences thus experienced.

To "replace one tree by another", from the corporate view hardly problematic and, above all, necessary, is thought of sharply different when the land is differently perceived and related to: *"One hectare of palm versus a hectare of native forest; an ecosystem where I hunt, where I fish, where I live, where I breathe tranquillity… I don't know how to argue that this is ecological"* (indigenous Awá, in an interview with UNIPA).

Lastly, as another research participant explained: as trees are being cut down, so are the myths that are bound up with the forest.[5] Deforestation dislocates local ways of being and relating to the environment. Beyond the centrality of plant and animal species to people's dietary patterns (i.e. in terms of food sovereignty), these plants and animals are also central to the exercise of traditional medicine, ceremonies, and inscribe landscapes with meaning and a sense of belonging. With the imposition of oil palm, these ways of relating to the forest are being abruptly disarticulated. Land conversion to oil palm, and the deforestation that has taken place to this end, has led to the dispossession of particular land uses and relations bound up with the land. These aspects will be returned to later (in this chapter as well as the next). Below, first the dispossession of land *as such* will be expanded on through a discussion of how, in Tumaco, the corporate sector amassed the lands necessary to establish and expand their operations.

Pushing the Agroindustrial Frontier

Over time, practices and means of land transfer and land use change in Tumaco have ranged from overt violence and direct coercion, to more indirect forms of coercion as well as more persuasive and nonviolent strategies and practices. A major example of the violent land dispossession that the Colombian palm oil industry has been associated with—the case of Jiguamiandó and Curvaradó (Chocó)—was presented in the previous chapter. With reference to that case, a member of Justicia y Paz explained:

> The situation, as they frame it, is that these extensive areas of land allocated to respective communities by the state are unproductive, hence these areas have to be made productive. The people are depicted as in no way susceptible to being persuaded into putting their lands to productive use in the industrial way pressed for; thus it is deemed necessary to resort to paramilitary groups to dispossess people, evict them from their lands. Since, allegedly, the people themselves are incapable of doing so, these lands must be *made* to produce.

As will be demonstrated, although in Tumaco (Nariño) the same "need for productivity" logic applies, the situation there differs somewhat from that of the Chocó, where the dispossession that took place occurred after 1993—hence after Law 70, on the basis of which rural Afro-Colombian communities mobilized to solicit collective titles to their lands, was promulgated. In contrast, in Tumaco oil palm was first established in 1959, albeit on a very small scale. It was from the 1970s and, increasingly so, from the 1980s onwards that the palm oil industry started to expand exponentially. During most of the industry expansion in Tumaco, legal recognition and protection of Afro-Colombian and indigenous communities therefore did not yet exist as it does today. From the analysis that will be developed below, it follows that both the absence *and* subsequent introduction of the respective legal provisions are reflected in the dynamics of land transfer and land use change in Tumaco over time.

Quasi-Legal Land Transfers and Industry Expansion

From the companies' point of view, the establishment and expansion of oil palm plantations in Tumaco have always proceeded through legal means. However, the allegations that permeate the views and testimonies put forward in interviews with local activists, people from affected communities, and representatives of the latter cast serious doubt on such claims. Regarding the initial stages of industry development (1960 to the early 1980s), the image that emerges is that of a set of land transfers which *on the face of it* appeared to be legal but in a significant number of cases are claimed to have been negotiated or enforced in a context of intimidation, misleading practices, and implicit and explicit threats.[6]

Amongst these are, for instance, denunciations of corporate practices whereby people who were reluctant or unwilling to sell their lands in effect were forced to do so as a result of palm oil companies buying up (or appropriating) bordering plots of land, as a consequence of which people ended up being encircled by the company. Even for people with no intention to cede their lands, with access to their land increasingly prohibited or blocked, in the long run there was practically no other option than to sell. Another strategy or practice alleged to have enabled expansion of the palm oil project that in effect forced people to sell or leave their land involved the unleashing of company horses and buffalo which ruined the soils and subsistence and commercial crops of families and individuals bordering with oil palm plantations.

In addition, companies are accused of the illegal taking of forest support systems in cases where agreement was reached on the transfer of a number of hectares corresponding to a family production unit or part thereof. Family production units are a basic reflection of the species diversity of the forest and interact with the forest they border with. The forest as such constitutes a support system that forms an integral part of traditional models of production. The companies, on top of the hectares agreed upon, appropriated this forest support system. Incompatible with palm, these forests not only lost their social, ecological, and cultural values but ceased to exist entirely.

Moreover, as land came to be treated as a commodity in a region where this was still largely alien to local culture, especially in the early stages of corporate land acquisition the prices paid for the land were often low. Cordeagropaz's Social and Business Coordinator, for instance, acknowledged that *"these lands were practically given away"*, ascribing this in part to local people not having an accurate notion of the monetary value of their lands. Above all, he asserted that:

> One has to put the land in its context; the value and the concept of land change a lot from place to place. Lately the value of land has increased [. . .] But in my view the value of the land has also increased precisely due to the palm. To have a half-abandoned field covered in some vestiges of crops and weeds is worth nothing. But today, to have land along the main road *has* value.

Hence, only the *exchange* value of land counts. It is of course important not to idealize or otherwise reify the relation that Afro-Colombian, indigenous, and peasant societies hold to their land and natural environments, or treat them as passive bystanders in processes of land use change. Economic motives were not wholly absent from the minds of local inhabitants. In this regard, both the lived reality of socioeconomic hardship and the lure of money that gradually began to assume a more central place in local culture must be taken account of. But, at the same time, this must be placed in critical perspective. The economic model that arrived to the Colombian Pacific disregarded local forms of production and values ascribed to the land. In the process, many people were misled and at times pressured into selling their lands through practices that are at best questionable and more often tread the illegal.

"Me Vende O Le Compro a La Viuda"[7]: Violence, Force, and Illegal Land Acquisition

In addition to the above-mentioned practices, direct force and threats by private armed actors were, and continue to be, used to "compel" people to sell their lands (see also Corte Constitucional, 2009b: 26). Palm oil critics in the local population claim that it was the palm oil industry that triggered the first wave of violence and forced displacement in Tumaco. *"People have never been willing to say that the first assassinations, the first assassins, had to do with the oil palm business. [. . .] That to the people they said, 'either you sell me your land or I will buy it from your widow, or your heirs'.*[8] *[. . .] Why haven't the people been willing to narrate these stories? Because the person that speaks pays with his life"* (Afro-Colombian grassroots leader). Other locals, however, dispute the claim that the majority of lands occupied by the palm oil sector were illegally appropriated, and contend, instead, that most lands were legally obtained. Hoffmann (2007) has reflected on this matter by stating that divergent explanations of a situation often coincide with dissimilar experiences of daily reality. People whose lives and daily routines are closely entangled with the palm oil industry, whose lands border with the oil palm plantations, or who have grown wholly dependent on the industry's economic and social infrastructure, are in no position to take a stance in opposition to the sector. At the other end, there are the critics of agroindustrial incursions into the region: the community leaders, local activists, and ethnic-territorial organizations that represent or support the dispossessed in their struggles (2007: 194–195).

Still, that indeed pressure was exerted over communal lands in order to consolidate nuclei of palm oil production, and that this may have been accompanied by violence, force, and assassinations, was at least acknowledged—albeit cautiously—by one local official:

> Within this process [of the first phase of industry expansion], from what is being told, some rather unorthodox practices took place. And perhaps pressure was exerted over these lands in order to consolidate the productive nuclei of these companies. But personally I wouldn't be able to provide strong evidence to say what did or did not occur exactly. What is certain is that indeed some force was used and, at some point in the 1990s, I recall, there were even the deaths of several leaders of the Process of the Black Communities. Who was responsible for these killings, I couldn't say either, but fact is that it did occur. And as a consequence, one way or another, amongst certain sectors the crop is met with a level of aversion. (Mayoral advisor in Tumaco)

Most of the palm oil-related violence, forced displacement, and cases of illegal taking of land are claimed to have taken place in the 1980s and '90s. Although in this an element of guerrilla violence is certainly not absent—especially in more recent years (see Noguera and Salgar 2016)—in connection to the palm oil industry such violence and threats are claimed to have been mostly carried out by paramilitary groups, with complicity (by commission or omission) of Colombia's public armed forces.[9] But much of this history remains unclear, and covered in silence (on the widespread fear to denounce and resist in Tumaco, see also Salgar Antolínez 2016). Regarding an alleged paramilitary backing of the palm oil industry, a legal advisor to the Alto Mira y Frontera community council—closely involved with the communities there since' 98—for instance explained that no inquiries from this angle were made, but that this connection has always been strongly suspected. On the paramilitary link, as well as activity by other armed groups, he said: *"There is a principle here that says, we'd say: 'where there are paras, there is palm'. There is this principle. And not just paras, there was also the guerrilla. And not just illegal armed groups, public forces, too. Going to Candelillas, or Imbilí, one runs into camps of the public forces. There is always at least a backing there, and, if not a backing, a symbolic message: don't interfere".*

Community leaders are especially hard-hit by the violent repression of "obstacles" to development and the defence of territorial autonomy.[10] To place such violence and repression in its proper context, it is important to note that Colombia's constitutional reform in 1991 and the corresponding expansion of the legal framework in the area of ethnic and cultural diversity, for the first time, provided Afro-Colombian communities with the instruments, institutional basis, and symbolic support to revisit the dispossessions suffered up to that point. Communities thus began to organize to reclaim illegally appropriated lands, to question the proclaimed property limits of palm oil companies, to halt ongoing land dispossession, and to recuperate traditional subsistence and production models. Particularly, the assassinations of Francisco Hurtado in 1997 (an Afro-Colombian community leader and outspoken critic of the palm oil sector), and Yolanda Cerón in 2001, are engraved on people's minds and, when brought up in interviews, were resolutely linked to the fact that both stood up against the imposition and expansion of palm oil. As such, contrary to paramilitary and official claims that Sister Yolanda Cerón was assassinated by paramilitaries for sympathizing and collaborating with the guerrilla, critics of this account assert that Sister Yolanda was silenced for accusing Colombia's public forces of complicity in the violence and coercion carried out by paramilitaries, for her active role in the support of Afro-Colombian communities organizing to seek the collective titling of their lands, for denouncing palm oil related land dispossession, and for accusing the local palm oil sector of financing paramilitary groups (VerdadAbierta.com 2014a).

Awá resistance to an encroaching palm oil industry, too, has been accompanied by threats, forced displacements, and "disappearances". In fact, for indigenous Awá in Tumaco, the processes that accompanied the expansion of the agroindustrial frontier constituted the first frontal clash that gave rise to the need to organize in defence of Awá territory, livelihoods, and culture. Indigenous Awá of resguardo La Brava narrated how lands were bought, obtained through misleading practices whereby people signed away their land without understanding what transpired; whereas in other instances, land was simply taken. "*He who had an ID was left with one, only one hectare [around the house]. If not, everything was taken [. . .]. Based on a terrible lie, for several kilos of rice, some sardines, mackerel, all of this land was invaded, all of it*" (indigenous Awá). As such, it was in response to the environmental destruction, violence, and land dispossession at the hands of "*the abuse that is palm*" from the early '80s onwards that Awá communities began to demand the recognition of their existence as an indigenous people and their presence in these forests, which in 1990 culminated in the creation of the UNIPA.

Industry Expansion Through the Incorporation of Small Growers

The practices by which the ground has been prepared for palm oil production, as addressed up to this point, all carried a more or less manifest element of imposition. Oil palm cultivation in Tumaco, however, is not unanimously rejected by small-scale agriculturalists within the local population (see Figs. 5.2 and 5.3), and neither does industry expansion rely exclusively on imposition, coercion, and force. Increasingly, industry expansion has taken the form of oil palm cultivation by small-scale agriculturalists who have entered into so-called "Strategic Alliances" with palm oil companies. The promotion of small grower involvement in the palm oil production chain sits comfortably with Colombia's push for agricultural modernization and adheres to developmental rhetoric along the same lines. Tumaco is argued to lack the type of "*strong, serious, and well-organized productive activities*" that can improve a situation where many people lack access to clean water, decent housing, sewer systems, basic sanitation, connection to the electricity grid, and basic health services (Cordeagropaz's Social and Business Coordinator). As opposed to the perceived unproductivity and inefficiency of small-scale, traditional models of agriculture,

Fig. 5.2 Small grower oil palm plantation in Tumaco

the corporatization and industrialization of agriculture is presented as a crucial step toward dealing with these issues. "Serious" productive activity is needed so that people can stay on their land, yet work with "enhanced knowledge", geared towards products with a guaranteed commerce:

> I can have 50 hectares of land but not have the means to cultivate them. To cultivate them well. And what I produce does not have an accepted market. And I have 50 hectares. I remain worshipping the land, it becomes a sacred element, I sanctify the land, idealise it. (Cordeagropaz's Social and Business Coordinator)

In many interviews with industry proponents, the leadership of indigenous and Afro-Colombian collective territories is blamed for blocking their communities access to enhanced options for social well-being and a better quality of life if resisting agroindustrial projects like palm oil; to

Fig. 5.3 Small grower oil palm plantation in Tumaco

diverge from a capitalist logic of productivity tends to be dismissed, in no uncertain terms, as living in the past.

As noted by Mondragón Báez (2002), global economic integration has globalized the agricultural problem, too. Pressures on peasant, indigenous, and Afro-Colombian economies have further intensified now that producers must compete not just in a national context but in an aggressive, highly competitive global market economy. This means that only a limited set of agricultural crops is constructed as "productive alternatives", conditional on agroindustrial models of production. According to the Executive Director of Cordeagropaz, 2500 families had shifted to cultivating oil palm by 2012. But Tumaco's rural communities stand divided when it comes to the acceptance of oil palm as a "productive alternative". Before delving deeper into the whys and the hows of small growers opting for palm oil, local tensions in view of the Strategic

Alliances formed around palm oil production will be briefly addressed first.

Strategic Alliances: Undermining the Figure of the Collective Territory?

Palm oil critics within the local population insist that industry expansion through small grower involvement is yet another strategy to force a neoliberal logic of capitalist development onto territories where resistance to such models persists. As discussed in Chap. 3, Colombia's constitutional change in 1991 and the corresponding advances vis-à-vis the formal recognition of cultural and ethnic diversity led to the allocation of collective land titles to Afro-Colombian and indigenous communities. The limits thus set on corporate private property have affected the dynamics of agroindustry expansion in Tumaco. On the new dimension of struggle and conflict over land that these dynamics implied, the legal advisor to the Alto Mira y Frontera community council stated the following:

> The companies, in view of the fact that they could not enter due to opposition by community leaders, began to use a new strategy, that of forming alliances with the peasants. They sidestepped the leadership, the Junta of the community council, and went directly to the base, to the community. Telling them how palm oil was the best option. And in a region like ours they managed to sell this idea. A region like ours, the Pacific with its high levels of poverty, whatever shiny little mirror they hold up to the people[11] will always have an effect, a huge effect. So this is how the second impetus to the conflict was set in motion; by creating alliances, associations on the margins of the community council. The company no longer fights with the community council, but works its interests through the associations of small growers so that the latter oblige the community council to opt for palm.

Critics argue that entering into direct dialogue and alliance with a select number of individuals or small grower associations within the collective territories, rather than consulting the entire community council, violates the requirement of prior consultation and undermines dynamics of collective decision-making. As previously addressed (see Chap. 3), indigenous and Afro-Colombian communities have the fundamental right to be informed and consulted prior to the implementation or undertaking of any project or activity that may affect their social, economic, and cultural integrity (Amparo Rodríguez 2014).

Many community leaders and inhabitants of the collective territories expressed their concern and frustration with practices that display contempt for the type of projects envisioned by the communities *themselves* (i.e. what, how, and for whom to produce). They deplore that companies, the Colombian State, and international aid arrive with fully elaborated projects and production models that are not in accord with the cultural, economic, and ecological rationalities of local people. It is not that people are against any type of activity that would serve the market economy. As stated by an Afro-Colombian community leader: *"Projects can be brought, can be undertaken, but these projects should spring from the communities"*. But more often than not, "ready-made" models are imposed, rather than involving local communities in the design and implementation of projects. Thus, a one-way traffic dynamic determines that *"you cultivate palm or you cultivate nothing. Or else the government does not give you the resources"*.

In rejecting the type of crops and production models pushed for by neoliberal dictates of development and capitalist criteria of productivity, palm oil critics differ markedly from small growers of oil palm. What drives small-scale agriculturalists to opt for the cultivation of oil palm and express pride in their achievements as *empresarios* of this crop? The next session delves deeper into these processes and the corresponding play of power in the politics of palm oil harm.

Closing the Gap: Incorporating the Small Grower

Contrary to local critics of palm oil, small growers manifest an acceptance of the productivist discourse that is centred on a notion of progress achieved through agroindustrial development—one that naturalizes the neoliberal (re)configuration of social relations and human interaction with the natural environment. As one small grower explained:

> I don't think that I have to live my life the way my parents or grandparents did. Those were different times, different conditions. Perhaps when my father lived, when my grandfather lived, first of all the crisis that we have today did not exist, crisis in every sense of the word. The globalization that we live today did not exist, there was not so much of this market competition that exists today. I would say that probably my grandfather lived a calm life, because he had his subsistence absolutely guaranteed. But perhaps he never imagined that the world would become so globalized and come to demand such extreme preparation in every sense of the word; personally, commercially, culturally, politically… and that he who was prepared would fare better. Perhaps my grandfather never… well, he died without knowing this. And so did my father. But we are a different generation. With us globalization makes its appearance, the neoliberal opening, free trade agreements. With us, other symptoms of life appear. When I was young we had fish close by, shellfish, very close. I would go and grab them, and it cost me nothing. Today this doesn't exist anymore. So from this point of view, today, already from when I was born, the necessity of education changed; today one has to attend primary school, go to college, go to university, and perhaps a very select number of privileged persons in our country will have the honour to be doctors as you will be. But one should consider these things a challenge in life. But this also requires having the means to finance all these wishes, so that all such aspirations can become reality.

In describing their decision to opt for palm, most of the small growers start off by pointing out the precarious conditions under which rural populations live. The provision of basic services—sewerage, electricity, potable water, health services, schools, and so on—is largely absent. As such, what for most of us are taken-for-granted aspects of life, many people struggle for on a daily basis in places like Tumaco; to sustain one's family, send one's children to school, having access to medical services, and so on, none of this is given. Small growers thus state that it is crucial to create the conditions in the rural zone that enable people to stay on their lands, cultivate the land, and live a dignified life. Without improved living conditions, they say, people will get involved with illicit activity or leave the rural zone to *"become an obstacle to the city"*:

> The important thing is that we do not neglect the countryside. If we do, trust me, we will go down a path... truly towards tragedy. If the government does not help the rural to cultivate licit crops, what will happen? (Small grower)

Many are aware of the forces that are at play in a context of global economic integration and consider participation in the competitive market economy the best option given their situation. Thus, echoing the agroindustrial developmentalist discourse, small growers, too, argue that the rural zone has to be made productive, *"hay que ponerlo a producir"*. But what does it mean to put the land to "productive use"? And what crops and production model fit the corresponding view of productivity? Small growers are aware that under current economic arrangements not all crops lend themselves to being "cash crops" and are often critical of this, yet decide to go along with the dictates of the underlying economic structure, because they view it as the only viable way out of socioeconomic hardship.

> Palm, this is a necessity. This we are certain of and we want to continue working the land in this way. Also with other products, exactly, but the paths we have followed in life have taught us that one cannot undertake economic activities that do not have a guaranteed commerce. For this reason, we stake on palm. Palm already has a guaranteed commerce, other products don't. (Small grower)

As such, when small growers of oil palm stress that palm is their only alternative, they do not refer to restrictions related to local soil conditions. On the contrary, people insist that the soil is "very strong" and "apt for a diversity of crops". They explain that any crop can take root, but that many "lack utility". Traditional production models and the crops that are more in accord with local culture and the territorial vocation of the zone are not considered feasible in terms of long-term improvements in the conditions of life. To mention but a few, the *borojó* fruit and *chontaduro* (peach palm), both native to the zone, as well as coconut, plantain, and papaya, are mentioned as suitable crops for subsistence but "doomed to fail" as commercial products. Instead, when cultivating oil palm, people know that the companies will buy their fruits. This guarantees them a regular income.

The conceptualizations of harm articulated by small growers in this regard diverge from those put forward by palm oil critics. The latter problematize the cultural, environmental, and social impacts of the agroindustrial production model of palm oil and reject capitalist criteria of productivity and competition. Small growers of oil palm, in contrast, tone down these harms significantly and instead tend to emphasize the socioeconomic marginalization to which they have historically been subjected. During a small grower reunion, one of the small growers put the matter as follows:

> What has happened? The campesino has been forgotten by the nation. With products such as rice, cacao, and cassava this precariousness could not be overcome. And so palm arrived and showed a better quality of life. Later the coca arrived and also showed a better quality of life. *[Some people laugh].* No, serious! It is like this! If the State does not give me the opportunities, one has to think of other ways out. We need to live in dignity; before this was not possible.

In palm oil, small growers have found the crop and sector to overcome this marginalization. Critics within the local population and NGOs, on the other hand, claim that small growers are misled by a discourse that has "planted the idea of palm in their minds", and that they are sold the illusory idea that they will become successful and equal business partners of the large companies. There is a notion that there is "a discourse that buys" the local small grower, which, I would argue, is not wholly accurate. Instead, it is my contention that a better understanding of small grower involvement in palm starts from a Gramscian focus on the operation of power and a *material reading of ideology*. Thus, ideology is understood as an active, structuring force in its own right rather than a form of false consciousness or mere reflection of the economic base; and lived practices as interwoven with beliefs and ideas that are themselves material forces (Ekers and Loftus 2008;

Hall 1996). To flesh out this idea further, it is necessary to consider the origins of the small grower of oil palm in Tumaco some 40–50 years.

The first small growers were locals that worked in the corporate oil palm plantations or had their own lands in areas surrounding the companies. Some were both plantation worker and smallholder. As such, they observed closely the arrival and gradual expansion of the palm oil industry. Copying (on their own initiative) the example of the corporate project, on a very small scale and in a nontechnified way, they started to collect seeds to grow their own oil palms. Gradually, more people followed in their footsteps. Thus, the small grower experience in Tumaco is to a considerable extent based upon *lived practice*; at first, growing involvement of local agriculturalists in the cultivation of oil palm was significantly shaped by positive first-hand, direct and indirect encounters with the activity. It was only towards the late 1990s that palm oil companies, together with local authorities and public institutions, began actively to promote small grower involvement in the palm oil business. It is at this point that a discourse of palm oil as the only viable legal and productive alternative for the local agriculturalist starts to assume a more prominent place and involves seeking to convince people that it is in their best interest to opt for palm.

With the creation of Cordeagropaz (see Chap. 3) and the formation of small grower associations, the palm oil sector and the Colombian State increasingly arrived at compromises with small growers. This is manifest mostly in financial and technical support for small grower projects.[12] In addition, the negotiation power of small growers has somewhat improved, which has led to less exploitative prices being paid for oil palm harvests. As such, rather than through sheer imposition, industry expansion through small grower involvement suggests that capital is willing (but also forced) to make concessions towards the interests and aspirations of local subjects. At the same time, processes of negotiation, concession making, and compromise discipline the peasantry into an entrepreneurial mind-set. While the stated objective of Strategic Alliances is to close the social and technological gap between large companies and the small producer, it is only when organized into associations and with projects that abide by specific technical and productive criteria, that small growers are granted access to the loans necessary to commence their projects. As such, there is a push towards more technologically advanced, capital- and energy-intensive models of agricultural production; the "right" way to grow oil palm corresponds with a particular set of technical, productive, and associative criteria. Hence, industry expansion through Strategic Alliances is drawing more and more territories into a neoliberal capitalist restructuring of agriculture. Cordeagropaz thereby functions as a bridge between the agroindustrial bloc and the small grower.

These processes call attention to the fact that power is not exclusively exercised by reliance on coercion, violence, and direct imposition, but works also through persuasion, compromise, and the accommodation of subaltern demands and aspirations. This gradually naturalizes an agroindustrial pathway of accumulation and the corresponding set of social and socioecological relations. For palm oil critics within affected communities, however, industrial palm oil production clashes with the territorial and cultural vocation of the Pacific coast region and long-held local conceptions of land. This, too, asks for further elaboration.

The Commodification of Land and Consumerist Path to Development

At the beginning of this chapter, the categorization of the territories of the Colombian Pacific as *baldíos* was highlighted, noting that such decontextualized understandings of land contrast sharply with a relational view of land wherein the history of human presence and the ecological value of a territory assume central importance. A strong connection to the land, central to the lives of many people the world over, is intricately interwoven with the human histories, ecology, and the biophysical and climatic conditions of these spaces.[13] An activist from Afrodes touched upon this when reflecting on how the history of colonialism, the slave trade, and the struggle for liberation have shaped Afro-Colombian culture and these communities' relation to the land. When erstwhile enslaved Africans spread out over the Colombian Pacific, they had to endure adverse climatic and natural conditions. *"They had to struggle against everything that comes with tropical humid forests full of plagues, viruses, and a great many things. These were inhospitable places, and they had to adjust their ways of life to these conditions and vice versa*". Strong ties to the territory thus developed; these are socionatural spaces where human ways of being are constructed upon the characteristics of an environment and where, in the process, an environment comes to bear the imprints of particular ways of being. Deforestation, the loss of land, displacement of traditional means of subsistence and systems of production, and an increased dependence on capitalist models of production and market economies alter the local landscape physically, socially, and symbolically, and, with these processes, the social and cultural realities constructed upon these landscapes also change. As such, in local culture, the land is not exclusively valued for its monetary value.[14]

Also running through the perspectives articulated by palm oil critics within the local population of Tumaco is a notion of autonomy, with which the land is so strongly associated. As stated by an Afro-Colombian community grassroots leader:

> In the conception of wellbeing and wealth that arrived to the Pacific from the beginning of the previous century, people are poor because they lack these and these things. I was born and raised along a river, and I tell you this: I lacked a laptop and the internet, for the rest there was nothing I lacked, I had everything, but this I lacked. Not that lacking these things hurt me all that much, because the most fundamental I had: affect, food, uncontaminated water, the recreation one wished for, clean air, clean food. I did not need to go the cinema, no, because the stories my grandparents told me *were* like a movie. So this wealth that comes from the culture, the territory, the ancestry, from the legacy of the past, this is what made us rich; we did not lack these things. With this emerged palm as a large-scale economic project and forced us to change this whole concept. That I have some land and they tell me: "your land is not productive. Come, I can make it produce and give you work". The people sold their land and became labourers, receiving a monthly pay that was much less than what they previously got out of their plot of land. Now one has a wage, now one can buy a fridge, a television, but this person

> ceased to have land. In other words, one stops being free in the productive sphere, one is no longer autonomous.

There is a general view that in being without land, *or without effective control over how the land is used*, one stops being free in the sphere of production—which is interwoven with many other spheres of community and family life. Therefore, to cede or lose control over the land is experienced as a loss of autonomy that impedes individuals and entire communities to give direction to their own projects of life. This loss of autonomy is a recurrent theme. In relation to palm oil, it is the company that is considered to be in charge of a person, of a community. It is the palm oil company that determines over people's life; the people are no longer in control of their own lives (inhabitant of the Alto Mira y Frontera community council).

In addition, it is claimed that the presence and growing influence of the palm oil industry in the heart of Afro-Colombian and indigenous territories has displaced a sense of community and the collective dynamics bound up with traditional systems of production significantly. Many palm oil critics ascribe the rupture of the social fabric of their communities, the disintegration of families, and reduced levels of solidarity and collective efficacy to the types of transition brought by the industry. Two local women from the PCN (*Proceso de Comunidades Negras*) deplored the loss of cultural forms such as the *minga*—the collective work action whereby people go from finca to finca and work united—and communal dynamics. They told, *"before, we produced for us, for the community, a production centred on sharing. It was considered offensive to sell a crop to another person; it would be a gift. Nature is life, from nature we eat, we share. Palm brutally changed this"*. Projects as palm oil are therefore experienced as forms of outside interference that disregard local culture and that fragment communities. Moreover, it is emphasized that these are not isolated incidents, but ongoing and systematic processes.

An ONIC consultant also brought up the topic of the *minga* and explained that what can take one family up to an entire month of work, together, communities manage to do in no more than 2 hours. This leaves time for the people to sit down with each other, to have some *chicha*[15] and talk a while, simply talk! But with the proletarianization of the rural population, he added, this type of relation is disappearing:

> Our black and indigenous communities are being converted into rural proletariat. They become workers, subordinates, people enslaved from 6 to 6. When people from the interior of the country arrive to a reunion like this and see forests, they say that the issue is that 'these blacks and Indians are lazy'. When for instance they arrive to the sea and see that the fishermen are playing domino at 10 in the morning, [they say] 'well of course these people do not progress, look, playing!' But they never ask this man at what hour he left to go fishing. This man left at 2 a.m. in the morning. With these monocultural schemes this type of relation disappears. And this has a very strong impact. With this, another notion of development starts to reign; the notion of consumerism as development.

Conceptions of land that treat the land as a commodity, or mere physical location or object, thus dismiss the social relations and practices, cultural forms, existential meaning and value bound up with the land for many rural populations. Although the expansion of Colombia's legal order vis-à-vis the recognition and protection of ethnic and cultural diversity to some degree has allowed to halt the dispossession of land and of the ways the land is used and related to, there are certain limitations that inhere in the formalization of land ownership.

The Formalization of Land: Bringing Order into Chaos?

Colombia's progressive Constitution, extensive jurisprudence and the legal instruments in place to protect ethnic and cultural diversity, seem to have opened up the legal and political space to challenge hegemonic notions and practices of legality that exclude from meaningful debate and the ambit of juridical and political action those types of harm that disproportionately affect Afro-Colombian and indigenous communities. However, many of the social and environmental harms associated with palm oil persist regardless. Some of the key limitations or friction points that inscribe land titling procedures require critical examination in this regard—without denying the importance of collective land titles. About the collective titling of land, an Afrodes activist said: *"Collective titling was necessary not because we grant any importance to a title* per se *but because, from a legal point of view, one needs a document so that the property form can be respected. We lived without titles all our life"*. To halt ongoing processes of land and cultural dispossession, land titles were a necessity.

Still, the mobilization of law as the site from which to challenge the social and economic relations and practices that threaten communities' cultural and territorial integrity comes with the severe limitation that *ownership* and *property limits* by far dominate the discussion. Largely absent, in contrast, is substantive debate on profoundly divergent conceptions of land, ways of being, and economic production and subsistence. In addition, the questionable character of past processes of land transfer and dispossession gets pushed to the background. Several conflicts that at the time of this research were ongoing can substantiate these claims.

First, there is the conflict between the Alto Mira y Frontera community council and palm oil company Palmeiras, in relation to 800 ha of land that Palmeiras had planted with oil palm in 1997. Incoder had initially excluded this area from the collective title received in 2005; however, the Office of the Inspector General intervened and ruled that Palmeiras' presence on these lands was illegal and that the company had acted in bad faith by establishing oil palm on this land in 1997. Accordingly, in 2006, Incoder reversed its 2005 decision and included the 800 ha in the Alto Mira y Frontera collective title. Palmeiras appealed, and 30 August 2013 the Administrative Tribunal of Cundinamarca ruled in favour of the community council.

Palmeiras' Managing Director at the time of this research claimed that the community of Alto Mira never laid claim to the lands in question and that this dispute was invented by the Inspector General from behind a desk in Bogotá; it was not the community itself, he said, that challenged Incoder's initial decision to exclude these 800 ha from the collective title and allocate them to Palmeiras. The conflict that ensued, in his view, exemplified a more frequent pattern whereby community leaders say things that they have been *told* to say by third parties, NGOs included, arguing that not so much the communities themselves, but "external forces" in Tumaco, are behind the public accusations and legal actions against companies.[16]

Another case involves a longstanding conflict between Bajo Mira y Frontera and palm oil company Palmas de Tumaco, which allegedly has been illegally expanding its operations beyond its own property limits since 1998 (JPCCERT 2012). After a change in the corporate management team, in 2008 the community council decided to (re-)enter into dialogue with the company in order to halt the ongoing processes of corporate expansion onto collective territory (community leader Bajo Mira y Frontera). Four years on, at the time of this research, technical and legal procedures had still not clarified and established the disputed property boundaries, although in 2011 Incoder ruled in favour of the company.[17] The community council therefore saw itself forced to solicit precautionary measures to prevent the displacement of families from the disputed land, which it was granted through a court ruling in 2012 (JPCCERT 2012).

For the affected communities, it is the defence of life, socionatural spaces of existence, ways of being, and self-determination that are at the heart of these conflicts, but these lengthy processes hardly allow for substantive debate in recognition of ethnic and cultural diversity. It is possible to argue—although perhaps at the risk of somewhat simplifying matters—that what dominates the discussion is a property regime that reduces the struggles in question to a set of decisive cut-off points. For Afro-Colombian communities, this relates to whether a specific dispute over land has its origins before or after 1993. This logic is perhaps clearest articulated in an interview with the Director of Sustainable Development at Fedepalma. Initially, all of the territories in this rural zone were *baldíos*, he said, that at some point were allocated as private property to the palm oil companies or this or that Afro-Colombian or indigenous community or individual. He then reflected:

> The whole matter rests on the moment these situations took place, in order to determine what rights apply. Better said, if palm is planted on collective lands it depends on whether the occupant of this piece of land has acted in good or bad faith. If things occurred before the whole process

> of collective titling commenced, then one has acted in good faith. If the activities took place after this date, knowing that this concerned a collective territory that had been titled as such, well then one has acted in bad faith and none of the investments that were made will be acknowledged.

Hence, a temporal criterion is decisive in ascribing a property status to the land. In effect, this means that the complexities—and long duration—of the social and cultural politics of affected communities are reduced to juridical understandings of space. This, I would argue, facilitates a shift from true dialogue on the messy history of land transfers and industry expansion, and on divergent conceptions of land, development, and ways of being, to the "orderly" realm of property rights.

Discussion: Power, Legality, and the Contestedness of Harm

In this chapter, I discussed the practices and discourses that have accompanied and facilitated land use change to palm oil production in Tumaco, Nariño. It has followed that the processes and practices of industry establishment and expansion are wide-ranging: from the legal to the illegal and from outright violence and coercion through to indirect forms of imposition and more consensual forms of power. As has been pointed out, in terms of the cultural constructs, legal categories, and discourses that have been deployed, mobilized, and exploited in this context, agroindustrial expansion in Tumaco was significantly aided by (i) the classification of the lands of the Colombian Pacific as *tierra baldía*, (ii) the depiction of both the region and its populations as marginal and underdeveloped, and (iii) imaginations of the frontier as ungoverned spaces where illegality reigns. Regarding the processes that followed, the conceptualizations of harm that emerge from the industry proponents' point of view problematize neither the deforestation per se, nor the subsequent land conversion. Instead, they argue that *some* deforestation and "serious" productive activity were essential to develop the region and its people, and to prevent greater social and environmental harm. In contrast, affected communities and palm oil critical NGOs view deforestation as an environmental harm in itself. Whether the deforestation was legal or illegal to them makes little difference with regard to the social, cultural, and ecological impacts consequently caused.

Regarding the dispossession of land, since the mid-1990s, processes of land transfer and land use change have taken on a different character. Although corporate expansion onto collective territory is alleged to be ongoing, over the whole, the illegal taking of land, forced sale through intimidation and threats, and violent dispossession are no longer the primary means of agroindustry expansion in Tumaco. Partly in response to the collective titling of Afro-Colombian and indigenous land, the palm oil industry has had to find other ways to expand its operations. Through Strategic Alliances between companies and small growers of oil palm, the agroindustrial production model and related criteria of productivity are thus expanding over collective territory. Critics within the affected communities argue that these practices impede their exercise of cultural, territorial, and economic autonomy as, in effect, decisions regarding what, how, and for whom to produce are externally imposed. As a corollary, alternative ways of being, conceptions of land, and local models of subsistence and production are disqualified and debilitated.

As such, those affected experience not only the dispossession of land *qua land*, but of *their ways of using and relating to the land*, too. In green criminological critique of constructions of "nature" as external and inferior to the human, and of conceptions of crime and harm that exclude the environment and the nonhuman from the criminological imagination, emphasis is placed on the interactions and interconnectedness between the natural and the social, the nonhuman and the human, insisting that our (human) being—social, cultural, and biological—is intrinsically bound up with the natural world (South 2008). It is crucial to elaborate further on the extent to which Colombia's constitutional safeguards and legal framework are able to effectively challenge the unequal power relations conducive to the environmental degradation and type of land use change that lead not just to the dispossession of land as such, but also to these broader experiences of dispossession (i.e. of "being" in its multiple dimensions). Thus, the next chapter, centred on the harms associated with the phases of oil palm cultivation and the processing of oil palm fruits, will critically interrogate the seeming paradox that, in a country that presents itself as pluri-ethnic and multicultural, an array of social and environmental harm persists almost uninterrupted and maintains large parts of Colombia's indigenous and Afro-Colombian in extremely precarious conditions.

Notes

1. A practice referred to as forest reserve subtraction, enabled by article 3 of Law 2 of 1959.
2. Although palm oil companies have certainly also been held accountable for illegal deforestation in Tumaco (see, e.g., Tribunal Superior de Distrito Judicial de Cali 2013).
3. Secondary forests are forests that have been (significantly) disturbed by activities like hunting, logging, and clearance for agriculture. That the timber industry has caused serious disturbance is rarely denied by people within the local population. But even if one accepts that there are indeed cases where the palm oil industry has "retaken secondary forest", multiple testimonies confirm that palm oil-related deforestation also destroyed primary forest. In addition, for palm oil, the stripping of a territory is *total*, which means that serious, additional harm is generated through such deforestation.
4. On this trip, I joined a group of biologists from the Andes University and Fundación Panthera. Panthera works amongst others with camera traps to examine the levels of biodiversity in and around palm oil plantations that may interfere with important wild life corridors and habitats.
5. "Myth" does not refer to mere fantasy or superstition here, but to narratives that have their basis in native knowledge and belief systems and thus give expression to a particular worldview.
6. See also Hoffmann (2007: 191) who, based on local testimonies, states that after an initial phase of bona fide land deals—even if against exploitative prices—the use of threats and coercion gradually started to assume a more prominent place in the expansion of the palm oil industry in Tumaco.
7. "Either you sell to me or I'll buy from your widow". Among marginalized groups in Colombia, this is an expression often heard with reference to paramilitary involvement in the forced dispossession of land.
8. Whether or not this precise expression was used in Tumaco is not the point. What is important is what the phrase *symbolizes*, which is the

collective memory of processes of violent dispossession of land and ways of life.

9. The analysis of the role of governments and power elites in the violent repression of oppositional forces and in facilitating or initiating land grabs can draw on, as well as add further insights to, existing criminological work on state crime (e.g. Green and Ward 2004; Barak 2015). It is beyond the scope of this study to do so here.
10. With regard to Afro-Colombian community leaders assassinated in the process of the defence, titling, and recuperation of collective land, see, e.g., VerdadAbierta.com 2014b; Noguera and Salgar 2016.
11. The expression used by this respondent—"*cualquier espejito que le brillen a la gente*"—in essence accuses the palm oil industry of misleading or deceiving people into cultivating oil palm by creating the illusion that this is their way out of poverty. The origins of the expression can be traced back to the time of the colonization of the Americas and refers to the deception of indigenous peoples by Spanish conquistadores. Surprised to see their own reflection in the mirrors brought to them by the Spanish, indigenous people thought that the mirrors were valuable goods. As such they were deceived into exchanging gold for mirrors worth exponentially less. I would like to thank David Rodríguez Goyes for pointing out the historical content of this expression.
12. Financial support includes, for instance, small grower access to Incentives for Rural Capitalization programmes, which means that, rather than having to repay a loan in full, 40% of the loan will eventually be cancelled (i.e. there is a 60% repayment obligation).
13. In times of growing disconnection (see Mol 2016; Brisman and South 2014), an insightful and beautiful read that brings into view how a connectedness to the land is neither some faraway nor bygone reality is James Rebank's (2015) autobiography "The Shepherd Life", a powerful, down-to-earth description of an enduring shepherding way of life in the English Lake District.
14. Of course, considerations of the economic value of land are not absent and indeed are gaining in importance. But overall, there is a notion that the economic value of land should be geared towards the community and not towards individual, private gain.
15. A traditional drink, fermented or nonfermented, produced on the basis of corn, other cereals, or fruits.

16. Such arguments seek to undermine the legitimacy of respective denunciations. See also Chap. 5.
17. This decision was vehemently opposed by the interviewed community leader, due to an alleged lack of transparency on the part of Incoder and allegations of a fraudulent interplay between Incoder and the company: "*They staged this from Bogotá. The field visit they carried out was a simulation; to get some coordinates to simulate. This was already fixed*".

References

Amparo Rodríguez, G. (2014). *De la consulta previa al consentamiento libre, previo e informado a pueblos indígenas en Colombia*. Bogotá: Grupo Editorial Ibañez S.A.S.

Barak, G. (Ed.). (2015). *The routledge international handbook of the crimes of the powerful*. Abingdon: Routledge.

Brisman, A., & South, N. (2014). *Green cultural criminology: Constructions of environmental harm, consumerism, and resistance to ecocide*. Abingdon: Routledge.

Corte Constitucional. (2009a). *Auto Nº 004 de 2009. Protección de los derechos fundamentales de las personas y los pueblos indígenas desplazados por el conflicto armado o en riesgo de desplazamiento forzado, en el marco de la superación del estado de cosas inconstitucional declarado en la sentencia T-025 de 2004*. Bogotá: República de Colombia.

Delgado A., Ruiz S., Arévalo L., Castillo G., Viles N., Calderón J., Cañizales J., et al. Eds. (2007). *Plan de Acción en Biodiversidad del Departamento de Nariño 2006–2030 – Propuesta Técnica*. Pasto: Corponariño, gobernación de nariño (Secretaría de Agricultura), IAvH, UAESPNN, Universidad de Nariño, Universidad Mariana y Asociación para el Desarrollo Campesino.

Ekers, M., & Loftus, A. (2008). The power of water: Developing dialogues between foucault and gramsci. *Environment and Planning D: Society and Space, 26*(4), 698–718.

Green, P., & Ward, T. (2004). *State crime: Governments, violence and corruption*. London: Pluto Press.

Hall, S. (1996). Gramsci's relevance for the study of race and ethnicity. In D. Morley & K. Chen (Eds.), *Stuart hall: Critical dialogues in cultural studies* (pp. 411–441). New York: Routledge.

Hoefle, S. W. (2006). Twisting the knife: Frontier violence in the central amazon of Brazil. *The Journal of Peasant Studies, 33*(3), 445–478.
Hoffmann, O. (2007). *Comunidades negras en el pacífico colombiano: Innovaciones y dinámicas étnicas.* Quito: IFEA, IRD, Ediciones Abya-Yala.
Juzgado Primero Civil (JPCCERT). (2012). *Medida Cautelar Previa No. 2012–00029.* Colombia, Circuito Especializado en Restitución de Tierras. Decided 25-10-2012, judge Eduardo Jacobo Martínez Rueda. Tumaco – Nariño.
Mol, H. (2016). Green criminology and (Constructions of) environmental harm: A review essay. *Critical Criminology, 24*(1), 145–150.
Mol, H. (2017). Agroindustry expansion through "strategic alliances": The shifting dynamics of palm oil-related dispossession. In D. R. Goyes, H. Mol, A. Brisman, & N. South (Eds.), *Environmental crime in Latin America: The theft of nature and the poisoning of the land.* London: Palgrave Macmillan.
Mondragón Báez, H. H. (2002). *La organización campesina en un ambiente de terror.* Bogotá: ILSA.
Noguera, S., & Salgar, D. (2016, September 8). El perdón de las FARC llegó a Tumaco? El espectador [Online], (Territorio). Available from: http://colombia2020.elespectador.com [Accessed 15 November 2016].
Ospina Bozzi, M. L. (2001). *La palma africana en Colombia: Apuntes y memorias, volumen 2* (2nd ed.). Bogotá: Fedepalma.
Passas, N., & Goodwin, N. (2004). Introduction: A crime by any other name. In N. Passas & N. Goodwin (Eds.), *It's legal but it ain't right: Harmful social consequences of legal industries* (pp. 1–27). Ann Arbor, MI: University of Michigan Press.
Rebanks, J. (2015). *The shepherd's life: A tale of the lake district.* Allen Lane.
Restrepo, E. (2004a). Biopolítica y alteridad: Dilemas de la etnización de las colombias negras. In E. Restrepo & A. Rojas, (Eds.), *Conflicto e (in) visibilidad. Retos en los estudios de la gente negra de Colombia.* Popayán: Editorial Universidad del Cauca, pp. 271–300.
Restrepo, E. (2004b). Un océano verde para extraer aceite. Hacia una etnografía del cultivo de la palma africana en Tumaco. *Universitas Humanistica, 58,* 72–87.
Salgar Antolínez, D. (2016, June 8). Tumaco: voces de un conflicto ajeno. El espectador [Online], (Territorio). Available from: http://colombia2020.elespectador.com [Accessed 15 November 2016].
Serje, M. (2012). El mito de la ausencia del estado: la incorporación económica de las "zonas de frontera" en Colombia. *Cahiers des Ameriques Latines, 71,* 95–117.

South, N. (2008). Nature, difference, and the rejection of harm: Expanding the agenda for green criminology. In R. Sollund (Ed.), *Global harms: Ecological crime and speciesism* (pp. 187–200). New York: Nova Science Publishers Inc.
Sykes, G. M., & Matza, D. (1957). Techniques of neutralization: A theory of delinquency. *American Sociological Review, 22*(6), 664–670.
Tribunal Superior de Distrito Judicial de Cali. (2013). *Referencia: 52835-31-21-001-2013-00012-01 Medidas Cautelares, Sala Civil Especializada en Restitución y Formalización de Tierras*. Bogotá: República de Colombia.
VerdadAbierta.com. (2014a, February 6). Las víctimas de Tumaco quieren la verdad. [Online], (Justicia y Paz). Available from: http://www.verdadabierta.com [Accessed 2 May 2014].
VerdadAbierta.com. (2014b, March 2). Cómo reparar los daños de la guerra en el pacífico nariñense. [Online], (Justicia y Paz). Available from: http://www.verdadabierta.com [Accessed 26 July 2014].

6

Reaping the Fruits

People that work palm demolish the being that God has created – nature. Large drainages, they don't care, harming whatever, from where all these riches that God has given us spring, from where all the fruits spring. Because the only thing they want is palm
(Inhabitant of Bajo Mira y Frontera).

In industry discourse, oil palm is praised as a "social and ecological crop" (Fedepalma 2006). Whether palm oil production is really all that social and ecological differs greatly according to what, and whose, criteria are followed. In this chapter, I will show that industry and government constructions of the social and ecological character of palm oil are incompatible with the socioecological and economic rationalities of local palm oil critics in Tumaco; a bud rot epidemic moreover exposed that the agroindustrial model of palm oil production is likewise incompatible with the biophysical properties and ecological dynamics of local ecosystems. Interviews with affected small growers and local palm oil critics will be drawn upon to show how this epidemic has brought yet another round of social and environmental harm upon the region.

Regardless of some social and environmental compromises being forged, throughout this chapter, I will demonstrate that the political and economic

---

Parts of this chapter have also appeared in Spanish, in an article written for the journal *Crítica Penal y Poder* (Mol 2016).

H. Mol, *The Politics of Palm Oil Harm*, Palgrave Studies in Green Criminology, DOI 10.1007/978-3-319-55378-8_6

arrangements, and entrenched power asymmetries, underpinning palm oil harm are left intact; any concessions (e.g. vis-à-vis the recognition of cultural and ethnic diversity) remain deeply embedded in existing power configurations, attitudes to nature, and the dominant economic model. In spite of reforms that, at least in theory, should be more open to alternative conceptions of development, being, and human relationships with our environments, hegemonic notions and practices of legality are kept in place. As a result, a whole variety of social and environmental harm persists, and it is increasingly difficult for communities to withstand pressures to put their lands "to productive use" in accord with neoliberal dictates of "development" and capitalist criteria of productivity.

Local Versus Industrial Models of Agricultural Production

The perspectives of the various actors that have a stake in the politics of palm oil harm are permeated by different constructions of "green", the criminological implications of which have been spelled out by Lynch and Stretesky (2003), addressed in Chap. 2. By reflecting on local models of production and subsistence in the Colombian Pacific, and contrasting these with the agroindustrial production model implemented by the palm oil industry, below I analyse the constructs and realities of harm linked to the corresponding land use change. The social and environmental effects of a growing "metabolic rift", discussed in Chap. 2, thus clearly surface.

Local, Traditional Models of Production: "Mira el trabajo que hace ese árbol"

The ways in which the inhabitants of the Colombian Pacific over time have come to utilize and relate to their territories are intrinsically bound up with the region's rich biodiversity and ecology; soil characteristics, vegetation cover, species diversity, hydrology, and climate conditions have fed into and shaped local ways of life, means of subsistence, transport systems, housing, and cultural artefacts. Subsistence and production in the Colombian Pacific have traditionally been built on a cultural logic of *multi-optionality* (ONIC consultant), which rests on combining fishing, hunting, gathering, forest harvesting, and nonindustrial forms of agriculture. Palm oil is argued to have disrupted the corresponding natural and cultural dynamics of the land, and with that the dynamic interplay between these.

The agricultural model that has long prevailed in the region, but is now under increasing pressure, is that of integrated farming. The arrival of the palm oil industry is by many claimed to have given the first impetus to the transition to a different logic of agricultural production. In integrated farming, a variety of traditional crops[1] exist interspersed with natural vegetation. Neither the cultivation of a single crop (monocropping), nor the use of agrochemicals is part of traditional systems of production. Decomposing underbrush, fallen leaves, and—amongst others—the shells of the cacao fruit serve as fertilizers. In addition to these, *tierra de hormiga* —the soil of anthills—was described as a natural fertilizer. Moreover, ideally, not all arable land is under constant production, thus allowing the soil to lay fallow, which enables nutrients to be replenished; unthinkable in an agroindustrial model of production that is organized around the capitalist imperative to leave no area "unproductive".

> The territory should be preserved, […] protect all this biodiversity that gives the land its dynamic, that allows it to produce". To say that the most important thing is that people grow palm and the economy recuperates is a vision that doesn't respect nature, doesn't respect the natural environment, it doesn't respect a thing, only money for the sake of money. An agroindustrial project promoted by the Colombian State, versus an ancestral agroforestry project promoted by the communities, there is this confrontation. An economy of scale versus an artisanal economy so to say, but one that guarantees people their life in their territory, their cultural life. In inverted commas: their "dignified poverty". (Afro-Colombian grassroots leader)

Impediments to the enactment of local ways of being and social and economic organization are at the centre of conceptualizations of harm that emerge from the perspectives of palm oil critics. A research participant from Guapi, at the time working for the Environmental Research Institute of the Pacific (IIAP), stated:

> The cultural aspect is very important, the traditions and values, in the way of producing, in what is produced. With palm oil this would change significantly because it just isn't the same as a campesino producing his *papa china*, his *ñame*,[2] his corn. The way of producing, the relations, practices, the lived experiences, these feed into the elaboration of songs, poems. With palm, as a worker of a palm company, these conditions are very limited, very hard. It completely changes one's life. I think this is something irreversible; to revert or go back is very difficult.

To reiterate, agroindustrial models of production and the integration of local rural economies into a global market economy are not necessarily perceived as harmful and hence rejected by all local actors. It is moreover important to note that traditional systems of production and local cultural forms and practices more broadly are not static phenomena. But this does not take away from the possibility, and reality, of a clash between different systems of production and the cultural frameworks in which these are embedded. For those who experience this clash, agroindustrial production is perceived to dislocate local, culturally specific social and economic forms of organization. This is not limited to palm oil but extends also, for instance, to growing pressure to cultivate grafted cacao (*cacao injerto*) rather than the local, traditional variant. On this matter, an inhabitant of Bajo Mira y Frontera who insisted to cultivate neither palm nor grafted cacao said that the latter is finishing off the native cacao variant in the region and stated that he wished "*to work culturally with my ideas, and that they let me work that way in peace*", without loans. Leading me through his finca of cacao interspersed with a variety of tree species, he pointed at the ground cover of fallen leaves and fruit shells over which we walked, forming a natural layer of vegetation fertilizing the soil: *"Mira el trabajo que hace ese árbol" ["look at the work that this tree does"]*. The bordering plot, in sharp contrast, consisted of abandoned rows of dead oil palm—an open, desolated site that in no way resembles the density and "work in action" of the plant diversity and vegetation cover of traditional models of production.

The Agroindustrial Monoculture and the Threshold of Harm

With the exception of some small-scale agriculturalists that cultivate several oil palms amongst a broader variety of commercial and subsistence crops, palm oil production generally occurs on the basis of cultivation in monocultures. It is above all this industrial production model and insertion into a global capitalist economy that are fiercely opposed by palm oil critics.[3] Still, the corporate executives interviewed for this research all argued that, in one way or another, an oil palm plantation resembles a forest, around which several economic, environmental, and cultural benefits are produced—thus echoing the discourse advanced by Fedepalma (2006). A former executive of a palm oil company, for instance, sustained this argument with reference to the process of photosynthesis through which carbon dioxide is stored, on the basis of which he argued that "*[a]s such, in fact, it is a forest landscape. Well then, that it does not have the same connotations as a tree that is without harvesting, yes, but it really is a tree*".

However, critics argue that vast plantations of a single tree species do not remotely resemble the socionatural spaces constituted by the highly diverse forests of the Colombian Pacific (see the previous chapter). In addition, the environmental exigencies of monocultures are high. It is important to note that as a result of the region's climatic, geographical, and ecological features, the soils of the Colombian Pacific are relatively poor in nutrients. This means that the circulation of organic matter is absolutely vital to retain the nutrient flow and the resiliency of the ecosystem. "*In poor soils, the richness is in the accumulation of organic matter, the circulation of matter in the forest*" (ONIC consultant). Deprived of these conditions, the use of external inputs—fertilizers and pest control—becomes a necessity.

In contrast, in corporate and industry discourse, oil palm is *praised* as a crop that with some water and fertilizer, to paraphrase a corporate executive, can be cultivated where other crops will fail, even in the poor soils of the Colombian Pacific. External inputs are viewed as a taken-for-granted part of production and become naturalized rather than problematized. The susceptibility of monocultures to disease is thus framed as a risk to be managed.

At the regulatory level, there is an unquestioned acceptance of the monoculture model of production, too, reflected for instance in the fact that no environmental permit is required for the oil palm plantation itself; an environmental permit is only required for the processing plant (where the oil is extracted from the fruits), and for the construction of roads. A coordinator at the regional environmental authority, Corponariño, pointed out that, on these points, all palm oil companies in Tumaco have "legalized" themselves. Fact is, however, that environmental legislation to this end came into effect with *Law 99 of 1993*, and that the palm oil industry had already been expanding significantly in the decades prior to this legislation. Asked for the environmental impacts of oil palm plantations *as such*, the answer was that, consistent with the official view, Corponariño maintains that *all* agroindustrial activities necessarily produce a number of consequences and that oil palm in this regard is simply "one more crop". Corporate claims that "*[w]hat is important [...] is to develop strategies to impact less*", as "*[t]here will always be an impact on the environment*" (former agronomic director of a palm oil company), likewise uphold the corresponding managerialist view.[4]

In contrast, from the perspectives put forward by its critics emerges an entirely different conception of palm oil production as a source of serious harm, including a variety of systemic harms that are inherent to agroindustrial production more generally. Amongst the harms most mentioned is palm oil's impact on soil moisture and nutrient cycling, due to the large quantities of nutrients and water the crop demands: "*Where you sow palm, if it is on soft terrain, the soils will dry and become hard like a rock. The palm absorbs all the water and nutrients from the soil, leaving the soil poor; you can no longer grow stuff other than palm*" (community leader Bajo Mira y Frontera). While claims that palm would leave the soil arid and sterile are discarded by corporate and industry actors, a more ambiguous image emerges from the small growers. Whereas some deny such claims, for instance based on successfully growing other crops on lands previously cultivated in palm, there are also more concerned small growers:

> Palm was designed genetically to have a high productivity, but with the use of high volumes of [chemical] fertilizers. And we are aware that not all of this is assimilated by the palm. Some of it also evaporates. Some of it ionizes and goes to the land, and this land will become unproductive. Us small growers, we must seek to prevent that one day our lands become unproductive, and one way to do this is by lowering the use of agrochemicals.[5]

Regarding accusations pertaining to the contamination of soils, groundwater, rivers, and water streams due to the application of agrochemicals, corporate actors and representatives of the industry emphasize that there is a significant shift underway towards the use of organic pest control and that the use of agrochemicals is limited these days; moreover, where the use of agrochemicals is still necessary, emphasis is put on the *authorized* nature of such use. In the words of a company official: "*The theme of agrochemicals doesn't worry me. That is, we use glyphosate, which isn't a very dangerous product. Well, it is the same that is being used to control coca but we use it very specifically, and it isn't a product that is prohibited*". The problem with agrochemicals is thus ascribed not so much to the products per se, as their inadequate, nontechnical application. From the viewpoint of Corponariño, too, provided that treatment is targeted and involves legal products applied in minimum and authorized quantities, such use is "non-injurious" and not problematic (coordinator at Corponariño). Accordingly, a much used fertilizer, Urea, is not considered problematic so long as the person who applies the product is trained to do so, observes the technical instructions, and does not apply the substance in excessive doses. By the same token, it is argued that, *if regulated appropriately*, glyphosate is an adequate product that can be used safely. Furthermore, the application of glyphosate to oil palm is held against the social and environmental destruction caused by the use of glyphosate in the aerial fumigation of coca:

> If applied in line with the doses indicated, at the right moment and the right crop, there are no major impacts. But when applied with planes, as the Ministry of Defence does to eradicate the coca, well… These planes simply have the coordinates, so that close to the crops the latch is opened,

> and since this happens at a high speed the latch opens *before* the crops, and is closed after passing. Before there are oil palm crops, plantain, cacao, and forest. And after, too, there are crops, forest, rivers, pasture. These crops are affected, the forests are affected, and the river is also affected. This application is anti-technical, inadequate. [...] This is the most serious problem there is, because this is killing licit crops, this is affecting the forest, the rivers, everything. And the same glyphosate is applied to the palm to clear the area around the palm, but because this is done manually, it is a technical application of the chemical. This is an aspect to be taken account of. What is more harmful? The glyphosate applied to coca, or the glyphosate applied to palm? Analysis and conclusion. (Coordinator at Corponariño)

Hence, from a legalistic and technicist reading of the matter, any potential issues are located at the individual and case-specific level rather than ascribed to the systemic need for chemical substances. The legal formalism upheld by the palm oil industry and in official discourse, and the criteria and thresholds corresponding to the "authorized, technical use" of "minimum quantities" of "legal chemical substances" are oblivious to the needs and subsistence patterns of local communities. For one thing, if one considers the vast extensions of plantations, then the use of the so-called minimum quantities of agrochemicals in *relative* terms obscures the fact that with thousands of hectares cultivated in palm, absolute figures are not so minimal. And furthermore, to mention but one aspect, many local communities lack access to clean water, which means that access to uncontaminated rivers and water streams becomes all the more important—not to mention the integrity of nonhuman life, and the cultural significance of the river in the region. In the everyday lives of communities inhabiting the Pacific coast region, rivers are a means of transport, source of subsistence, spaces of recreation, and houses are constructed on or nearby the riverbanks. In short, "*impacts that in one way or another concern the water, impact directly on local culture*" (member of Justicia y Paz); the river carries social, cultural, and symbolic values (Oslender 2008).

Abundant rainfall also enters the equation here. The companies and representatives of the industry make reference to the region's "natural irrigation system"—a view also advanced by Corponariño—as a major advantage of the region. Critics, on the contrary, argue that the rain that pours down onto oil palm plantations washes agricultural runoff into the groundwater and adjacent rivers. A consultant from the ONIC for that matter pointed out the "madness" to establish monocultures and use a chemical fertilizer like Urea in regions like the Pacific, saying that the rainfall exacerbates the ecological and social consequences associated with the use of agrochemicals. In terms of soil and water contamination, the *processing* of oil palm fruits is also claimed to have caused massive environmental harm in the zone, affecting subsistence patterns, plant and animal life, and human health (for bathing in polluted rivers, and consuming the water and contaminated fish). On the presence and operations of the palm oil industry in the region, an Afro-Colombian community leader thus said:

> The run-offs of the companies ended up in the river. The fish also died. Water streams dried up. This all constituted a grave problem for the community. There was no entity of control that would look after this and exercise control. On the contrary, companies were granted permission. That is to say, they cultivated palm and afterwards received permission. And so the misery began, this was when the misery for families living in the zone began. (Community leader Alto Mira y Frontera)

Today, treatment installations for the solid and liquid residues of the extraction process are in order and—in theory at least—regulatory entities exercise oversight over the processing plants. Yet, as mentioned previously, in the initial stages of industry presence and expansion, no such regulatory framework existed. Corponariño acknowledges that before Law 99 of 1993, palm oil companies "*discharged directly into the Mira River, the Caunapí River, and were contaminating*", but that with Law 99, from 1993 on "*a process of legalization and coordination between Corponariño and the companies started, and the companies were given a deadline in order to start implementing the different [treatment] systems. Little by little, the companies complied, until in the end they were all operating legally*". Notwithstanding the improvements that over the years have been made in this part of the production chain, enormous harm has been brought about in the past. But whereas some of the environmental risks and harms of palm oil production are acknowledged, more often, fundamental points of contention are sidestepped and/or altogether dismissed. In some ways, compromises are forged.

Capital's Compromise with Nature: Accommodating Environmental Needs

In the previous chapter, I elaborated on the notion that capital is willing, and forced, to make concessions towards the interests and aspirations of local subjects. In this section, it will be argued that this extends to the "natural" realm: capital must also accommodate the "needs" of local ecosystems and ecological processes and, as such, forge *environmental* compromises. The bud rot epidemic, which will be discussed in the last part of this chapter, is an alarming case in point of what happens when nature is appropriated and transformed in disregard of local ecosystems. The need to be attentive to environmental conditions and vulnerabilities is to some extent recognized by the industry. For instance, a corporate executive said:

> These are perennial crops that one cannot afford to rob their ecosystem. The ecosystem must be maintained. I think this obliges us to yield to the very environment, to not attack it, trying to regenerate the biodiversity.

Thus, the planting of *plantas arvenses* around the borders of plantation lots (denominated as "beneficial weeds") and use of the fungus *Beauveria bassiana* are mentioned as examples of biological methods used to control plagues. What these and other control measures share in common is that they reflect an overriding logic that does not seek to intervene less, or radically alter our interactions with or actions upon nature and the nonhuman, but to improve the techniques of *environmental management* in perceivably more sustainable ways. The palm oil industry has been forced to adopt—and has embraced *on its own terms*—"good" environmental and agricultural practice. In no particular order, the consequent measures taken by the industry are driven primarily by motives to

(i) preserve the natural conditions of production; (ii) reduce, manage, or contain resistance from local subjects and NGOs; (iii) meet export requirements; and (iv) conform to global conventions and current sustainable development discourse. Especially, the last two points have found expression in Fedepalma's "ample exercise" at the national interpretation of the principles and criteria of the RSPO[6] (Director of Planning and Social Development at Fedepalma)—a process that is considered a crucial guide towards improving the social and environmental sustainability of the sector. This, in turn, should improve the position of Colombia's palm oil industry in gaining access to markets that demand compliance with high social and environmental standards (Fedepalma 2011: 13). In the words of the Director of Planning and Social Development at Fedepalma: "*Ultimately, this has an impact on the market, which is to say: the companies that aren't certified would come to be barred from the market*". There are, as such, strong economic incentives to engage in efforts that make the Colombian palm oil industry (appear) more sustainable. "*This is the focus that Fedepalma is currently engaging, promoting this type of initiatives so that companies realize this: that if they don't join in on this, the market will close its doors. And not only the export market*" (ibid.).

On the one hand, such processes of RSPO certification carry a strong hint of "green washing"—an important topic for green criminological analysis (see, e.g., Lynch and Stretesky 2003; Brisman and South 2014: 86). Green washing, in short, refers to a corporate strategy to ease environmental unrest and convince concerned consumers, NGOs and local people of the environmentally friendly character of corporate practice. The environmental measures and objectives of palm oil companies thereby continue to operate within an unchallenged agroindustrial capitalist model of production. That said, we should not altogether discard the possibility that some of the measures thus implemented can push for modest improvements in production practices. However, most important for the discussion here is that, rather than a crude instrumentalism, in the environmental domain, too, more hegemonic, negotiated relationships are entered into. While, to an extent, this takes the sting out of the contestation around palm oil harm and gradually naturalizes a given constellation of social relations and human ways of interacting with the environment, as already noted, there are also segments within the local population that do *not* accept the type of social, economic, and human–environment relations—and associated development narrative—that are thus sought to be naturalized. Below, the corresponding constructions, practices, and realities of harm will be elaborated on.

"Dreams Destroyed" Versus "Dreams not Dreamt"

Significant parts of the local population in Tumaco consider as problematic the development narrative put forward by industry proponents. In their view, palm oil may well be a source of development (as economic gain) for corporations, some workers, and some public officials, but not for their communities or the country as a whole. In the words of a representative of the Alto Mira y Frontera community council, "a country that devastates territories, a country that displaces persons, [...] that forces people to change their cultural forms of making beneficent use of the land and comply with international or corporate recipes instead, to me, that is not development". This notion—that people are forced to change their ways of being and seeing—runs through the conceptualizations of harm that emerge from the perspectives of (local) palm oil critics and is underpinned by different understandings of what constitutes "development". To further illustrate these tensions (and the corresponding views and realities of harm), this section starts by sketching the situation lived by indigenous Awá of La Brava and Peña La Alegría.

Encircled by Palm: Restricted Mobility and Routine Social Practice

Inhabitants of La Brava and Peña La Alegría, within the span of a few decades, have been confined to ever more restricted areas; something that Awá of UNIPA and La Brava say was initially provoked by the invasion of the palm oil industry in the '80s. While before the region could be peacefully traversed and families lived dispersed and sometimes at considerable distances from

Fig. 6.1 Road leading through oil palm plantation owned by Astorga (photo by author)

each other, different Awá resguardos have now become increasingly isolated and disconnected. To reach the resguardos of La Brava and Peña La Alegría, first one has to cross the river Caunapí. Having crossed this river, the route then leads through the oil palm plantation of Astorga (see Fig. 6.1), which occupies some 4000 ha. The journey takes about 30 min. That is, if travelling by motorbike. Both the ferry to cross the river Caunapí and the road that runs through the plantation are privately owned by Astorga. This means that movement is restricted and effectively controlled by the company; to use the company's infrastructure requires permission and is bounded by the time limits set by the company. Territories have moreover been drastically reduced in size; La Brava and Peña La Alegría, in 2000 and 2010, respectively, obtained collective titles to what *remains* of Awá ancestral land. Consequent limitations on movement, access, and exit, thus as it were, confine these

Fig. 6.2 Resguardo Peña La Alegría (photo by author)

communities in their territories. Peña La Alegría, completely encircled by oil palm, has grown wholly dependent on the palm oil company (see Figs. 6.2 and 6.3).

The deforestation that has taken place to establish the oil palm has radically altered the landscape, which has been stripped of the natural ecosystem that forms the basis of Awá traditional systems of subsistence, cultural, and spiritual forms (see Bisbicús et al. 2010). Around these two Awá resguardos, plantations of oil palm have replaced what were once biodiverse forests. Hunting activities have diminished to a minimum due to the loss of fauna. Fishing, too, has waned as a consequence of the contamination of rivers and water streams, which interviewed Awá ascribe both to chemical run-off from oil palm plantations and coca-related problems—cultivation, laboratories, and indiscriminate aerial fumigations presumably meant to eradicate the coca (see, e.g., Corte Constitucional 2009: 156–157).

Fig. 6.3 Facing the other direction, oil palm as far as the eye can see (photo by author)

But environmental degradation also places severe limitations on subsistence and the enactment of cultural practices *within* collective territories. This, however, is not so much the direct result of palm oil operations but primarily linked to coca-related activities and attendant oil spills. Again the convergence of problems in the region (see Chap. 4) surfaces when a member from UNIPA explains:

> We have contamination due to the fumigation, contamination due to the maintenance and agrochemicals needed by oil palm growers in Awá zones, but on top of the contamination from the [agrochemical] inputs used for the coca crops, the spraying, on top of this comes the contamination from the oil that is spilled… I don't know how the Awá manage to survive in the territory. And how the forest and woodland endure.

All of these factors are moreover said to place extreme pressure on the water in the region, in terms of water streams running dry. On this issue, Peña La Alegría suffers most extreme: "*Peña La Alegría [...] has a small part from where the water springs when it rains, but if it doesn't rain the people remain without water. They have to ask the municipality for help, to bring them water by tank*" (UNIPA member). In addition to the resulting heightened exposure to disease, perversely, these water shortages result in the need to be supplied with water *in a region that stands out for its vast river network*. As previously pointed out, water, in regions like the Colombian Pacific, is simultaneously a literal means of subsistence (i.e. as a liquid to consume and as a "basket" of fish and the like) and infuses culturally specific ways of being. The water itself as well as the landscapes through which it flows is imbued with meaning and central to whole ways of being; moreover, indigenous Awá from La Brava point out the important function that waterways have in *connecting* communities, and in enabling the provision of the necessary materials to set up projects. On the part of affected communities, there is no shortage of productive, cultural, and environmental initiatives that are envisioned to improve people's life projects and local environmental conditions. What *is* lacking are the economic resources and essential infrastructure (over land and over water) to autonomously enrol the type of activities that are in accord with local culture and territorial vocation. This means that, coupled with the fact that the traditional means of subsistence—hunting, fishing, food gathering, and agriculture—are thwarted or even completely disabled, the experienced conditions leave communities with little other choice than to subsist by cutting the remaining commercial woods:

> Here basically, large trees, the streams practically dried up, timber species there are none anymore. Here, people subsist from day to day by finishing the few woods [*palitos*], balsas, that still remain, because there simply is no other way.[7] In view of the surge in crops for illicit use at one point, there was only fumigation and forced eradication. People no longer eat the few animals that remain. There simply has not passed much time, 10 years and this will simply be a myth of everything that existed for example some 20 years ago. Things are running very fast in terms of finishing off all this biodiversity and the very diversity of people's customs. This is the most,

> let's say, it is as if practically annihilating… this is practically a project of annihilation of the thinking of a people and all the riches that exist here. Of the environmental, the natural, the cosmological, the spiritual, all of this basically. (Indigenous Awá)

Hence, in a context of social and economic marginalization, environmental degradation, and territorial fragmentation, indigenous and Afro-Colombian communities are being impeded to effectively exercise the autonomy they are formally granted. Notwithstanding the allocation of collective land titles and cultural rights, prevailing power asymmetries are left intact. These dynamics lay bare yet another dimension of the ways in which the dispossession of specific social, cultural, and productive *uses* of land is ongoing, even if land tenure formalization may have been partially successful at halting the dispossession of land *qua land*. But for industry proponents on the other hand, the shift away from traditional land use patterns represents a benign and inevitable transition towards more efficient and lucrative ways of using the land. Therefore, what for some is felt like a push towards acculturation, others explain as the success story of the transformative power of palm oil. Below, each of these positions will be addressed.

Agroindustry and the Push Toward Acculturation

From the perspective of corporate actors and industry proponents more broadly, the majority of people from Colombia's Pacific coast (and rural zones in general) lack an entrepreneurial mentality driven by motives of accumulation, which is deemed essential to progress socially and economically. This logic is, for instance, manifest in the following statement:

> Fishing, logging, mining, these are given to me by nature. I don't grow fish, I don't grow wood, I don't grow gold. These have been the three predominant vocations in the Pacific. And people thought that neither the fish, nor the wood, nor the mining would ever face depletion. In the economic rationality of a fisher the question is: why would I accumulate if tomorrow I go out, fish, eat, and sell? The same occurs with wood: I cut the wood for the house, the rest I sell. The same with gold. So, people

> were never producers, they have always been extractors. Let's involve them in a mentality of accumulation, of the capitalist type: accumulate in order to grow and enrich ourselves. This rationality isn't there in the mind of a miner. If you look at these three, surrounded by all this wealth, these are the poorest sectors of the Pacific! (Cordeagropaz's Social and Business Coordinator)

But in indigenous and Afro-Colombian culture, to accumulate has never been an organizing principle; to this very day, the drive to accumulate is by many perceived as a disarticulating and destructive logic (socially, culturally, and ecologically). In local accounts, Afro-Colombian culture is presented as—until relatively recently—tending to revolve around living life by the day: "*Before we lived with the tide, life and production responded to the phases of the moon. When I was little, we woke up to live the day, to resolve the problems of that day, not of the following week*" (Afro-Colombian activist). Likewise, another person stated: "*Our people… The thing is that ours is not a culture of accumulating. 'I have today'. For me, to accumulate is not my principle of life. For me, life of the people of the Pacific revolves around pleasure, permanent pleasure, joy* [alegría], *to be content, to share*".

Of course, there are those within the local population that hold a positive conception of the type of agroindustrial capitalist development that has arrived to the region and that is fast transforming it. But for others these processes are perceived as negative imposition instead. For the latter, as mentioned previously, the "development" that has arrived to the Colombian Pacific is neither of the type envisioned by the people, nor something they can benefit from. In the words of an Afro-Colombian woman: "*The development that has arrived is not for us, it is for others. We, in the environments where we live, are unprepared for this kind of global development*". Those who benefit, she said, tend to be the ones that have studied, that have prepared themselves, "*but we are at a disadvantage, and it is a violation to come at us to impose ideals upon us that weigh down on, rather than potentially support, our knowledges*".

The perceived imposition of a model of development that negates local proposals for autonomously conceived projects is widespread amongst those that are critical of palm oil, which also finds expression in the notion that the industry constitutes a "strategy of acculturation" (Afro-Colombian activist). It is not *change* that people object to, contrary to what corporate executives and industry representatives claim. "*Of course with time all things evolve and change, but I mean, naturally or in keeping with the dynamic of a people, of the territory*", said an Afro-Colombian native from Guapi. What is objected to is the imposition of projects that are not in accord with, or that are oblivious to, the very life projects envisioned by the communities; a community leader of Alto Mira y Frontera in this sense emphasized that the development that arrived to the region is neither sustainable nor sincere. The agroindustrial, capitalist development of the land has not led to significant improvements in the deplorable socioeconomic and environmental conditions experienced in Tumaco, and may well be said to have *exacerbated* these conditions. The Colombian State is viewed critically for its role in maintaining this reality:

> For 20 years there has been talk of changing an attitude because a people like the black community, a people of the seas, rivers, and water streams, is living in bad conditions–bad health, bad alimentation, bad education. But to this very moment this same people continues to resist, but without having received a minimum from the State. That is to say, a minimal investment by the State so that this situation could change. But they sure spent money, a lot! And they say: 'We have invested a significant amount of money in the black classes'. But how did they invest this money? In projects that weren't designed with us. And this denigrates a working class, because to all likelihood we will be parasites or lazy... It turns out that the illusion of investment is indeed upheld by the State, but to us the money does not arrive. (Community leader, Alto Mira y Frontera)

Money that is supposedly invested in the communities is misappropriated, spent primarily at the institutional level, on (technical) intervention by second-level organizations, or at any rate does not arrive to the base, many argue, and the projects that do arrive are often not built up *from* and *with* the communities. Some claim that this situation has led communities to grow so dependent on external aid that a level of passivity is taking hold, that is:

> We are being distracted in the productive theme and they are, so to say, anesthetizing us in our social struggles. I'm not saying not to get involved in these productive projects but let's not lose sight of the fundamental issue. This is impeding us to decide over our future. *Lay down* the terms, not receive them. [...] A development project is a community project. But this development project bears no resemblance whatsoever to whom we are. I don't see anything here, or only very minor things that strengthen our identity, our thinking, and that capacitate us to our own benefit. To be other is impossible. And all the more so when it comes to culture; to want this culture of ours to be of a different type is impossible. [...] These monocultures generate this type of conflict: wanting to make of us a culture that we are not. (Afro-Colombian grassroots leader)

A different version emerges from the corporate and industry perspective, according to which the palm oil industry is depicted as a key driver of social and economic progress whilst being respectful of cultural diversity, rather than a driver of cultural annihilation.

The Transformative Power of Palm and the Law as "Obstacle to Development"

The managing director of a palm oil company in Tumaco said the following after pointing out the improved quality of life of local small growers of oil palm there:

> I lived fascinated by the case of Tumaco. Well, Fedepalma has created a new federation slogan called "The transformative power of palm", and 15 days ago when I was in Bogotá I told Jens Mesa[8] how great the slogan appears to me, because we already witnessed what oil palm is capable of. Palm is capable of developing a people. We've seen it in Indonesia and Malaysia, where it has done exactly the same. Personally I don't understand why we have so many enemies, because we have enemies all over the place. Some NGOs think that we are the worst crop in the world. I don't know why. I don't know what caused them to think this, because I think we have the best crop in the world.

That said, various corporate and industry actors claimed that the full potential of the palm oil industry cannot be materialized under current conditions, in which an allegedly far-reaching legal framework is held to have a paralysing effect on the development of industrial activity. Although admitting that Colombia's enormous wealth in cultural and ethnic diversity warrants respect and protection, it is held that it is in the national and local communities' interest that respect for cultural difference is combined with efforts to convince these communities of the need to participate in a competitive global market economy and accordingly make their lands (more) productive. "*Because, look, overall these populations are lacking, but nobody makes them realize that they are lacking because they live according to their own culture, according to their standard. Hence they are not led to dream*" (former agronomic director of palm oil company).[9] Increased productivity, geared to a specific set of commercial products that are competitive in the global market, is viewed as an absolute must for economic prosperity, but the terrains deemed suitable to this end are often "the theatre of this type of social conflict"'.

> It's not that I'm saying that I'm OK with invasion, I *don't* agree that these people are culturally violated. Of course not, right? But the thing is that we must think in production. In many cases some resguardos have regained lands – I know this from examples of cattle breeders here in Nariño – and so they told the rancher, who had something, let's say, in the order of 2,000 hectare: "No, this is our land". They fully invoke the legal question. Well this rancher is a big producer, and as an outcome of legal circumstance he gets expelled. These lands went from vast production to not producing anything. Having these lands, well then let us instruct the man who lives there, the indigenous communities, to produce well, to be competitive, because we need to think in this. In this globalized world, facing the 21st century, we cannot be thinking as 200 years ago. [...] Here in Colombia, for sure you have noticed, there are many discussions in terms of respect for ethnic groups. Well, splendid. But let's look at it from a realistic point of view: the world is globalized, and if the world is globalized, then we must think in some very specific products (ibid.).

Considering that many of these products will have to be grown on lands historically inhabited by Colombia's ethnic groups, "*it is essential to rethink this model; to respect ethnic groups so that they may become productive. [...] This is not invading them in their cultural being. No. It's teaching them to work more competitively*" (ibid.).

A patronizing view that communities must be taught to improve their conditions of life by adapting to the spirit of our times goes accompanied by complaints from corporate executives and representatives of the palm oil industry that Colombia's legal and institutional framework vis-à-vis land tenure and cultural rights stands in the way of business efforts that can contribute to the social and economic development of marginal zones. Cordeagropaz's Social and Business Director insisted that without the proper instruments to give *useful* substance to Law 70, communities are no more than contemplating the land. Fedepalma's Director of Planning and Social Development likened Law 70 to a "straitjacket", an obstacle to development that has generated zones where industries are unable to undertake activities to the benefit of socially and economically disadvantaged communities. To quote more at length from another corporate executive:

> I think this has been detrimental for the Pacific. There is a very complex ideological notion to this. The black communities have enormous extensions of land, *unexploited*, they don't exploit these lands. The Pacific is a zone that could thrive economically; it has very good economic potential because of its ports into the Pacific. I'm not saying this for the sake of palm oil. It may as well be other crops. But the black communities do not allow any type of activity other than cultivating subsistence crops [*pancoger*]. What are the consequences? The Pacific has been condemned to economic failure. No company can go there to do a single thing for the black community. One cannot buy lands; one cannot establish anything. So they are doomed. From an ecological point of view, it is perhaps very interesting. The *micos* [little monkeys] there will live forever, and all that, but the people will continue in absolute poverty, in absolute poverty. The thing is, these romantic visions, things are more complex. If you don't act someone else will. In the Pacific there is gold. The government does not grant a licence to anyone to extract this gold. So who will exploit it? Illegal actors, paramilitaries... And this *does* end up killing people. By the same token, if you condemn the Pacific by not allowing any palm oil company to operate there, what do they grow? Coca. And this generates violence.

Yet another corporate director warned that "*Tumaco will remain stuck in the 20th century for a long time ahead until the laws change and communities are enabled to do something different [with the land]*". In his opinion, what communities see as a political achievement has in effect condemned them to indefinite poverty.

The "mistaken notion of food security" is targeted along the same lines. When local subjects denounce the palm oil industry for the threat it poses to people's food security and sovereignty,[10] they engage in such critiques from particular socioeconomic, ecological, and cultural realities. Theirs is a *contextualized* critique that points out the social, economic, ecological, and cultural significance of local models of production and the crucial importance of having access to healthy environments. Against this stand the disembedded claims from industry proponents that (i) palm oil is a source of food, in that it is used to elaborate food products; (ii) the palm oil industry attends equally to both the food and biofuels market; (iii) oil palm cultivation does not displace subsistence crops; and (iv) generally, in regions as Tumaco, malnourishment is linked to bad eating habits rather than agroindustrial activity. It is claimed that the palm oil industry has the potential to *enhance* food security by capacitating regions to produce a given crop that is competitive in the domestic and global market:

> Food security is not about having everything that goes into one's plate available right there and then; food security implies that regions are capacitated to produce a set of specific crops that lend themselves for export. And with this, I buy what is missing from my plate so that I can complement my daily calories. This is what food security means. Food security is not about having five thousand poor agriculturalists with one hectare cultivating cassava and all that, this is nonsense. These are the lies that people are being fed in Latin America. Latin America has to be serious about this, because food security implies that a population is able to purchase the complements to their daily diet. [...] Food security in these zones is achieved through a variety of products that are central to the international market, and with agriculturalists organized accordingly in producer associations; something in which Colombia and Nariño especially are lacking. This is the only way one manages to be competitive. For me, food security is to be competitive. (Former agronomic director of palm oil company)

Overall, what emerges from the corporate and industry perspectives is a general acceptance of some cultural expressions, but outright dismissiveness of cultural difference that manifests itself in the productive sphere. Accordingly, in the encounter between the neoliberal dictates of development and productivity on the one hand and alternative ways of being and social and economic organization on the other, the recognition of cultural and ethnic diversity does not extend to the so-perceived "backward" elements or overly radical demands that correspond to nonconformist ways of using and relating to the land. In the discussion section of this chapter, I reflect on this by drawing on the notion of "neoliberal multiculturalism" (Hale 2002).

The Economic and Environmental Viability of Small-Scale Cultivation

From the discussion thus far it follows that, for its critics, palm oil is not a viable project.[11] But as indicated, in view of the integration of more and more small growers into the structures of the palm oil business, the politics of harm in the context of palm oil production entails more than a binary opposition between large industry players on the one hand and palm oil critics on the other. Accordingly, I return once more to the small grower, addressing both the reality of harm of the small grower as such, and the tensions that exist within the local population of Tumaco as regards the contestation around palm oil.

On small grower aspirations and gains, in Chap. 5 the acceptance by small growers of a productivist discourse that (i) normalizes a capitalist pathway of accumulation and (ii) is organized around a select number of cash crops which are deemed economically feasible was pointed out. On the whole, small growers emphasize the positive social and economic impact that oil palm cultivation has had on their lives, for example:

> Let me assure you that those of us here who are oil palm cultivators know its favourable impacts. It is a product that creates prospects. I cultivated 12 hectares in this project. I was harvesting 20 tons of fruit every 20 days. This allowed for a good entry into sustaining one's family; one experienced that

> this was a way to educate our children and at the same time live communally in the countryside. (Small grower)

Especially during "the first cycle of palm", the sector flourished and people lived well, another small grower said.[12] In fact, the standard of living in zones of small grower involvement in the cultivation of oil palm was repeatedly claimed to be much higher than in zones where no such cultivation takes place, which is perceived as a faithful reflection of the crop's beneficial impact from the economic point of view.

However, the economic viability of palm oil for small growers, under current economic arrangements and power relations, is questionable, more than anything in view of the debts, dependencies, and risks that small growers are pulled into. It should be emphasized that oil palm is a capital-intensive, slow-maturing crop that is costly in establishment, maintenance, and processing. Small growers explain that from the point of establishing the oil palm until it starts to produce, one hectare costs up to 12,000,000 Colombian pesos. The loans obtained by small growers are based on 7,800,000 Colombian pesos per hectare.[13] This means that small growers often do not have the financial means to apply the amount of fertilizers on the basis of which plantations would start to produce after 2–3 years. As a consequence, they indicate that their oil palms tend to mature much slower, taking up to 5 or 6 years in some cases. This further increases the burden of the debt assumed. Moreover, in order to obtain a loan, small growers must be organized into producer associations. Even if the debt of each individual is known, ultimately, the responsibility falls on the association as a whole,[14] and so small growers express that this raises concern as to whether all will work the same way to return the money. The consequent pressure of being indebted is acutely felt:

> When the credit is in one's own name it is rather straightforward to say: I owe the bank 6 million and I will have to work hard for these 6 million. But when working collectively, well one sees this sum reaching 430 million and believe me, this is frightening. (Small grower)

The embeddedness of the palm oil industry in the global economy further adds to the fact that the structures and conditions of involvement are subject to forces that do not allow for small grower autonomy or equality of terms, let alone a small grower-controlled process; yet the latter *is* something that small growers frame as an objective for the future. Many are intent on enhancing their position as independent producers. Small growers in Guapi, for instance, indicated that they want to organize their involvement in palm oil as "*a community project, avoiding that the corporations or large players enter. This also requires having processed products, not just the raw material*". In Tumaco, too, small growers indicate that they are working towards a collectively owned extraction plant, rather than having to negotiate a fair price with the companies in the area.

For such reasons, various NGOs problematize the incorporation of small growers into the palm oil industry, signalling that indebted small growers are locked into inequitable social and economic relationships which leave them highly exposed to the uncertainties bound up with both the industry itself and things such as adverse weather conditions.[15] The way things stand, it is claimed that small growers of oil palm are effectively handing the control of their lands over into corporate hands:

> It is almost as if not even the crop itself belongs to the people. The only thing the people do is handing over their land and labour power. I mean, where do you get the resources to grow palm? To make drainages, which you constantly have to make; to buy seedlings that are expensive; to buy fungicides, weed control? There are huge costs involved. And in addition, as a 'peasant' farmer, how are you going to wait the 5 years it takes to get the first harvest of this crop? (Member of Justicia y Paz)

In itself, palm oil is not necessarily considered a bad thing (leaving aside the environmental aspect for a moment). The problem is that under current economic arrangements there are no other (i.e. more beneficent) ways to relate to its production: companies are in full control of the production process and commercialization, and it is with them that the added value of the palm oil supply chain ends up. "*The production chain is totally controlled. And the worst link in the chain, the one that suffers most, is the impoverished small grower that enters into this business*" (ibid.).

Many small growers are conscious of the power imbalances they are subjected to in building their subsistence on cultivating oil palm. But at least with this crop, they say, people *have* where to sell their fruits. "*In this sense one feels very insecure to practice other types of agriculture. One ends up with palm because they [the companies] will buy your fruit*" (small grower). However, small growers also insist that over the years their negotiation power has improved: "*I think that, before we were organized into associations, the large corporations abused the small grower. Taking advantage, because they bought the fruit at the price they felt like*" (small grower). Hence, organized small growers were gradually able to negotiate better prices for their product and, in 2006, gained insight into the process whereby the price per ton of fruit was being established.

> Having figured this out, we sat down with them and said: 'Look, we know how the price is being set and you are not paying us a fair price. Start paying us a just price'. And so we began to negotiate. And we were more or less about to arrive at an agreement. Because the truth is that we didn't reach that point. We never really reached the point of agreement. Because whilst we were in this process, the downward spiral set in, the palm started to die due to the disease. (ibid.)

In terms of palm oil's *environmental* viability—even if environmental considerations are not at the centre of small grower conceptualizations of harm—concerns were raised in relation to the use of agrochemicals. That small growers have uttered the need to lower the use of agrochemicals out of fear that their lands may become unproductive was previously noted in Chap. 5. There is, however, a second reason in view of which reliance on agrochemicals is problematized, which relates to the difficulties that this reliance generates to small growers who wish to practice more integral farming methods, allowing them to work organically within a diversified system of commercial crops, subsistence crops, and animals. "*Perhaps from the industry perspective they think this is a waste of time. But this is very important because there [in the finca] is where the food is, it is life*" (small grower). On the other hand, there are also small growers who, even if somewhat apprehensive about the use of agrochemicals on oil palm, say that the real issue lies with the glyphosate used for the eradication of coca:

> The indiscriminate use of agrochemicals is not exclusively palm related. Here for instance, many agrochemicals have been used for other activities, including illicit ones. For instance, for the past 10, 12, 15 years we have been indiscriminately fumigated with the famous glyphosate. And this is contaminating, too. Studies have found that for the aerial fumigation of one hectare, whether licit or illicit –here they are fumigating more our licit than the illicit production– 6 gallons of glyphosate are needed. 6 gallons! In the past 10 years, 400,000 hectares have been fumigated in our region. If we assume that for fumigating one hectare 6 gallons of glyphosate are needed, we are talking of 2,400,000 gallons of glyphosate. I say, this has to cause some impacts; impacts that we didn't cause. They have brought this upon us, imposed it on us, poured it out over us. So why… this should also be subjected to scrutiny, rather than saying this or that of palm. At least one can observe that the palm is showing clear, concrete, real, and tangible results. (Small grower)

Overall, small growers recognize that there are certain problems with palm oil, but ultimately emphasized the social and economic gains to be had from palm oil in the midst of the many difficulties people in the region are confronted with. Thus, in view of the coexistence of support and rejection of palm oil in Tumaco, leaders of small grower associations are somewhat frustrated with what they call the "bitter enemies" of palm, with reference to some community leaders within the juntas of Alto Mira y Frontera and Bajo Mira y Frontera. In response to the view that, with palm oil, communities become led by individualist dynamics revolving around the palm oil business rather than community needs, a small grower countered:

> The argument that palm oil would disarticulate in my opinion lacks substance. I think quite the opposite. Look, our associations, of small producers, today we know each other better, today we act as a family; the members of the associations and our families know each other. I am so proud when I go to the *vereda* [rural settlement] where I have my parcel

> and greet the members of the family. It gives me such pride for instance that when I'm ill, someone here [from the urban centre of Tumaco] sends a car to take me to the doctor; this is brotherhood, this is solidarity, this is to have a sense of collaboration, of belonging, to be as brothers amongst each other. And it is our organization that allows for this, this is the level we have reached. So one wonders, is this disarticulating?

To reiterate, small growers hold a different concept of the difficulties they are faced with, and they construct, and accept, other ways of overcoming these. They seek to manoeuvre their way within the very social, political, and economic arrangements they are drawn into. Consequent tensions manifest themselves strongest between the leadership of small grower associations and juntas of Afro-Colombian community councils. Mention is made of cases where juntas have actively sought to slow down the cultivation of palm on collective lands. The latter argue that they must do so, in order to protect people from disaster and to comply with internal regulations that set limits on the permitted extension of monocultures (Bajo Mira y Frontera community leader). But generally, in view of the socioeconomic marginalization in the collective territories, juntas tend not to take a resolute stance that forbids people to grow oil palm:

> We cannot tell the people 'don't cultivate this crop' when we have nothing to offer them in return. But if we had more productive projects on offer in accord with the socioeconomic conditions, politics and culture of the people, we would. But for now, let's say, we leave them free to choose the crop available to them for their subsistence. This is to survive; this is not even to live well, but to survive. (Community leader, Alto Mira y Frontera)

But ultimately, critics see the palm oil industry as part and parcel, and hence yet another manifestation, of a more fundamental set of injustices and entrenched power dynamics. It is instructive to elaborate on this point by way of reflecting on what a public official in Tumaco (also a former president of Palmasur) had to say about persistent local opposition to palm oil and the internal divide this creates within communities.

In addition to suggesting that "historical referents" may have generated a certain level of aversion against palm (see p. 137)—i.e. the force and violence that occurred at the time of initial industry establishment and expansion—the emergence of small grower associations is put forward as another possible source of tension. These associations, most of which are organized around oil palm, might be perceived as threatening the autonomy of the governing bodies (the juntas) of the collective territories:

> When confronted with producer associations that gain a certain degree of autonomy, a certain degree of power, normally these governing bodies are no longer, let's say, that autonomous anymore; they will have to negotiate, or enter into dialogue, with these associations.

The threat to food security by production in monocultures—admittedly a legitimate reason for concern—is mentioned as a third source of possible tension:

> [P]erhaps one of the rejections may also be, and this goes not only for oil palm but for any product, is that if we work monocultures, well then logically we have a serious problem in terms of food security and autonomy in the territory. But if anything has done serious damage in the theme of food in the region, it has been coca. And here we do have several studies to show. Before the coca arrived we had sufficient food production, for the local market, perhaps not to commercialize and all that, because there was no organized process, but local markets were supplied. Then the coca arrived, and with that the illusion of money, and people abandoned their subsistence crops. When the coca was finished, hunger prevailed: territories with hunger. And because the aerial spraying, the fumigation, does not discriminate, it is the worst thing we can have. It kills everything. What is more, it does more damage to subsistence crops than to the actual coca. [...] If anything has done damage in the area of food security, it is coca. And monocultures of whatever type as well. And for this reason the advice is that we do not depend on monocultures, that we diversify.

To sum up, the explanations for opposition to palm oil are sought in (i) past occurrences of violence; (ii) power struggles within the local population from a perceived loss of autonomy; and (iii) fear that food security is at risk. While there may well be an element of truth to these views, arguably, they are also mostly surface-level interpretations of much more entrenched (and disavowed) dynamics of a reality that lends itself to a rather more critical reading.

To begin with, if indeed opposition has its logic in past episodes of violence, then the "historical referent" called upon by the above-quoted mayoral advisor seems mistaken. That is, acts of violence and coercion linked to palm oil production should be placed in a historical frame of reference that has a much longer timeline; any repression and force that have taken place in connection to the palm oil industry are the prolongation of a historical continuum of dispossession and subjugation experienced by Colombia's indigenous and Afro-descendant peoples. Second, the direct lines between small grower associations and palm oil companies may certainly be perceived as eroding the sovereignty of the governing bodies of community councils, but, arguably, beyond this also epitomize a persistent undermining of the dynamics (and sense) of the collective and the effective reach of cultural and collective land rights. Lastly, the remarks about the risk to food security fail to address issues of food *sovereignty*. This leads back to the crucial matter that notwithstanding the rhetoric of the "need to diversify", communities lack the economic resources to diversify their means of subsistence in accord with local culture and existing social relations and practices, and, furthermore, the dictates of neoliberal capitalism actively impede such options. Interestingly, missing from the reflections of this official is the bud rot epidemic: a factor that would appear a rather obvious reason for the continued rejection of palm oil by its local critics and further add to tension around the palm oil industry in Tumaco. In what follows next, the final part of this chapter, this epidemic and the way it has been handled are discussed.

The Bud Rot Epidemic: The Materiality of Nature

From 2005 onwards, cases of bud rot[16] increasingly started to affect the oil palm in Tumaco and over the span of several years developed into an epidemic that by 2011 had culminated in the loss of some 29,000 ha of oil palm, at which point the Colombian Agricultural Institute (ICA) declared a phytosanitary emergency. Due to ongoing problems of infection, in August 2012 this emergency declaration was extended for another year. Although absolute agreement on what causes the bud rot is lacking, abiotic conditions are thought to play a decisive role in the onset of bud rot. In Tumaco, high humidity levels and extended periods of cloudy weather, disturbances in soil nutrients, and a vast monoculture model of production thus heightened the vulnerability of *Elaeis guineensis* (African oil palm) to biotic pathogens as *Rhynchophorus palmarum* (South American palm weevil) and *Phytophthora palmivora* (a fungus). Bud rot (see Fig. 6.4) is as such believed to be caused by the interplay between climatic factors, soil properties, and agronomic practice, and their interaction with the genetic properties of a crop.

The bud rot epidemic in Tumaco—how it came about, how it was dealt with, and how it stood at the basis of another round of environmental and

Fig. 6.4 *Pudrición de Cogollo*, i.e. bud rot (photo by author)

social harm—is a manifest and alarming example of the role played by the *materiality of nature* as a key factor in shaping and influencing processes of capitalist accumulation (Castree 2003; Sneddon 2007). Both human organization and the materiality of nature, as Scott has noted (1998: 7, 19–22), intervene with "ideal" visions of the management, manipulation, and control of ecological processes and conditions. To draw on the work of Tsing (2005), global processes and the top-down implementation of capitalist models of production do not meet the local without alteration or resistance. Of key importance here is that in the friction of encounter between global designs and local realities, natural conditions, too, play a central part. Yet thus far, criminology, green criminology included, has largely failed to account for the materiality of nature in its analyses of environmental crime and harm. Green criminology's coherence is at stake if, on the one hand, it is critical of the type of anthropocentrism that reduces nature to something that can be mastered and used instrumentally to our likings, yet at the same time implicitly reinforces notions of nature as a passive acted-upon space that has no bearing on processes of capital accumulation and concomitant harms and conflict. The aim here is to give a modest impetus towards rethinking this omission.

In Tumaco and the Magdalena Medio, the incidence of bud rot (*pudrición de cogollo*) has assumed epidemic proportions. A corporate executive of a palm oil company pointed out the link between high humidity levels and such uncontainable outbursts of bud rot:

> Bud rot is produced by a complex of fungi, and humidity favours the action of fungi, making them more violent. This then combined with the presence of a plague, *Rhynchophorus palmarum* –an insect– and this aggravated the situation. In the Llanos [Colombia's plains], the disease manifested itself in the 1990s, but in the Llanos there is a period of summer that lasts some four months and this breaks the cycle of the fungi and allows the plant to recuperate. So in the Llanos, although the disease occurs, plants recover. [...] In the Atlantic coast the situation is similar to the Llanos, large periods of summer, as a result the cycle of diseases is shortened, and so the disease is not that severe.

Asking whether, in the light of these conditions, one could argue that the Magdalena Medio and Tumaco are actually not that apt for palm, the answer was that these zones are referred to as “marginal”; the north of Latin America has high levels of biodiversity, which is of much benefit in many ways, but also leads to a greater susceptibility to diseases.

It is safe to conclude that in Tumaco, this “susceptibility to diseases” materialized. This provoked a grave socioeconomic crisis, the consequences of which will be felt for many more years to come. At the time of conducting this research, 3 years after the epidemic peaked, small growers pointed to the serious subsistence problems suffered in the zone:

> The situation is critical. Perhaps he who is working, the companies or what have you, don’t realize, but those who live this situation first-hand know. In my zone nobody would pass the day without eating because we had food security. Today, there are people who, if they have breakfast, won’t have lunch, because there is no way. We have barely begun to contemplate how to deal with this. If things go well we will be sowing palm by the end of next year, if things go well, some, not all”. (Small grower)

How are the consequent harms conceptualized from the perspectives of the different actors involved? That is to say, wherein lies the harm? Is it ascribed to the preparatory stages and production practices leading up to the epidemic; the epidemic itself; or the way the epidemic has been dealt with? Palm oil proponents (public officials, corporations, representatives of the industry, and small growers) tend to view the bud rot epidemic as an “incidental thing”, a “phenomenon beyond anyone’s expectation”, unfortunate and unforeseen. Thus, bud rot is something that happened *to*, not because of, the palm oil industry. Its occurrence moreover changes nothing about the necessity to (re)establish the same type of productive project. As one industry representative put it:

> For being the most viable crop, it became one of the… almost the only alternative. The other options were highly unviable. So that when the oil palm fails, Tumaco fails. But again, if it weren’t for palm, Tumaco would have been an endless failure. There was no other alternative. (Executive Director of Cenipalma)

From the corporate and industry perspective in particular, the focus lies with managing the incidence of disease and pest problems under current conditions and objectives, rather than shifting to a production model that is more in accord with the biophysical properties of local ecosystems and climate conditions. And although the problems associated with agricultural production by monocultures are recognized, the exposure to destructive outbreaks of diseases gets attributed primarily to the sole dependence on a *single crossbreed* of a given crop. As such, the solution is sought in a greater genetic diversity of oil palm species and enhanced varietal resistance *within a monocrop model of production*.

Conceptualizations of harm by palm oil critics, on the other hand, centre principally on problematizing agricultural production in vast monocultures and the consequent deterioration of natural barriers and ecosystem resiliency, thus challenging in a much more fundamental way the type of relations and practices that are conducive to the onset of disease and pest problems in the first place. Noting that devastation was highest in zones where deforestation had been most extensive and plantations most industrialized and vastest, the problem is located in the mismatch between regionally specific climate and ecological conditions on the one hand, and one-size-fits-all and profit-oriented industrial production models on the other. Community leaders say they knew, and warned their people, that one day this would hit the zone. Some see this in terms of nature striking back; "*nature is so good that when man does not want to obey her, she strikes back*" (inhabitant of Bajo Mira y Frontera). There are also persons within the local population that think of the epidemic as a curse, as something of supernatural origin, to revenge the death of those that were assassinated in the process of defending the land. Either way, bud rot is seen as a *symptom* of all that is wrong with palm oil, not a mere (and unfortunate) outcome.

Eradicating the Infected Palms: A New Round of Harm

In 2011, the ICA declared the municipality of Tumaco to be in a phytosanitary emergency (ICA 2011). While companies by then had largely eradicated their plantations, there were still some 16,200 ha of infected oil palm—mostly pertaining to small growers—that had to be eradicated to avoid that bud rot would continue to spread to newly planted oil palm (Corte Constitutional 2013). Various methods can be deployed to this end: manually with conventional, nonmechanized tools or by chainsaw; mechanically by use of an excavator; or the injection of a chemical substance called MSMA—*monosodium methanearsonate*, an arsenic-containing herbicide commonly referred to as Master. As the cheapest option, a process of oil palm eradication through MSMA injection thus commenced. Community leaders, in response, have accused the government of exposing the people and environments in affected zones to a dangerous toxic substance, without prior consultation of communities and all on the basis of an economic-reductionist calculation.

A small grower who, from an economic point of view, confirmed the need to eradicate with Master and highlighted also that studies indicate it is safe to use the product, calculated that the total volume of Master required exceeds 200,000 l (the dose injected per palm is 100 cm^3, and on average one hectare has 130 palms). Cautious of the substantial amount of herbicide to be applied in the entire trajectory of eradication, he said to agree with those who ask for a study into the environmental impact of this process to be carried out. But above all, he resolutely stated, infected palms have to be eradicated as soon as possible: since 2010, eight new projects carried out by six small grower associations have been initiated, together reaching some 2600 ha of newly planted oil palm. These continue to be at risk so long as infected palms are not eradicated:

> The thing is that those who ultimately started to demand the urgent process of eradication from the government, were *we*, those who are already cultivating again. Because we put it like this: they say that the palm that we are cultivating now is a little tolerant to the disease. Tolerant but not immune. What this means for us is that, if they would put us in a room with 20 persons of which one has the flu, in the end all 20 of us will get ill. No matter how strong our immune system. Therefore, what we are saying is that if there are 16,000 hectares that still need to be eradicated,

> and us small growers have already planted two thousand new palms, then eradicate please, because our two thousand hectares will die. (Small grower)

But critics within the affected territories claim that the use of MSMA has damaged soils, flora, fauna, and water sources, and caused adverse health impacts: including allegations that a young child died due to Master-related intoxication and that various persons have shown symptoms of poisoning (nausea, vomiting, and diarrhoea). In addition, cows and horses are said to have died (testimonies given at public hearing on 25 February 2013, see Annex, and in interviews with community leaders; see also Corte Constitucional 2013).

None of the above-mentioned impacts have been corroborated, but the critical issue remains that no prior consultation has taken place regarding the process of eradication. On this ground, representatives from Alto Mira y Frontera and Bajo Mira y Frontera submitted a *tutela* action that sought a halt to the use of MSMA for the eradication of infected palms and to demand the observance of communities' territorial autonomy, integrity, and corresponding right to prior consultation. On 20 November 2012, a ruling in favour of the communities considered that their collective and territorial rights had been infringed. During the public hearing/consultation process that took place as a result, a public advocate from the National Ombudsman for Human Rights reiterated that the Colombian State has a responsibility to monitor from the moment of design through to implementation and subsequent phases any megaproject that affects Afro-Colombian or indigenous communities and territory, or has the potential to do so: "*And, please, don't tell me that the palm is not a megaproject. We are dealing here with a national megaproject that, in this case, impacts on the communities of the collective territories of Alto Mira y Frontera and Bajo Mira y Frontera*". He further stated that palm oil cannot be considered a community project but *arrived to* Tumaco at different junctures instead, and that the principle of prior consultation of the community *as a collective* has neither been observed during the different phases of oil palm establishment, nor in the process of eradication, as in both cases small growers were approached *individually*.

For the ICA, as well as the Ministry of Agriculture (El Espectador 2013), the declared phytosanitary emergency takes precedence over communities' right to prior consultation. On 22 May 2013, the Constitutional Court overturned the previous rulings, considering that the events in question have not affected the communities of Alto Mira y Frontera and Bajo Mira y Frontera in their existence as an ethnic group, and that no evidence supports the suggestion that the used substance is injurious or dangerous to human health, animals, or environment (Corte Constitutional 2013).

Reactivating the Economy, or Reactivating the Palm Oil Time Bomb?

But conflict is not limited to the eradication process. As a consequence of the bud rot epidemic, thousands of families in Tumaco lost their livelihoods, some of them depending exclusively on palm oil as their source of subsistence. After the bud rot, many families were thus left with nothing but dead palm and high debts. Unable to pay off their loans, small grower debts were bought off by the FONSA; available to small growers that have suffered losses due to climate-related problems, phytosanitary, or public order issues and that consequently face financial distress, in which case they are given a 7-year grace period during which no payments have to be made. This then allows them to solicit new loans and start a new project.

However, the renovation of oil palm plantations is a controversial matter and mired in difficulties for many small growers. On the one hand, small growers express that they want to renovate their palm, so as to regain their livelihoods. Yet the overwhelming majority of small growers also express a level of ambiguity towards the renovation of their palm; now doubly (if not threefold) indebted, small growers will generally have to pay off their loans with fewer hectares than before. The reason for this is that new projects may not exceed 9 ha, a measure that should ensure that people dedicate at least part of their lands to subsistence crops for direct consumption.[17] Indebtedness—and *accumulating* debt in particular—as such instils small growers with feelings of anxiety, and not without reason, if we take a closer look at the renovation process.

Renovation consists in replacing monocultures of *Elaeis guineensis* (African palm) with monocultures of a crossbreed between *Elaeis guineensis* and *Elaeis oleifera* (American palm)—an interspecific hybrid referred to as OxG that should be more resistant to bud rot. Hybrid oil palm thereby resembles what Levidow and Paul (2011) refer to as a "techno-fix". A techno-fix seeks to fix sustainability problems through technological innovation, and as such "performs, facilitates, and naturalizes a specific development pathway" (Levidow and Paul 2011: 31). But hybrid oil palm, as a monoculture, necessitates the continued dependence on external input of nutrients, weed and pest control. In the words of an ONIC consultant:

> But look, look at the logic of these people! What will happen? A hybrid is not going to respond to all of the problems. The wonder of the hybrid: once again a monoculture, and once again an explosion of fungi, bacteria, and insects.

Indeed, small growers mentioned that new cases of bud rot have been affecting the hybrid: this sometimes implied the loss of a few trees, sometimes several hectares. What results is a feeling that one cultivates with risk. Although uncertainty as to how the hybrid in Tumaco will behave led one corporate executive to liken the zone to a laboratory, what is certain is that the hybrid is more demanding in labour than the *guineensis*, and also in terms of external inputs has higher production costs.[18] This is primarily so because the crop must be manually pollinated. On the difficulties this comes with, a small grower said:

> Okay, how do I buy the pollinizer? The thing is that one kilo costs 162,000 pesos,[19] and [this kilo is] for so many hectares. One does not have all these hectares, but they don't sell this according to need or per gram. [...] And how should one store the pollinizer? So they say it is necessary to keep this in a refrigerator, and people are still a long way from having this. This is very difficult to manage. This is the part that terrifies me most in the new palm programme. Labour and costs, these 2 things are very worrying.

All in all, one senses an air of apprehension when talking to small growers of oil palm about their experiences and their expectations for the future.

"*Already for a long time, and for much more time to come, one feels vulnerable*" (statement during small grower reunion). But for those who have become disillusioned with oil palm, it is difficult to obtain a loan for anything other than oil palm. A community leader gave the example of a 60-year-old inhabitant of the Bajo Mira y Frontera community council, indebted for 50 million pesos:

> He said: 'I went to Cordeagropaz to solicit a loan to cultivate cacao or another thing and they told me no, but that they *would* have given it to me if it was for palm'. So we told him: 'You are 60 years old, already indebted for 50 million plus interest. Now they are going to give you another loan of 50 million pesos to start cultivating anew, knowing that these palms will die. With your age, you are not going to be able to pay this loan, which basically makes you irresponsible in that you will leave your children behind with a disaster'. And he said: 'I am aware of this, but I don't have any other way out' (community leader of Bajo Mira y Frontera).

All of this provokes distress in those within the population that already experience palm oil as a threat to their cultural, physical, and territorial integrity. With this new episode of palm oil production, they say, misery will start all over again (community leader Alto Mira y Frontera). Others hold a more optimistic view of palm but are concerned nonetheless. "*If we cultivate we have a problem, if not, we have more problems*" (small grower). Thus, it seems that what is promoted as a social and ecological crop has locked local subjects into a situation that is characterized as highly uncertain, chaotic, and worrisome.

Discussion: Power, Systems of Legality, and the Contestedness of Harm

This chapter has illustrated how different ways of being, of relating to the environment, and of organizing the productive sphere, correspond to different conceptualizations of harm. The legal formalism, economic reductionism, and technicist rationality adhered to by corporate actors and industry representatives are largely incompatible with local social relations and practices, environmental conditions, and cultural life. Neither are the ecological dynamics of local ecosystems accommodated to the extent that we can speak of oil palm as a "social and ecological crop" (Fedepalma 2006). Supposedly, since Colombia's constitutional change in 1991, a space for dialogue between different conceptions of life, development, and ways of being has been opened up. But in reality a whole variety of legal and illegal harms persist. The grim reality is that communities are not able to truly exercise the cultural and territorial autonomy they were granted. An inhabitant of Bajo Mira y Frontera put it like this: "*We have all these years of living here, and yet they are coming at us as if we were some meddlers [sapos]*". The word *sapo* (literally: toad) has a derogatory meaning here, in this case in the sense of "meddling" in political and economic affairs that should not be interfered with. As such, the perception conveyed by this local Afro-Colombian man is that the natives of the zone—who have constructed their livelihoods upon these lands and environments—are treated as intruders, meddlers or informants by external actors from the government, companies, public armed forces, and illegal armed groups.

In view of the subordination of social, cultural, and environmental considerations to the neoliberal dynamics and economic interests tied to industrial, capitalist development, it is instructive to examine Colombia's expanded legal framework in the light of what Charles Hale (2002) refers to as "neoliberal multiculturalism".[20] Under neoliberal multiculturalism, the legal and political framework does not—and does not *seek*—to fundamentally challenge hegemonic social, cultural, political, and economic configurations; rather, a limited degree of cultural recognition is paralleled by the foreclosure of more radical demands that are geared toward the reconfiguration of prevailing social, cultural, political, and economic conditions and relations.

In the addressed context, a proclaimed recognition of ethnic and cultural diversity is not matched by the existence of the material infrastructure essential to give meaningful expression to cultural and territorial autonomy.[21] As a result, communities are increasingly forced to leave their lands to search for other ways to subsist or, alternatively, are pushed to accept the very productive projects that they oppose so vehemently. Thus, although having formal ownership over their lands, many of the communities in question become exposed to a *veiled* imposition of agroindustrial production models geared to (globally) competitive cash crops on Afro-Colombian and indigenous collective land. Without serious (re) distributive politics and environmental ethics, the effect of Colombia's expanded legal order and—on the face of it—encompassing political framework in the domain of ethnicity, therefore, seems to be that communities are inserted much more effectively into capitalist relations of production.

As such, it can be argued that we are dealing not merely with the denial of rights but with a far more complicated process of the simultaneous affirmation and exclusion of cultural difference. To draw on Borras and Franco (2012), a de facto state-corporate control over how communal lands are used and related to demonstrates that we ought to look beyond the "bundle of rights" and focus on the "bundle of powers" instead. Seeing rights—whether human or environmental—as a terrain *traversed* by the operation of power rather than a terrain that lends itself for radically challenging power, criminologists should not uncritically celebrate the creation of new forms of rights or the extension of rights beyond humans. Chapters 5 and 6, in particular, have demonstrated how a criminological perspective informed by a broader and at the same time more nuanced engagement with harm can enhance our understanding of the play of power in the context of agroindustrial palm oil production. Lastly, the analysis of the bud rot epidemic in the final sections of the present chapter exemplifies once more the hitherto addressed dynamics of power and corresponding practices, constructions, and lived realities of harm,[22] which, seen through the bud rot epidemic, as it were put the social and environmental injustices that infuse the addressed context under a magnifying glass.

Notes

1. Including but not by any means limited to coconut, borojó, cacao, cassava (*yuca*), and plantain.
2. *Papa china* is a type of potato; *ñame* is known as yam, a root crop.
3. In addition, there are some crop-specific issues which entail that oil palm does not easily lend itself to cultivation in a diversified farming system.

Even those who claim that the latter is possible, acknowledge that *in the long run* such diversification cannot be maintained. A small grower of oil palm, for instance, explained that in an initial phase palm can coexist with other crops, but only if one accepts that the oil palm is the number one crop and that, in the end, only the palm will remain; when the oil palm matures, it will eliminate the other crops. This is so for reasons of space (i.e. the roots of the oil palm spread horizontally), water demands, and due to restricted sunlight coming through.

4. Within green criminology, White (2011: 68) has usefully distinguished between unintentional and nonintentional harm in this regard; negative effects that are *known* yet accepted as forms of "collateral damage" correspond to the latter category.
5. But organic fertilizers are expensive, and indebted small growers cannot afford to produce less.
6. The RSPO, the Roundtable on Sustainable Palm Oil, is a global network of palm oil companies, retailers, and industry representative bodies across the supply chain and, to a lesser extent, NGOs.
7. This contrasts sharply with a corporate view of deforestation as a tendency of "coastal culture" (see Chap. 5).
8. Jens Mesa Dishington is the Executive President of Fedepalma.
9. Compare this to the view that "*the arrival of oil palm ends with all our dreams, because they put the idea in people's mind that the only product that allows to subsist is palm*" (community leader from Alto Mira y Frontera).
10. Both terms are drawn upon in the local context, but the thus-articulated critique corresponds by and large to the food *sovereignty* concept. Although subject to debate—see Jansen (2014) for a critical review of the food sovereignty framework—"food security" requires that people have access or the means to purchase sufficient food. When food security is threatened, proposed solutions tend to be framed in terms of capitalist criteria of heightened productivity and free-market competition. "Food sovereignty" requires that people are able to exercise autonomy in meeting their dietary needs, and that they have access to and are able to produce the foods that fit their (cultural) dietary patterns. As such, from the point of view of food sovereignty the target of critique is the agroindustrial model of production and neoliberal capitalist relations and practices.
11. Even palm oil's strongest critics do not deny that its cultivation can be economically lucrative, and that, initially, the employment it generated gave a boost to Tumaco's economy. But the environmental, social, and

cultural costs at which this comes are considered to exceed the economic gains by far.

12. The cycle of oil palm to which this small grower refers came to an end when the outbreak of bud rot started to take its toll from 2005 onwards.
13. The mentioned sums, at the time of this research, corresponded to more or less 6780 and 4410 US dollars, respectively. Considering that the minimum wage in Colombia at that time was set at 566,700 Colombian pesos—i.e. 320 US dollars—it is obvious that the loans that small growers have to assume are dizzying to say the least.
14. This is arguably an effective way to compel individual associates to discipline each other into "good, responsible entrepreneurs" that deviate as little as possible from the productivity standard on which loans are based.
15. For example, a member of Grupo Semillas pointed out that small growers have lost their entire livelihoods in the floods and landslides that occur during Colombia's winter season, which is notorious for its heavy rainfalls.
16. The bud is the growing point of the oil palm, located at the top of its trunk.
17. In a remarkable twist to the story, from the industry perspective it was stated on various occasions that, "having learned from their past mistakes", the bud rot epidemic "has convinced small growers of the importance to diversify their crops". Thus, the exclusive cultivation of oil palm in the past is framed as a choice, freely decided by individual small growers. Arguably, this depoliticizes a context marked by marginalization, a lack of options other than palm, and the force of ideology.
18. Also, the hybrid is said to take at least 1.5 years extra before starting to produce, which for indebted small growers is yet another difficulty to deal with.
19. Roughly 54 US dollars.
20. The concept will be more extensively taken up in the concluding chapter.
21. This material infrastructure encompasses economic resources as well as ecological conditions.
22. Referring here to the lived realities of small growers of oil palm and affected communities at large.

References

Bisbicús, G. T., Paí Nastacuas, J. L., & Paí Nastacuas, R. (2010). *Comunicación con los espíritus de la naturaleza para la cacería, pesca, protección, siembra y cosecha en el pueblo indígena Awá de Nariño*. Bogotá: Programa Somos Defensores.

Borras, S. M., Jr., & Franco, J. C. (2012). Global land grabbing and trajectories of agrarian change: A preliminary analysis. *Journal of Agrarian Change, 12*(1), 34–59.

Brisman, A., & South, N. (2014). *Green cultural criminology: Constructions of environmental harm, consumerism, and resistance to ecocide*. Abingdon: Routledge.

Castree, N. (2003). Commodifying what nature? *Progress in Human Geography, 27*(3), 273–297.

Corte Constitucional. (2009). *Auto Nº 004 de 2009. Protección de los derechos fundamentales de las personas y los pueblos indígenas desplazados por el conflicto armado o en riesgo de desplazamiento forzado, en el marco de la superación del estado de cosas inconstitucional declarado en la sentencia T-025 de 2004*. Bogotá: República de Colombia.

Corte Constitucional. (2013). *Sentencia T-300. Vulneración de los derechos de participación, de libre determinación y de consulta previa de los grupos afrodescendientes que habitan en las Comunidades Alto Mira y Frontera y Bajo Mira y Frontera, en el proceso de erradicación de palmas africanas por el método de confinado por inyección*. Bogotá: República de Colombia.

El Espectador. (2013, February 12). Tutela ata manos al ICA para erradicar grave enfermedad fitosanitaria. *El Espectador* [online], (Economía) 12. Available from: http://www.elespectador.com [Accessed 15 October 2013].

Fedepalma. (2006). *La Agroindustria de la Palma de Aceite en Colombia*. Bogotá: Fedepalma.

Fedepalma. (2011). *Anuario Estadístico 2011/Statistical yearbook 2011. La agroindustria de la palma de aceite en Colombia y en el mundo/The oil palm agroindustry in Colombia and the world, 2006—2010*. Bogotá: Fedepalma.

Hale, C. R. (2002). Does multiculturalism menace? Governance, cultural rights and the politics of identity in Guatemala. *Journal of Latin American Studies, 34*(3), 485–524.

ICA. (2011). *Resolución 004750 de 2011*. Bogotá: ICA.

Jansen, K. (2014). *Food Sovereignty: Re-peasantization/Dispossession/Agro-ecology versus expanded reproduction*. Conference paper at the International

Colloquium 'Food Sovereignty: A Critical Dialogue', January 24, 2014. The Hague: International Institute of Social Studies.
Levidow, L., & Paul, H. (2011). Global agrofuel crops as contested sustainability, Part II: Eco-efficient techno-fixes? *Capitalism Nature Socialism, 22*(2), 27–51.
Lynch, M. J., & Stretesky, P. B. (2003). The meaning of green: Contrasting criminological perspectives. *Theoretical Criminology, 7*(2), 217–238.
Mol, H. (2016). "De respetar a las etnias para que sean productivas": Agroindustria, Daño Social y Ambiental, y Multiculturalismo Neoliberal. *Crítica Penal y Poder, 10,* 53–82.
Oslender, U. (2008). Another history of violence: The production of "geographies of terror" in Colombia's Pacific coast region. *Latin American Perspectives, 35*(5), 77–102.
Sneddon, C. (2007). Nature's materiality and the circuitous paths of accumulation: Dispossession of freshwater fisheries in Cambodja. *Antipode, 39*(1), 167–193.
Scott, J. (1998). *Seeing like a state. How certain schemes to improve the human condition have failed.* London: New Yale University Press.
Tsing, A. L. (2005). *Friction: An ethnography of global connection.* Princeton: Princeton University Press.
White, R. (2011). *Transnational environmental crime. Towards an eco-global criminology.* London: Routledge.

7

Conclusion: To Miss the Forest for the Trees?

I have always dreamt of a better Pacific, less violence. That really in Colombia the national government no longer imposes on the Pacific what it wants and what its businessmen want, but that it actually manifests a sense of humanity with this population that has been historically assaulted, that every day has less opportunities and is given less opportunities. So that this region and its inhabitants will have, that we are going to have, a better tomorrow and a better quality of life
(Afro-Colombian from Guapi).

In sharp contrast to government and industry depictions of palm oil as a source of progress and prosperity, for many inhabitants of Colombia's Pacific coast palm oil is not considered to generate the conditions for a better tomorrow. While some of the practices linked to the palm oil industry fit the most conventional definitions and understandings of crime, many of the social and environmental harms discussed throughout this book do not fit legalistic definitions of crime. Thus, in order to advance a criminologically relevant, critical engagement with harm (theoretically valid and politically indispensable), this study examined the play of power in the politics of harm in the context of palm oil production in Colombia's Pacific coast region. This has involved the analysis of practices, constructions, perceptions, and lived realities of harm, attending to the perspectives of corporate executives, industry representatives, public officials, NGOs, local palm oil critics, and small growers of oil palm. In this final chapter, I draw up the conclusions of this analysis.

H. Mol, *The Politics of Palm Oil Harm*, Palgrave Studies in Green Criminology, DOI 10.1007/978-3-319-55378-8_7

Before embarking on this, it is instructive to go back to the view expressed by a palm oil industry representative, that "to centre on palm is to miss the forest for the trees", previously discussed in Chap. 4. Palm oil critics, according to this view, miss the bigger picture if placing the palm oil industry at the centre of critique where this should rather go out to a host of other problems deemed much more serious in size and nature.

However, although there are many problems that converge in the region, the palm oil industry cannot be absolved of responsibility for the harms it produces at present, nor for its share in past cycles of crime and harm the impacts of which linger on in the present. At the same time, agroindustrial palm oil production does not stand on its own but is part of a bigger picture of globally entrenched social and environmental injustice; here we *should* be careful not to miss the forest for the trees. While it is at all times important to be attentive to local dynamics and particularities, these local realities must be placed in their broader cultural and political economy framework. The focus of this book has been with one region, country, and industry, yet pivots around the notion that this region, country, and industry do not exist in a vacuum but are part of a wider constellation of social, political, and economic forces, and that palm oil—as an agro-commodity—is part of global patterns of production and consumption. The Colombian palm oil industry operates in a national policy framework that pushes for the modernization of rural Colombia (Tenthoff and Eventon 2013), which, in turn, cannot be understood in isolation from an international political economy geared to extractivist patterns of accumulation (Cotula 2012; Veltmeyer and Petras 2014). Thus, from Lampong, Sumatra, where oil palm plantations expand to the detriment of the economic, ecological, and cultural centrality of *repong damar* agroforestry systems (Colchester et al. 2006); to Alberta, Canada, where boreal forests, birds, fish, and human populations are paying with their life and health for economically highly lucrative tar sands (Smandych and Kueneman 2010); to the Amazon in Brazil, where rainforest and indigenous inhabitants are seemingly expendable in the face of a by-and-large western appetite for meat (Boekhout van Solinge 2010), lands are grabbed, ecosystems destroyed, and traditional land uses displaced and undermined to enable the expansion of agribusiness and large-scale mining.

The analysis that has been developed over the course of this book also suggests that a criminological focus restricted to a legalistic concept of crime risks missing the forest for the trees. The local realities of harm addressed in this study are to a significant extent the outcome of lawful practice and business as usual. Some will argue that these harms exceed the scope of criminological study. In fact, even within critical criminology—if anything, centrally concerned with questions of power vis-à-vis crime and crime control—the concept of harm, and the need for harm perspectives, is contested. Yet, the discussions in Chaps. 4–6 demonstrate that there exists *a thin line and dynamic interaction* between the illegal and the legal, coercive and consensual dynamics of land use change, and overt versus more veiled forms of imposition. To address the full complexity of such matters is where the theoretical and political rationale for a harm approach within criminology must be sought. In other words, reluctance to move the analysis beyond the illegal or "evidently criminal" dimensions of these continuums may rule out a comprehensive and theoretically accurate understanding of the power dynamics bound up with criminology's core organizing referents—crime, harm, injustice, and rights. In the closing thoughts of this chapter, I will argue that this neither requires us to abandon the concept of crime nor to conflate the categories of harm and crime.

Harm, Systems of Legality, and Why Contest Matters

Starting from the notion that harm is contested, and that this contestation takes place within criminology as well as within the social domain, Chap. 2 laid out this study's focus on the discursive and practical dimensions of the politics of harm in the context of palm oil production. Drawing loosely on Foucault's (1991) ideas regarding the "economy of illegalities", this politics encompasses the continuum of legal harm, tolerated illegal harm, and nontolerated illegal harm. Below I reiterate and discuss some of the main findings of the corresponding analysis.

"The Implementation of Death": From Crime to Tolerated Illegality

In Chap. 4, it was noted that in grappling with the politics of harm in Colombia's Pacific coast region, one is confronted with the need to disentangle the complex and varied linkages that exist in practice and discourse between the harms endured by human populations and environments there, the operations of the palm oil industry, and the presence of armed actors and illicit economic activity in the region. I argued that protagonists of the palm oil industry mobilize and exploit the "messy" reality that consequently inscribes the contested grounds of the regions where the industry operates, drawing attention to the discursive strategies thereby deployed. The case of Jiguamiandó and Curvaradó—located in the northernmost department of the Colombian Pacific (Chocó)—was described to introduce these discussions, considering that the "disappearances", massacres, selective assassinations, and violent land expulsion in Jiguamiandó and Curvaradó, in the eyes of critics of the palm oil industry, are generally taken to exemplify the excesses linked to palm oil, while industry protagonists invoke the case to argue the contrary.

Three principal strategies, through which protagonists of the palm oil industry seek to dissociate the presence and operations of the industry from the violence and dispossession it has been associated with, were then discussed. To begin with, alleged crimes and harms are externalized. Forced displacement, for instance, is variously explained within the framework of counter-insurgency operations; clashes between paramilitary forces and guerrilla groups; or relegated or ascribed to "common delinquency" or the illicit economic activities engaged in by illegal armed groups. As the Colombian State and the palm oil industry absolve themselves of blame or any kind of responsibility for these crimes, in effect, the latter become *tolerated* illegal harms whose link with legal business is denied.

Second, allegations of harm are undermined or delegitimized by reference to political ideology and affiliation, or by suggesting that such allegations are the product of a presumed infiltration by subversive forces. Both the externalization and the delegitimization of harm and crime, for that matter, call to mind Stan Cohen's (2001) notion of "interpretive denial", meaning that in order to avoid accountability, events are given a (radically) different interpretation, either in terms of what is taking place or who is held to be responsible for this. Hence, even when the occurrence of some form of crime or harm is acknowledged, this is explained as unrelated to the palm oil industry, as not really about palm oil harm but a matter of political preferences, or such accusations or manifestations of opposition are attributed to outside interference and manipulation rather than believed to reflect the sentiments of local people themselves.

Third, a strict legal–illegal binary is called upon, on the basis of which harmful practices are relegated to an exterior realm presented as disorderly and ungoverned, as spaces where illegality reigns and the state is deemed absent. On such accounts, violence and illegality are destabilizing forces working exclusively against the interests and the regular functioning of legal institutions and structures, rather than existing *intertwined* with institutional structures and legal business. In contrast, critics of the palm oil industry, even in cases where they do not hold the latter directly responsible for the climate of fear and the crimes and violence committed in regions which the industry operates, nonetheless accuse the industry of "fishing in troubled waters". In other words, at the end of the day, companies are still held to exploit the opportunities opened up for legal business by the actions and presence of illegal actors.

Of course, the blurred line and active interface between the legal and the illegal, and the illegal practices of legal industries, is a field of study well established in critical criminology (e.g. Passas and Goodwin 2004). In addition, there are insightful analyses of the ways in which the powerful deny (Cohen 2001) or "other" their crimes (Jamieson and McEvoy 2005). The ways in which armed conflict, illicit economies (e.g. related to the narco trade), and agribusiness in Colombia interweave in (material) practice as well as discursively can further add to these discussions.

From Accumulation by Dispossession, to Dispossession via Consent?

Despite accusations (and documented cases) of palm oil-related forced displacement, land transactions negotiated in a context of violence, intimidation, misleading practices, and implicit and explicit threats, in Chap. 5 it followed that land use change to palm oil production is not always the product of violent imposition and coercion but may also have its basis in forms of power that work through persuasion and consent. In Tumaco, the existence of a substantial group of small growers that have opted to cultivate oil palm suggests that Gramsci's (1971) concept of hegemony carries relevance for the analysis of the play of power in the politics of harm in this context. In Gramsci's understanding of hegemony, in order for a dominant class to entrench its position of power and privilege and preserve the prevailing social and economic relations and conditions, it is crucial to gain the "consent" of subordinate groups to such ways of social, economic, and political organization and the corresponding reproduction of unequal power configurations. Coercion and consent must thereby not be seen as opposites, but as existing intertwined and in different combinations (Buttigieg 1995; Hall 1996). In addition, although the process of achieving or maintaining hegemony rests principally on persuasion, compromise, the granting of concessions, and the accommodation of subaltern demands and aspirations, as Buttigieg (1995) has noted, this should not lead one "to underemphasize the extent to which these are *uneven relations of power* that strengthen and help perpetuate the grip of the dominant classes over the state as a whole" (1995: 27, emphasis in original).[1]

Thus considered, industry expansion through Strategic Alliances displays a pathway of accumulation that gradually naturalizes a constellation of social and economic relations and forms of human interaction with the natural environment that is much more amenable to the political, economic, and cultural project of neoliberalism. The notion that consent in this context is constructed upon a material basis rather than a mere ideational product (Eagleton 1991: 112–113) and asks for a material reading of ideology was addressed in the outline of how the small grower experience in Tumaco started and evolved.

Small growers see oil palm cultivation as an economic activity that allows for *dignified* conditions in the rural zone, allowing them to stay on their lands rather than leave for the urban zone. They cultivate oil palm to overcome the social and economic marginalization they have historically been subjected to; if not palm, then another crop, and if need be coca. Most small growers are well aware of the fact that the available alternatives are limited to cash crops that are lucrative and competitive at the domestic and global market economy. Thus, although not uncritical of the palm oil industry and their position in it, small growers generally accept a productivist discourse that is centred on progress through agroindustrial development, and the corresponding neoliberal (re)configuration of social and socioecological relations this implies is gaining ground in the zone. As a corollary, via consenting small growers, oil palm plantations are thus also expanding on and around collective Afro-Colombian and indigenous territories.

As such, although the use of force in land conflicts endures throughout Colombia (see, e.g., Maher 2015), the expansion of the palm oil industry through small grower involvement points at the same time to a shift in the operation of power from primitive accumulation, or accumulation by dispossession (Harvey 2003), towards what is more accurately thought of in terms of struggles for hegemony. The realities of harm as perceived and experienced by local palm oil critics thereby diverge from those of small growers of oil palm, yet *both* are immersed in and struggling against prevailing power imbalances and structural inequalities. Alongside tensions *between* different eco-justice approaches (White 2013), it thus follows that tensions exist also *within* each of these. Environmental justice in terms of the distribution of land access and land uses means different things to different rural communities.

For those that continue—or continue the struggle—to organize their lives on the basis of economic, ecological, and cultural rationalities that diverge from the neoliberal mind-set and capitalist criteria of productivity, while the *dynamics* of dispossession may well have changed, the lived reality of harm is largely the same. Albeit by different means, the violation of cultural integrity and autonomy and the dispossession of the *ways* in which the land is used and related to endure. In what follows, this dimension will be taken up in further detail.

Legally Undermining and Destroying Life: A Case of Hands-Off Criminology?

Critics of the palm oil industry view the Strategic Alliances between palm oil companies and small growers—especially where this occurs on collectively titled land—as yet another strategy to bring about the capitalist development of Afro-Colombian and indigenous territory. As such, it constitutes a form of industry expansion that is deemed exemplary of the contempt displayed time and again for the type of projects that communities *themselves* envision (i.e. what, how, and for whom to produce). Hence, while public officials and industry protagonists insist on the legal character of initial industry establishment, the resulting deforestation, and subsequent expansion of the palm oil industry in Tumaco, critics (within the local population and beyond), on top of questioning the legality of these processes, argue that the presence and livelihoods of local communities figured nowhere in the process of granting concessions for exploitation to the companies in question. The spread of agroindustrial palm oil production in the zone has increasingly displaced the social and socioecological relations, cultural forms, and meanings bound up with these lands and environments. The consequent dispossession of livelihoods and relations to the land has led to processes of social, economic, and cultural marginalization.

From the corporate and industry perspective, the establishment of oil palm plantations was a social and environmental necessity; the industry provides local communities with a viable economic alternative and alleviates pressure on the surrounding forest ecosystem. Thus, rather than a source of harm, the palm oil industry is presented as a counterweight to environmentally destructive practices (out of poverty or a presumed cultural inclination) and involvement with illegal groups and activities (e.g. coca cultivation). The result, however, is that vast monocultures of oil palm have displaced the multi-optionality that lies at the basis of local production and subsistence models. In view of the impacts this has on the livelihoods of affected Afro-Colombian and indigenous communities, and on communities' ability to enact cultural practices and beliefs, in Chap. 6 it was noted that there is a severe disconnection between the conditions and dynamics of life in these rural zones on the one hand, and the legal formalism adhered to by palm oil industry proponents on the other hand.

Legal or not, to the extent that the presence and operations of the palm oil industry in this region (and other regions) destroy and undermine human and nonhuman life, and given the fact that such practices—and the relations, structures, and processes underpinning them—are tolerated (accepted even) and fall within existing legal and regulatory frameworks, it takes a theoretically and politically disengaged criminology *not* to include the consequent harms as an object of study. In addition, even if the palm oil industry at present operates according to what is *largely* a legal state of affairs, current conditions cannot be dissociated from the illegalities that have taken place in the past; the harms experienced by affected communities may well exceed legalistic definitions of crime, but it is not possible to neatly separate the legal and illegal harms that inscribe the addressed context. The harm approach advanced in this study lays bare the limits of the types of criminological analysis that are more concerned with form than substance, in other words, that prioritize (i) crime over harm; (ii) tangible forms of dispossession over less tangible forms (e.g. a focus on dispossession by force and the taking of land *qua land* must be extended to the dispossession of the uses, relations, and meanings inscribed in the land); and (iii) the active violation of rights over the exertion of power *through* rights.

Heading for What Future?

One would expect that the legal recognition of ethnic and cultural diversity, and the collective land titles correspondingly granted to Afro-Colombian and indigenous communities, could halt the subjugation (and obliteration) of cultural difference and the imposition of "development". Yet as this study has shown, the agroindustrial capitalist development that expands over the Colombian Pacific coast region displaces local ways of being and forms of social, cultural, and economic organizing.

Arguably, the shift away from past discourses and practices of cultural assimilation is at most an *apparent* move forward. Underlying the persistent harms (legal and illegal) detailed in this study is a *reconfiguration* of colonial power instead. To elaborate on this, here I want to come back to the concept of "neoliberal multiculturalism" (Hale 2002) that was briefly referred to in Chap. 6.

Various scholars (e.g. Rodríguez-Garavito 2011; Hale 2002) have observed how the last decades have been marked by both a pervasive globalization of neoliberal economics and ideology, and the proliferation of national, international, and soft law in the domain of ethnicity and cultural difference. The analysis of the dynamics that underlie this convergence has led these scholars to challenge the common assumption that neoliberal doctrine is incompatible with demands for collective rights and the recognition of cultural difference (Hale 2002, 2005; Rodríguez-Garavito 2011; Brandtstädter et al. 2011). Hale (2002: 487), in this regard, has noted that "proponents of the neoliberal doctrine pro-actively endorse a substantive, if limited, version of indigenous cultural rights", and has coined the term "neoliberal multiculturalism" to refer to this. Whilst accommodating some element of cultural diversity and difference, and alongside a discourse of encounter, ultimately, the resistance of "non-consenting" segments is kept within acceptable limits; radical challenges to hegemonic social, cultural, political, and economic structures and relations are pre-empted (Hale 2002, 2004). Provided that the terrain of legal recognition and the inclusion of cultural difference is carefully designed, the granting of cultural rights and collective entitlements to land does not necessarily threaten the advance of the neoliberal project:

> "Even if large swaths of territory are excluded from the land market, regularization of land tenure pays off, both because the rest of the land becomes fair game for commoditization and because the existence of collectively owned property poses no direct challenge to the principle of private property or to the reign of market forces, but does achieve the key goal of replacing chaos and contention with an intelligible, predictable and market-friendly grid of property rights". (Hale 2011: 195)

Within a "restructured arena of political contention" (Hale 2005: 13), collectivities have access to cultural rights but lack the resources that are needed to exercise these rights *on their own terms*, which means that limits are set on the potential for transformative change.

The present study has confirmed that notwithstanding the collective land titles, cultural rights, and *de jure* territorial autonomy of Afro-Colombian and indigenous communities, only a limited degree of cultural difference is allowed for. From the analysis of the politics of harm vis-à-vis palm oil production, it follows that a thoroughgoing—and hence true—recognition of ethnic diversity and cultural difference must be integrated with a serious redistributive politics. Nancy Fraser (1997), for that matter, duly argues that contemporary tendencies to differentiate between a cultural and social politics rest on a false antithesis. But over and above this, the present study has also shown that we need to go still further. That is, struggles for land and the recognition of cultural diversity seek to put an end to class, ethnic, and racial systems of oppression, *but intersect also with the operation of power through human–nonhuman lines of differentiation and the human–environment nexus*. Hence, the fundamental dimension that is missing from Fraser's (1997) account is an environmental politics of reconnection (see South 2008, for the need to reconnect with nature). Yet nature, under capitalism, inevitably seizes to have value in and of itself (Castree 2003; Crook and Short 2014), and the structural forces that underlie extractivist patterns of capitalist accumulation, as well as the wider cultural framework these forces are embedded in, stand in direct conflict with a social, cultural, and environmental politics guided by principles of social, environmental, and cognitive justice. It is worthwhile to reflect on the future we are headed toward in the light of contemporary extractivism, and what the alternative could be.

Continuing Down the Extractivist Path

Over the course of the preceding chapters, various dimensions of what can be referred to as "clearance" (Smith 2008) have been addressed—e.g. ideological clearance through the figure of the *baldío*; physical clearance through deforestation and the expulsion of people from their land; and existential clearance by displacing uses, meanings, and ways of relating to land. Smith argues that "[short] of killing and doing bodily harm, [clearance] is one of the worst and most effective acts of cruelty and violence against a people", stating that it constitutes an act of ethnocide and "perhaps even genocide" (2008: 18). Although (still) controversial, it is indeed not unthinkable to think of the connection between extractivism and the destruction of physical and cultural life in terms of genocide.

Genocide tends to be predominantly perceived as racially motivated mass killing, or the intentional, physical annihilation of a people targeted *for who they are*. Thus considered, it is perhaps hard to see a link between extractivism, clearance, and genocide. But, as Short (2010) points out by tracing genocide's conceptual genealogy, a more appropriate use of the term brings into focus a variety of methods and political economic drivers that lead to the social death or cultural destruction of a people. The notion of a *cultural* genocide is, as such, intrinsic to the concept of genocide, which is moreover closely related to "ecocide" or ecocidal forms of environmental destruction (Higgins et al. 2013). Ecocide refers to the processes whereby such extreme damage is done to ecosystems that the ecological conditions to sustain life are exhausted, seriously impaired, or irreversibly destroyed. Extractivist practices, too, carry this potential. Such practices, in addition to, and through, the harm generated to ecosystems and nonhuman life, are prone to undermine the traditions and ways of being of human communities that the latter have built upon the targeted ecosystems and environments. In this light, the extractive industries play a key role in processes of ecocide, and of provoking an ecologically induced genocide in different regions of the world (Crook and Short 2014; Short 2010).

This dispossession of life and livelihoods, rather than a product of genocidal intent, is best understood as "a by-product of an incompatible expansionist economic system" (Short 2010: 842). That is to say, while there is no specific intent to destroy environments, animal species, as well as the physical and cultural life of human populations, the inherent tendency of capitalism to expand entails that "intent is invested in the structures themselves" (Crook and Short 2014: 311). That said, the destructive impacts of the extractive industries can certainly be considered *purposeful*. In the case of agroindustry expansion for instance, there exists a clear objective to replace existing rural economies and systems of subsistence—supposedly "unproductive" and "backward"—by an agroindustrial mode of capitalist production. Again, it is instructive to invoke White's (2011) distinction between unintentional and nonintentional here. It is clear from the views articulated by the protagonists of the palm oil industry included in this research that the push for palm oil rests on an unequivocal celebration of neoliberal ideology and capitalist social relations that are *known* to be at odds with the type of relations, practices, and beliefs in keeping with which large parts of the local population have long organized their lives. Regardless, the displacement of these ways of organizing social, economic, and cultural life is accepted as inevitable and necessary in the transition to what are seen as more viable economic and social modes of life. Under the banner of "development" and "progress", the flourishing of human and nonhuman life—*in all its diversity*—is thus actively impeded.

Moving to Post-extractivist Economies

South (2010) outlines a number of ways in which "the ecocidal tendencies of late modernity" are linked to existing and emerging forms of crime, harm, injustice, exclusion, victimization, and conflict. The exponential growth of the global palm oil industry over the last decades, and incentives for its continued growth into the future, does not give reason for optimism as regards palm oil's share in these ecocidal tendencies. As argued in Chap. 6, the pressure exerted by local populations, environmental NGOs, and the global rise to prominence of "sustainable development" discourse (Leopold 2010) means that in the environmental domain, too, more hegemonic, negotiated relationships must be forged. But the modest measures thus taken to improve the palm oil industry's social and environmental impact continue to function within a global, capitalist political economy, and hence the pace and impacts of contemporary ecocidal trends can at most be slowed down and attenuated. Chapters 5 and 6 detailed the social, environmental, and cultural impacts generated in the long trajectory from first incursions to the latest phase of industry expansion of the palm oil industry in the Colombian Pacific. Crucially, the final commodity purchased by the consumer obscures the social and the socioecological relations and the corresponding harms that inscribe this context, known as "displacement", one of six dimensions that give capitalist commodification its specific character, together with (see Castree 2003).[2]

Thus, the palm oil that has been extracted from the oil palm fruits and at some point, somewhere, is sold in the form of a chocolate bar or burned on the road by a vehicle that runs on blended biodiesel, obscures the fact that the monoculture model of production in which such commodities originate is simply unsustainable—socially and environmentally. The bud rot epidemic in Tumaco has shown with particular force how the resilience of an ecosystem lies in its diversity and the ecological embeddedness of each of its component parts, and that oil palm plantations *cannot* be equated to true forest landscapes. Whatever compromises are made, at the end of the day this is still an extractivist model of production that inevitably brings serious harm upon the natural and human environment.

The only way to put an end to the crimes and harms that inhere in extractivist patterns of accumulation is by breaking with a system that seeks to put each and every inch of nature to "productive use" and transition into post-extractivist agricultural regimes and economies instead (Gudynas 2013). We do not have to look far for the confirmation that such models of social and economic organization are possible and viable; we can draw on the economic, cultural, and ecological rationalities in accord with which many Afro-Colombian, indigenous, and peasant communities (seek to) organize their lives. Our "proximity to the edge of ecocide" (South 2010: 230) and our complicity in upholding a global economy that is inflicting a "slow industrial genocide" (Huseman and Short 2012) in the regions where such extractivist practices are taking place instruct us that allegedly backward beliefs and practices, which have their logic in notions of diversity and respect, may in fact be the progress that we so urgently need. What this requires is that we reconnect with nature, our sense of humanity, and start to think in terms of economic *degrowth*.

As argued by Acosta (2013: 80): "Efforts to move toward post-extractivism in the global South should go hand in hand with economic degrowth or, at least, stationary growth in the global North". That powerful ideologies and interests make this transition a difficult one should not distract us from the real need for this transition; the question is no longer *whether* or not, but *how* to organize the shift to post-extractivist economies (Gudynas 2013).

Closing Thoughts and Suggestions for Further Research

According to Reiman (2007: 239), "a theory of crime is a part of a theory of society". It is my contention that a critical understanding of society requires criminologists to ask not only what *crime* is, and what uses this category serves, but that it is necessary to integrate this with a "theory of harm". In this book, this has been pursued by examining the discursive and practical dimensions of the politics of palm oil harm. Regarding the theoretical rationale for the study of harm in green criminology, Lynch et al. (2013) have noted:

> The major assumption behind the harm approach is that documenting the harm will establish the validity of green criminology by making the empirical case that these harms have substantively significant social and economic consequences and therefore deserve serious study within criminology. (Lynch et al. 2013: 998)

Albeit from a somewhat different angle, this study, too, has insisted that green criminological perspectives on harm must do more than expose the "bads" of society and spell out clearly the *theoretical* (and political) relevance of a criminological focus on broader notions of harm. However, in contrast to Lynch et al. (2013), I do not see harm as necessarily a more scientific, objective focus of analysis. Rather, the theoretical relevance of "harm" for criminology, in my view, must be located precisely in the contest that exists around the constructions, practices, perceptions, and lived realities of harm. It is from this angle that the politics of harm—legal harm, tolerated illegal harm, and nontolerated illegal harm—in the context of Colombian palm oil production has been examined here.

It should be noted that at no point in this book, has harm been equated to crime. Rather than blurring these categories, the perceived task at hand for criminologists is to examine the power dynamics, the divergent realities, and the meanings bound up with the discipline's core concepts. For that matter, it is worth reiterating that the analysis developed over the preceding chapters calls attention to the fact that while rights on the one hand can be an instrument to challenge power, they are also a terrain through which power operates. Afro-Colombian and indigenous communities in Colombia are not simply confronted with the denial of their cultural and territorial rights, but with a far more complicated process of the simultaneous affirmation, inclusion, and exclusion of cultural difference. A harm perspective allows examining how power operates *through* rights and how rights can thus be a factor in the reproduction of inequality, suffering, and injustices.

In order to create a society led by principles of social and environmental justice, it is necessary to arrive at an encompassing, critical understanding of how society is organized and how this enriches and benefits some while working to the detriment of others. This book has sought to demonstrate that a critical engagement with the contestedness of harm is an appropriate object of criminological analysis and can be more thoroughgoing to this end than a narrow, legalistic concern with crime. Harm, as a concept that *investigates* social reality, allows for more reflexivity vis-à-vis criminology's core concern and critical engagement with matters of crime and crime control, and derived foci (e.g. rights and justice).

Along the lines set out in this book, four suggestions for further research emerge, three of which are principally centred on dimensions of power and domination that could not be addressed in this study. A first dimension concerns the harms and contention linked to the organization of labour and work conditions in corporate oil palm plantations. Although explored to some extent in interviews with trade union representatives (see Appendix), it was beyond the scope of this study to interrogate this dimension in any great detail, nor did the research design allow for this (concerns about the safety of research participants as well as my own also informed this decision).

Another component that has not been explored is the gender dimension of dynamics and impacts of land use change to oil palm in terms of community life, subsistence practices, and the division of labour. Such considerations have, for instance, been addressed by Lozano (1996), through a focus on gender dynamics in the social, cultural, and economic spheres of Afro-Colombian community life (from colonial times to recent incursions of capital into the Pacific), the gender division of labour within oil palm plantations, and the impacts of the palm oil industry on the lives of Afro-Colombian women more generally. Restrepo (2004), too, has stated the need for a more detailed analysis of the gender division of labour within oil palm plantations. Addressing the impacts of land use change to palm oil production from a green criminological focus on gender can connect with, draw from, and contribute to similar work in rural criminology, where gender relations are a central aspect of analysis (see Donnermeyer and DeKeseredy 2014).

Thirdly, vis-à-vis land access and use, and in terms of land ownership, Mondragón Báez (2002: 29–30) has argued that Colombia's peasantry *at large* has not been granted the legal protections that indigenous and Afro-Colombian rural communities achieved in the 1991 Constitution, claiming that this perpetuates the historical neglect, invisibilization, and social exclusion of the peasantry. This study's focus on the Pacific coast region, and the realities of harm of indigenous and Afro-Colombian communities there, has not filled this gap.

A final suggestion for further research is to explore the *chain* of criminogenic effects of the social and environmental harms that stem from palm oil production and the extractive industries more generally, in keeping with a green criminological line of work that theorizes the interconnection between environmental victimization and the broader genesis of crime (see Potter 2014). This could add another spatial dimension to the study of crime and harm linked to natural resource extraction. That is, in addition to the "on-site" manifestation of such crime and harm, it is essential to trace the "trail of crime and victimization" leading from these localities to the broader municipal, departmental, or national level. As Potter (2014) notes:

> [Environmental] victims often seem to be at risk of participation in offending behaviour and therefore becoming labelled as 'criminals'. It seems that they are also at some risk of becoming victims of (further) crime, such as when they seek to raise their voices in protest and are then victims of state or corporate violence or, more notably, when dispossession, dislocation or deprivation make them vulnerable to 'normal' criminal victimisation. (p. 16)

What thus ought to be brought into focus are the forms that the struggle to subsist takes by those that—dispossessed of their lands and/or means of subsistence—have been displaced from or seen themselves forced to leave their *veredas*, municipality, or department of origin, not infrequently ending up as the internally displaced living in the slums of Bogotá, Cali, and so on. Also in need of analysis are the ways in which these same persons may become the victim of subsequent crime—think of "social cleansing" (Graham 2016), hate crimes, police violence, and so on. If the trail of impacts of extractivist patterns of accumulation comes into focus, criminology can move closer and closer to fully exposing and theorizing the social, economic, cultural, and environmental devastation and deprivation that are the product of an inherently unjust and unsustainable global economic system and social order.

Notes

1. Reference to "the state as a whole" refers to Gramsci's notion of the integral state, which is composed of *political society* (the governmental, juridical, and administrative apparatus) and the organizations and institutions of *civil society* (the educational system, church, trade unions, etc.) (Buttigieg 1995). The legitimacy of existing social, economic, and political arrangements is rooted in the sphere of civil society; it is in this sphere that ideas and conceptions of the world circulate, and the ethos that underlies existing sociocultural, economic, and political principles is manufactured, naturalized, and consolidated, as well as challenged (Buttigieg 2005).
2. The other five being privatization, alienability, individuation, abstraction, and valuation.

References

Acosta, A. (2013). Extractivism and neoextractivism: Two sides of the same curse. In M. Lang & D. Mokrani (Eds.), *Beyond development: Alternative visions from Latin America* (pp. 61–86). Amsterdam and Quito: Transnational Institute and Rosa Luxemburg Foundation.

Boekhout van Solinge, T. (2010). Deforestation crimes and conflicts in the amazon. *Critical Criminology, 18*(4), 263–277.

Brandtstädter, S., Wade, P., & Woodward, K. (2011). Introduction: Rights, cultures, subjects and citizens. *Economy and Society, 40*(2), 167–183.

Buttigieg, J. A. (1995). Gramsci on civil society. *Boundary 2, 22*(3), 1–32.

Buttigieg, J. A. (2005). The contemporary discourse of civil society: A Gramscian critique. *Boundary 2, 32*(1), 33–52.

Castree, N. (2003). Commodifying what nature? *Progress in Human Geography, 27*(3), 273–297.

Cohen, S. (2001). *States of denial. Knowing about atrocities and suffering*. Cambridge: Polity Press.

Colchester, M., Jiwan, N., Andiko, S. M., Firdaus, A. Y., Surambo, A. & Pane, H. (2006). Promised land: Palm oil and land acquisition in Indonesia—implications for local communities and indigenous peoples. *Moreton-in-March: Forest peoples programme*. Bogor: Perkumpulan Sawit Watch.

Cotula, L. (2012). The international political economy of the global land rush: A critical appraisal of trends, scale, geography and drivers. *The Journal of Peasant Studies, 39*(3–4), 649–680.

Crook, M., & Short, D. (2014). Marx, Lemkin and the genocide-ecocide nexus. *The International Journal of Human Rights, 18*(3), 298–319.

Donnermeyer, J. F., & DeKeseredy, W. S. (2014). *Rural criminology*. Abingdon: Routledge.

Eagleton, T. (1991). *Ideology: An introduction*. London: Verso.

Foucault, M. (1991). *Discipline and punish: The birth of the prison*. London: Penguin Books.

Fraser, N. (1997). *Justice Interruptus: Critical Reflections on the "Postsocialist" Condition*. London: Routledge.

Graham, T. (2016, April 21). Colombia's 'social cleansing' phenomenon: Exterminating people like bugs. *Colombia Reports*. Available from: http://colombiareports.com/social-extermination-undesirables-colombia/ [Accessed 10 January 2017].

Gramsci, A. (1971). *Selections from the prison notebooks*(Q. Hoare & G. Nowell Smith, Eds. & trans.). London: Lawrence and Wishart.

Gudynas, E. (2013). Transitions to post-extractivism: Directions, options, areas of action. In M. Lang & D. Mokrani (Eds.), *Beyond development: Alternative visions from Latin America* (pp. 165–188). Amsterdam and Quito: Transnational Institute and Rosa Luxemburg Foundation.

Hale, C. R. (2002). Does multiculturalism menace? Governance, cultural rights and the politics of identity in Guatemala. *Journal of Latin American Studies, 34*(3), 485–524.

Hale, C. R. (2004). Rethinking indigenous politics in the era of the 'Indio Permitido'. *NACLA Report on the Americas, 38*(2), 16–21.

Hale, C. R. (2005). Neoliberal multiculturalism: The remaking of cultural rights and racial dominance in Central America. *Political and Legal Anthropology Review, 28*(1), 10–28.

Hale, C. R. (2011). Resistencia para que? Territory, autonomy and neoliberal entanglements in the 'empty spaces' of Central America. *Economy and Society, 40*(2), 184–210.

Hall, S. (1996). Gramsci's relevance for the study of race and ethnicity. In D. Morley & K. Chen (Eds.), *Stuart Hall: Critical dialogues in cultural studies* (pp. 411–441). New York: Routledge.

Harvey, D. (2003). *The new imperialism*. Oxford: Oxford University Press.

Higgins, P., Short, D., & South, N. (2013). Protecting the planet: A proposal for a law of ecocide. *Crime, Law and Social Change, 59*(3), 251–266.

Huseman, J., & Short, D. (2012). 'A slow industrial genocide': Tar sands and the indigenous peoples of Northern Alberta. *The International Journal of Human Rights, 16*(1), 216–237.

Jamieson, R., & McEvoy, K. (2005). State crime by proxy and juridical othering. *British Journal of Criminology, 45*(4), 504–527.

Leopold, A. (2010). The changing constellation of power and resistance in the global debate over agrofuels. *Innovation—The European Journal of Social Science Research, 23*(4), 389–408.

Lozano, B. R. (1996). Mujer y desarollo. In A. Escobar & A. Pedrosa (Eds.), *Pacífico: ¿Desarrollo o diversidad? Estado, capital y movimientos sociales en el Pacífico Colombiano* (pp. 176–204). Bogotá: CEREC and Ecofondo.

Lynch, M. J., Long, M. A., Barrett, K. L., & Stretesky, P. B. (2013). Is it a crime to produce ecological disorganization? Why green criminology and political economy matter in the analysis of global ecological harm. *British Journal of Criminology, 53*(6), 997–1016.

Maher, D. (2015). Rooted in violence: Civil war, international trade and the expansion of palm oil in Colombia. *New Political Economy, 20*(2), 299–330.
Mondragón Báez, H. H. (2002). *La organización campesina en un ambiente de terror*. Bogotá: ILSA.
Passas, N., & Goodwin, N. (2004). Introduction: A crime by any other name. In N. Passas & N. Goodwin (Eds.), *It's legal but it ain't right: Harmful social consequences of legal industries* (pp. 1–27). Ann Arbor, MI: University of Michigan Press.
Potter, G. R. (2014). The criminogenic effects of environmental harm: Bringing a 'green' perspective to mainstream criminology. In T. Spapens, R. White, & M. Kluin (Eds.), *Environmental crime and its victims: Perspectives within green criminology* (pp. 7–21). Farnham: Ashgate.
Reiman, J. (2007). *The rich get richer and the poor get prison: Ideology, class, and criminal justice* (8th ed.). Boston: Pearson/Allyn & Bacon.
Restrepo, E. (2004). Un océano verde para extraer aceite. Hacia una etnografía del cultivo de la palma africana en Tumaco. *Universitas Humanistica, 58*, 72–87.
Rodríguez-Garavito, C. (2011). Ethnicity.gov: Global governance, indigenous people, and the right to prior consultation in social mine fields. *Indiana Journal of Global Legal Studies, 18*(1), 263–305.
Short, D. (2010). Cultural genocide and indigenous peoples: A sociological approach. *The International Journal of Human Rights, 14*(6), 833–848.
Smandych, R., & Kueneman, R. (2010). The Canadian-Alberta tar sands: A case study of state-corporate environmental crime. In R. White (Ed.), *Global environmental harm: Criminological perspectives* (pp. 87–109). Cullompton: Willan Publishing.
Smith, A. (2008). Landscapes of clearance: Archaeological and anthropological perspectives. In A. Smith & A. Gazin-Schwartz (Eds.), *Landscapes of clearance: Archaeological and anthropological perspectives* (pp. 13–24). Walnut Creek: Left Coast Press.
South, N. (2008). Nature, difference, and the rejection of harm: Expanding the agenda for green criminology. In R. Sollund (Ed.), *Global harms: Ecological crime and speciesism* (pp. 187–200). New York: Nova Science Publishers.
South, N. (2010). The ecocidal tendencies of late modernity: Transnational crime, social exclusion, victims and rights. In R. White (Ed.), *Global environmental harm: Criminological perspectives* (pp. 228–247). Cullompton: Willan Publishing.

Tenthoff, M., & Eventon, R. (2013). *A 'veritable revolution': The land restitution law and the transformation of rural Colombia*. Amsterdam: Transnational Institute.

Veltmeyer, H., & Petras, J. (2014). A new model or extractive imperialism? In H. Veltmeyer & J. Petras (Eds.), *The new extractivism: A post-neoliberal development model or imperialism of the twenty-first century?* (pp. 21–46). London: Zed Books.

White, R. (2011). *Transnational environmental crime. Towards an eco-global criminology*. London: Routledge.

White, R. (2013). *Environmental harm: An eco-justice perspective*. Bristol: Policy Press.

Annex
List of Interviews and Site Visits

Industry Representatives

Semi-structured Interviews

Director of Planning and Social Development at Fedepalma
- Bogotá, 08-08-2012

Executive Director at Cordeagropaz
- Tumaco, 30-08-2012

Small grower of oil palm and representative of Palmasur
- Tumaco, 31-08-2012

Social and Business Coordinator at Cordeagropaz
- Tumaco, 12-09-2012

Executive Director at Cenipalma (*Centro de Investigación en Palma de Aceite*, Colombian Oil Palm Research Centre)
- Bogotá, 18-12-2012

H. Mol, *The Politics of Palm Oil Harm*, Palgrave Studies in Green Criminology, DOI 10.1007/978-3-319-55378-8

Corporate Executives

Semi-structured Interviews

Former agronomic director of a palm oil company with operations in Tumaco
- Pasto (Nariño), 29-08-2012

Managing Director of a palm oil company with operations in Tumaco
- Bogotá [Skype], 28-01-2013

Chief executive within a palm oil company operating in Colombia's eastern (formerly working for a palm oil company with operations in Tumaco)
- Bogotá, 11-02-2013

Corporate executive in a palm oil consortium with operations in Colombia's eastern plains and Tumaco
- Bogotá, 18-02-2013

Small Growers of Oil Palm

Semi-structured Interviews

Small grower from Bajo Jagua, community council Bajo Mira y Frontera
- Tumaco, 10-09-2012

Small grower and technical consultant of *Agromira*
- Tumaco, 11-09-2012

Representative, small grower association *Asociación de Palmeros de Guapi* (Asopalma)
- Guapi, 06-01-2012

Legal representative, small grower association *Asociación de Palmeros de Chilví* (Asopalchí)
- Tumaco, 17-01-2013

Small grower and member of small grower association *Agrofortaleza*
- Tumaco, 18-01-2013

Accompanied Field Visits to Small Grower Plantations, Attendance of Small Grower Reunions, and Informal Conversations

Field visit to small grower plantations with technician from Cordeagropaz
- Tumaco, 12-09-2012

Field visit to small grower plantations with representatives of Asopalma
- Guapi, 07-01-2013

Attendance of small grower reunion of Agrofortaleza
- Tumaco, 14-01-2013

Attendance of small grower reunion of Agromira
- Tumaco (Bajo Mira y Frontera), 15-01-2013

Field visit to small grower plantations with technician from Asopalchí
- Tumaco, 17-01-2013

Local Palm Oil Critics

Semi-structured Interviews

Interview with four representatives of the UNIPA (Unidad Indígena del Pueblo Awá)
- Pasto, 28-08-2012

Afro-Colombian grassroots leader and former representative of Recompas (*Red de Consejos Comunitarios del Pacífico Sur*, Network of Afro-Colombian Community Councils of the South Pacific)

- Tumaco, 30-08-2012

Afro-Colombian community leader, member of the governing body of Alto Mira y Frontera

- Tumaco, 30-08-2012

Afro-Colombian from Río Gualajo

- Tumaco, 11-09-2012

Legal advisor (1998–2008) to the Alto Mira y Frontera community council

- Tumaco, 11-09-2012

Afro-Colombian member of the Bajo Mira y Frontera community council

- Tumaco, 02-12-2012

Afro-Colombian woman, former member of the governing body of Bajo Mira y Frontera

- Tumaco, 15-01-2013

Afro-Colombian community leader, member of the governing body of Bajo Mira y Frontera

- Tumaco, 18-01-2013

Representative of the Alto Mira y Frontera community council

- Tumaco, 18-01-2013

Afro-Colombian community leader, member of the governing body of Alto Mira y Frontera

- Tumaco (Alto Mira y Frontera), 26-02-2013

Awá from Resguardo La Brava, two members of the community's governing body and two additional members

- Tumaco (Resguardo La Brava), 13-03-2013

Informal Conversations

Multiple informal conversations were held with an Afro-Colombian activist; a *Tumaqueño* living in the urban zone of Tumaco with a long trajectory in the Afro-Colombian social movement.

- Tumaco, period from September 2012 to February 2013

Two Afro-Colombian women from the Nupa and Alto Mira y Frontera community councils

- Tumaco (office of the PCN), 14-09-2012

Representative of Cococauca (*Coordinación de Consejos Comunitarios y Organizaciones de Base del Pueblo Negro del Pacífico Caucano*, Coordination of Community Councils and Grassroots Organizations of the Black Communities of the Colombian Pacific in Cauca)

- Guapi, 05-01-2013

Afro-Colombian member of the Bajo Mira y Frontera community council

- Tumaco, during field visit to Bajo Jagua (*vereda*), Bajo Mira y Frontera, 15-01-2013

Afro-Colombian community leader from Río Mejicano

- Tumaco, 18-01-2013

Former member of the governing body of the Alto Mira y Frontera community council

- Tumaco, 02-12-2012
- Tumaco, during field visit to Alto Mira y Frontera, 26-02-2013

NGOs, Grassroots Organizations, and Trade Unions

Semi-structured Interviews

Comisión Intereclesial de Justicia y Paz (Inter-Church Commission of Justice and Peace, a non-governmental human rights organization)
- Bogotá, 18-07-2012

Grupo Semillas (environmental NGO)
- Bogotá, 23-07-2012

Afrodes (*Asociación de Afrocolombianos Desplazados*, Association for Displaced Afro-Colombians, created in 1999 by and for displaced Afro-Colombians)
- Bogotá, 02-08-2012

Movimiento Cimarrón (movement created in 1982 in Buenaventura promoting Afro-Colombian rights, autonomous ethnic organization, and participation in democratic processes)
- Bogotá, 26-11-2012

ONIC (*Organización Nacional Indígena de Colombia*, National Indigenous Organization of Colombia)
- Bogotá, 30-01-2013

Fensuagro (*Federación Nacional Sindical Unitaria Agropecuaria*, National Federation of Agricultural Farming Unions)
- Bogotá, 07-12-2012

Sintraimagra (*Sindicato Nacional de Trabajadores de la Industria de Productos Grasos y Alimentos*, National Trade Union of Workers of the Fat and Food Products Industry)
- Bogotá, 22-02-2013

Public Officials

Semi-structured Interviews

Incoder (*Instituto Colombiano de Desarrollo Rural*, Colombian Institute of Rural Development)
- Pasto, 27-08-2012

Corponariño (*Corporación Autónoma Regional de Nariñol*), Regional Autonomous Corporation of Nariño (maximum departmental environmental authority in Nariño)
- Tumaco, 31-08-2012

Mayoral advisor in Tumaco
- Tumaco, 18-01-2013

Technical Secretary of "Productive Chains" of the Ministry of Agriculture
- Bogotá, 14-03-2013

Other

Field trip to a corporate oil palm plantation in Altamira (Casanare) with groups of biologists from the Andes University and the Panthera Foundation (Bogotá); specialized in wild cat—e.g. lions, tigers, jaguars, and leopards—conservation strategies.
- Altamira (Casanare), 19-11-2012 to 21-11-2012

Attendance of a discussion space/public reunion in relation to the process of prior consultation regarding the eradication of oil palms infected with bud rot, attended primarily by community leaders and inhabitants of Alto Mira y Frontera and Bajo Mira y Frontera, academic experts, representatives of the ICA, the Ministry of Interior, Fedepalma, Palmasur, and the Colombian Ombudsman for Human rights.
- Tumaco, 25-02-2013

Semi-structured interview with Gearóid Ó Loingsigh, investigative journalist

- Bogotá, 22-07-2012

Semi-structured interview with Afro-Colombian from Guapi, investigator at the IIAP

- Buenaventura, 27-08-2012

Attendance of the "Campaign Another Possible Pacific" (*Campaña "Otro Pazífico Posible"*): a bi-national workshop organized by the Process of Black Communities. Attended by members and representatives of Afro-Colombian communities and organizations from various zones of the Colombian Pacific coast, as well as Afro-Ecuadorian organizations and representatives

- Tumaco, 02-12-2012 to 04-12-2012

Semi-structured interview with members of Chiyangua y Chirará, local initiative in Tumaco that seeks to promote Afro-Colombian culture and traditions (in education, agricultural production, etc.)

- Tumaco, 05-12-2012

Index

H. Mol, *The Politics of Palm Oil Harm*, Palgrave Studies in Green Criminology, DOI 10.1007/978-3-319-55378-8

The manufacturer's authorised representative in the EU is Springer Nature Customer Service Centre GmbH, Europaplatz 3, 69115 Heidelberg, Germany. If you have any concerns regarding our products, please contact ProductSafety@springernature.com

Printed and bound by CPI Group (UK) Ltd, Croydon, CR0 4YY
01/10/2026
02225974-0001